access to history

CW00927184

From Second Reich to Third Reich: Germany 1918–45 for Edexcel

access to history

From Second Reich to Third Reich: Germany 1918–45 for Edexcel

Geoff Layton

HODDER EDUCATION

AN HACHETTE UK COMPANY

This high-quality material is endorsed by Edexcel and has been through a rigorous quality assurance programme to ensure that it is a suitable companion to the specification for both learners and teachers. This does not mean that its contents will be used verbatim when setting examinations nor is it to be read as being the official specification – a copy of which is available at www.edexcel.org.uk.

Study guides revised and updated, 2008, by Angela Leonard (Edexcel).

The publishers would like to thank the following for permission to reproduce copyright illustrations: AKG-images, pages 14, 110, 189, 210; © Archivo Iconografico, S.A./Corbis, page 102; © Austrian Archives/Corbis, pages 67, 74, 96, 112, 149, 165; Bauhaus-Archiv Berlin, page 80; © Bettman/Corbis, pages 4, 10, 81,115, 127, 164, 168, 172, 232; BPK Berlin, page 236; BPK Berlin/Kunstbibliothek, Staatliche Museen zu Berlin Photo: Knud Petersen, page 179; BPK/Staatliche Museen zu Berlin – Preußischer Kulturbesitz, Nationalgalerie. Photo: Jörg P. Anders, page 79; © Corbis, page 11, 181, 194, 222, 237, 244; Erich Lessing Archive/AKG-images, page 78; Getty Images, pages 63, 89, 197; Hulton-Deutsch Collection/Corbis, page 137, 180, 234, 243; Imperial War Museum, page 131; Mary Evans Picture Library, page 166; Mary Evans/Weimar Archive, page 39, 217; © Michael Nicholson/Corbis, page 227; Süddeutsche Zeitung Photo, page 90; Süddeutsche Zeitung Photo/Scherl, pages 103, 138; Yad Vashem Art Museum, Jerusalem/ Mrs Simenhoff, S. Africa, page 221.

The publishers would like to acknowledge use of the following abstracts: Hanseatische Verlagsanstalt for an extract from *Verfassungsrecht des Großdeutschen Reiches* by E. Huber, 1939; University of North Carolina Press for an extract from *The Nazi Voter: The Social Foundations of Fascism in Germany* 1919–1933 by Thomas Childers, 1986.

Every effort has been made to trace all copyright holders, but if any have been inadvertently overlooked the Publishers will be pleased to make the necessary arrangements at the first opportunity.

Although every effort has been made to ensure that website addresses are correct at time of going to press, Hodder Education cannot be held responsible for the content of any website mentioned in this book. It is sometimes possible to find a relocated web page by typing in the address of the home page for a website in the URL window of your browser.

Orders: please contact Bookpoint Ltd, 130 Milton Park, Abingdon, Oxon OX14 4SB. Telephone: (44) 01235 827720. Fax: (44) 01235 400454. Lines are open 9.00–5.00, Monday to Saturday, with a 24-hour message answering service. Visit our website at www.hoddereducation.co.uk

© Geoff Layton 2008
First published in 2008 by
Hodder Education,
An Hachette UK Company
338 Euston Road
London NW1 3BH

Impression number   5 4 3 2
Year   2012 2011 2010 2009

Cover photo: David Crausby/Alamy
Typeset in Baskerville 10/12pt and produced by Gray Publishing, Tunbridge Wells
Printed in Malta

A catalogue record for this title is available from the British Library

ISBN: 978 0340 965 818

Contents

Dedication

Keith Randell (1943–2002)

The *Access to History* series was conceived and developed by Keith, who created a series to 'cater for students as they are, not as we might wish them to be'. He leaves a living legacy of a series that for over 20 years has provided a trusted, stimulating and well-loved accompaniment to post-16 study. Our aim with these new editions is to continue to offer students the best possible support for their studies.

To Janet

1 The German Revolution 1918–19

POINTS TO CONSIDER

The purpose of this chapter is to consider the events that occurred in Germany during the final days of the First World War and the challenges faced by the new democratic Germany during its first months. These were dramatic, but difficult times for German politicians and the German people. The main areas are:

- The collapse of Imperial Germany and the abdication of Kaiser Wilhelm II
- The German Revolution: the establishment of the democratic republic and the failure of the Spartacist revolt
- The establishment of the National Constituent Assembly

Key dates

1918	September	Ludendorff conceded that Germany was defeated
	October 3	Prince Max of Baden appointed chancellor
	November 2	Grand Fleet mutiny at Kiel
	November 8	Bavaria proclaimed a socialist republic
	November 9	Kaiser fled to Holland
		Ebert appointed chancellor
		Germany proclaimed a republic
	November 11	Armistice signed at Compiègne
1919	January 1	German Communist Party founded
	January 5	Start of Spartacist uprising in Berlin
	February 6	National Constituent Assembly met at Weimar

1 | The Collapse of Imperial Germany

Key question
Why did Germany lose the First World War?

When war broke out in 1914 it was assumed in Germany, as well as in all the Great Powers, that the conflict would not last very long. However, by late September 1918, after four years of bloody war, Germany faced military defeat. The reasons for its eventual collapse go right back to the early days of August 1914, but the pressures had developed over the years that followed. The main factors can be identified as follows:

- Germany's failure to achieve rapid victory in the summer of 1914. The German High Command's strategy was built upon the notion of a quick victory in order to avoid a long drawn-out conflict with the Allies. By the autumn of 1914 the **Schlieffen plan** had failed to gain a rapid victory.
- Stalemate. Germany was forced to fight the war on two fronts – the east and the west. The balance of military power resulted in a war of stalemate that put immense pressures on **Imperial Germany**. The situation was made particularly difficult for Germany by the Allies' naval blockade, which seriously limited the import of all supplies. And, although the German policy of **unrestricted submarine warfare** at first seriously threatened Britain, it did not decisively weaken her.
- Strengths of the Allies. Britain and France were major colonial powers and could call upon their overseas empires for manpower, resources and supplies. Furthermore, from April 1917, the Allies were strengthened by America's entry into the war, which resulted in the mobilisation of two million men.
- Limitations of German war economy. Imperial Germany was totally unprepared for the economic costs of a prolonged war. It made great efforts to mobilise the war effort and arms production was dramatically increased. However, the economy was seriously dislocated, which wrecked the government's finances and increased social tension.

A chance for Germany to escape from the military defeat came when Russia surrendered in March 1918. This immediately enabled Germany to launch a last major offensive on the Western Front. Unfortunately, it was unable to maintain the momentum and, by August, German troops were being forced to retreat. At the same time its own allies, Austria, Turkey and Bulgaria, were collapsing.

The socio-economic effects of the First World War

In 1914, the vast majority of Germans supported the war and there were no signs of the country's morale and unity breaking down until the winter months of early 1917. Then, the accumulation of shortages, high prices and the black market, as well as the bleak military situation, began to affect the public mood. Social discontent thereafter grew markedly because of:

- Food and fuel shortages. The exceptionally cold winter of 1916–17 contributed to severe food and fuel shortages in the cities. It was nicknamed the 'turnip winter' because the failure of the potato crop forced the German people to rely heavily on turnips, which were normally for animal fodder.
- Civilian deaths. The number of civilian deaths from starvation and hypothermia increased from 121,000 in 1916 to 293,000 in 1918.
- Infant mortality. The number of child deaths increased by over 50 per cent in the course of the war years.

Key terms

Schlieffen plan
Its purpose was to avoid a two-front war by winning victory on the Western Front before dealing with the threat from Russia. It aimed to defeat France within six weeks by a massive German offensive in northern France and Belgium.

Imperial Germany
The title given to Germany from its unification in 1871 until 1918. Also referred to as the Second Reich (Empire).

Unrestricted submarine warfare
Germany's policy of attacking all military and civilian shipping in order to sink supplies going to Britain.

Key question
How did the war affect the living and working conditions of the German people?

Kaiser
Emperor. The last
Kaiser of Germany
was Wilhelm II,
1888–1918.

A cartoon drawn in 1918 by the German artist Raemaeker. It underlines the serious situation faced by **Kaiser** Wilhelm II, who is held by two ominous figures – war and starvation.

- The influenza epidemic. In 1918 Europe was hit by the 'Spanish flu', which killed between 20 and 40 million people – a figure higher than the casualties of the First World War. It has been cited as the most devastating epidemic recorded, probably because people's resistance to disease was lowered by the decline in living conditions.
- Inflation. Workers were forced to work even longer hours, but wages fell below the inflation rate. Average prices doubled in Germany between 1914 and 1918, whereas wages rose by only 50–75 per cent.
- Casualties. About two million Germans were killed, with a further six million wounded, many suffering disability. The emotional trauma for all these soldiers and their families was not so easy to put into statistics.

Social discontent, therefore, grew markedly in the final two years of the war. Considerable anger was expressed against the so-called 'sharks' of industry, who had made vast profits from the war.

Resentment grew in the minds of many within the middle class because they felt that their social status had been lowered as their income declined. Above all, opposition began to grow against the political leaders, who had urged total war. Faced with the worsening situation on the domestic front and the likelihood of defeat on the Western Front, the military leaders, Generals Ludendorff and Hindenburg (below and page 68), recognised the seriousness of Germany's position, and decided to seek peace with the Allies.

Profile: Erich Ludendorff 1865–1937

1865	– Born in Kruszewnia in the Polish Prussian province of Posen
1882	– Joined the Prussian army
1894	– Joined the General Staff and worked closely with Schlieffen
1914	– Appointed Chief-of-Staff to Hindenburg on the Eastern Front
1916	– Transferred to Western Front. Promoted to the post of Quartermaster General – virtual military dictator, 1916–18
1917	– Responsible for the dismissal of Chancellor Bethmann-Hollweg (1909–17)
1918	– Masterminded German final offensive
	– Proposed the theory of the 'stab in the back' (see page 5)
	– Fled to Sweden
1919	– Returned to Germany
1920	– Took part in Kapp *putsch* (see pages 39–40)
1923	– Collaborated with Hitler and was involved in Munich *putsch* (see pages 41–3)
1937	– Died in Tutzing, Bavaria

Ludendorff was a soldier of considerable ability, energy and enthusiasm. In the campaign in Belgium he showed considerable initiative and was sent, as Chief-of-Staff, to serve with Hindenburg on the Eastern Front. Here he played an important part in the major victories over the Russians. In 1916, the two men were posted to the Western Front and during the years that followed they were able to assume supreme command of the German war effort. By the end of the war, Ludendorff was effectively the wartime dictator of Germany and, when it was clear that Germany had lost the war, he tried to direct the control of the constitutional reform in October 1918. After the war, he dabbled in extreme right-wing politics and became associated with the activities of Hitler's Nazi Party whose racial views he shared. Later, he became disenchanted with Hitler and in his latter years became a pacifist.

> **Key term**
>
> *Putsch*
> The German word for an uprising (though often the French phrase, *coup d'état*, is used). Normally, a *putsch* means the attempt by a small group to overthrow the government.

The October reform

Once Ludendorff came to appreciate that an Allied invasion of Germany would lead to destructive internal disturbances, he pushed for political change. Ever since Imperial Germany had been created in 1871, it had been an **autocracy**. Now Ludendorff wanted to change Germany into a **constitutional monarchy** by the Kaiser's handing over political power to a civilian government. In other words, he aimed to establish a more democratic government, while maintaining the German monarchy.

Ludendorff's political turnaround had two aims. First, he wanted to secure for Germany the best possible peace terms from the Allies – it was believed that the Allied leaders would be more sympathetic to a democratic regime in Berlin. Secondly, he hoped the change would prevent the outbreak of political revolutionary disturbances.

However, Ludendorff had a third and a more cynical ulterior motive. He saw the need to shift the responsibility for Germany's defeat away from the military leadership and the conservative forces, which had dominated Imperial Germany, e.g. landowners and the army. Instead, he intended to put the responsibility and blame for the defeat on the new leadership. Here lay the origins of the **'stab in the back' myth**, which was later to play such a vital part in the history of the Weimar Republic. It was a theme soon taken up by sympathisers of the political right wing (see page 36).

It was against this background that on 3 October 1918 Prince Max of Baden, a moderate conservative, was appointed chancellor. He had democratic views and also a well-established international reputation because of his work with the Red Cross. In the following month a series of constitutional reforms came into effect, which turned Germany into a parliamentary democracy:

- Wilhelm II gave up his powers over the army and the navy to the *Reichstag*.
- The chancellor and his government were made accountable to the *Reichstag*, instead of to the Kaiser.
- At the same time, armistice negotiations with the Allies were opened.

What pushed Germany, in such a short space of time, from political reform towards revolution was the widespread realisation that the war was lost. The shock of defeat, after years of hardship and optimistic propaganda, hardened popular opinion. By early November it was apparent that the creation of a constitutional monarchy would not defuse what had become a revolutionary situation.

Key question
Why did Ludendorff support constitutional reform?

Key terms

Autocracy
A system where one person (usually a hereditary sovereign) has absolute rule.

Constitutional monarchy
Where the monarch has limited power within the lines of a constitution.

'Stab in the back' myth
The distorted view that the army had not really lost the First World War and that unpatriotic groups, such as socialists and Jews, had undermined it. The myth severely weakened the Weimar democracy from the start.

Reichstag
The German parliament. Although created in 1871, it had very limited powers. Real power lay with the Emperor.

Key dates

Ludendorff conceded that Germany was defeated: September 1918

Prince Max of Baden appointed chancellor: 3 October 1918

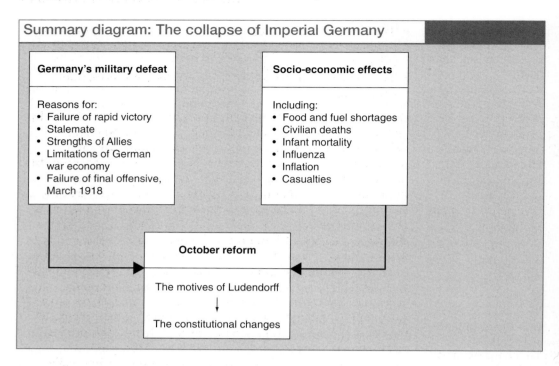

Summary diagram: The collapse of Imperial Germany

Germany's military defeat

Reasons for:
• Failure of rapid victory
• Stalemate
• Strengths of Allies
• Limitations of German war economy
• Failure of final offensive, March 1918

Socio-economic effects

Including:
• Food and fuel shortages
• Civilian deaths
• Infant mortality
• Influenza
• Inflation
• Casualties

October reform

The motives of Ludendorff

↓

The constitutional changes

2 | The German Revolution

On 29 October, a mutiny began to spread among some sailors who refused to obey orders at Wilhelmshaven, near Kiel. Prince Max's government quickly lost control of the political situation and by 2 November sailors gained control of other major ports, such as Kiel and Hamburg. These take-overs had been prompted by a real fear amongst the sailors that their officers were planning a suicide attack on the British fleet, in order to restore the honour of the German navy. The news of the Kiel mutiny fanned the flames of discontent to other ports, Bremen and Lübeck, and soon throughout Germany. By 6 November, numerous workers' and soldiers' councils, similar to the **soviets** that had been set up by the **Bolsheviks** in Russia, were established in the major cities of Berlin, Cologne and Stuttgart. In Bavaria, the last member of the House of Wittelsbach, King Louis III, was deposed and the socialist Kurt Eisner proclaimed Bavaria an independent democratic socialist republic.

By the end of the first week of November it was clear that the October reforms had failed to impress the German people. The popular discontent was turning into a more fundamental revolutionary movement whose demands were for an immediate peace and the abdication of Kaiser Wilhelm II. The disturbances were prompted by:

• The realisation by troops and sailors that the war was lost and nothing was to be gained by carrying on.

Key question
How and why did the October reform fail?

Key dates

Grand Fleet mutiny at Kiel: 2 November 1918

Bavaria proclaimed a socialist republic: 8 November 1918

Key terms

Soviet
A Russian word meaning an elected council. Soviets developed during the Russian Revolution in 1917. In Germany many councils were set up in 1918, which had the support of the more radical and revolutionary left-wing working class.

Bolsheviks
Followers of Bolshevism – Russian communism.

- The sense of national shock when the news came of Germany's military defeat – propaganda and censorship had really delayed the reality for too long.
- The increasing anger and bitterness over socio-economic conditions.

Coalition government
Usually formed when a party does not have an overall majority in parliament; it then combines with more parties and shares government positions.

Key date
Kaiser fled to Holland
Ebert appointed chancellor
Germany proclaimed a republic:
9 November 1918

Key question
In what ways was the left-wing movement divided?

Socialist republic
A system of government without a monarchy that aims to introduce social changes for collective benefit.

Soviet republic
A system of government without a monarchy that aims to introduce a communist state organised by the workers' councils and opposed to private ownership.

Prince Max would certainly have liked to preserve the monarchy, and possibly even Wilhelm II himself, but the Emperor's delusions that he could carry on without making any more political changes placed the chancellor in a difficult position. In the end, Prince Max became so worried by the revolutionary situation in Berlin that on 9 November he announced that the Kaiser would renounce the throne and that a **coalition** left-wing **government** would be formed by Friedrich Ebert. It was in this chaotic situation that Philipp Scheidemann, one of the provisional government's leaders, appeared on the balcony of the *Reichstag* building and proclaimed Germany a republic. (Actually, an hour later Germany was also declared a 'soviet republic' – a statement crucial for the shaping of the next few months of the German Revolution.) It was only at this point in the evening of 9 November that the Kaiser, who was in Belgium, accepted the advice of leading generals. In that way, the Kaiser did not formally abdicate, he simply walked away and went into exile voluntarily in Holland.

The left-wing movement

A genuinely revolutionary situation existed in Germany in early November 1918. However, the revolutionary wave that swept Germany was not a united force. In fact, the left-wing movement behind it consisted of three main strands (Table 1.1).

Table 1.1: The German left-wing movement

	Moderate socialists	*Radical socialists*	*Revolutionary socialists*
Party names	SPD (German Social Democratic Party)	USPD (German Independent Social Democratic Party)	Spartacists (Spartacus League)
Aim	To establish a **socialist republic** by the creation of parliamentary democracy	To create a socialist republic governed by workers' and soldiers' councils in conjunction with a parliament	To create a **soviet republic** based on the rule of the workers' and soldiers' councils
Leaders	Friedrich Ebert Philipp Scheidemann	Karl Kautsky Hugo Haase	Rosa Luxemburg Karl Liebknecht

The SPD (German Social Democratic Party)

The SPD represented moderate socialist aims and was led by
Friedrich Ebert and Philipp Scheidemann. It dated from 1875.
In the election of 1912 it had become the largest party in the
Reichstag with a membership of over one million. Its fundamental
aim was to create a socialist republic, but being wholly committed
to parliamentary democracy, it totally rejected anything that
might have been likened to Soviet-style communism.

The Spartacists

On the extreme left stood the Spartacus League (otherwise known
as the Spartacists), led by Karl Liebknecht and the Polish-born
Rosa Luxemburg, one of the few women to be prominent in
German political history (see profile, page 9).

The Spartacists had been formed in 1905 as a minor faction of
the SPD. By 1918 it had a national membership of about 5000.
From 1914, they had opposed the war and they were deeply
influenced by Lenin and Bolshevism. They had come to believe
that Germany should follow the same path as Communist Russia.
The fundamental aim of the Spartacists was to create a soviet
republic based on the rule of the **proletariat** through workers'
and soldiers' councils.

The USPD (Independent German Social Democratic Party)

The USPD had been formed in 1917 as a breakaway group
from the SPD. It was led by Hugo Haase and Karl Kautsky.
Although the USPD was a minority of the assembly in the
Reichstag it had a substantial following of 300,000 members.

The USPD demanded radical social and economic change as
well as political reforms. However, as a political movement, it was
far from united and internal divisions and squabbles seriously
curtailed its influence. The main disagreement was between those
who sympathised with the creation of a parliamentary democracy
and those who advocated a much more revolutionary democracy
based on the workers' councils.

Ebert's coalition government

Because of the different aims and methods of the socialist
movement, there was a lack of unity in Ebert's coalition
government. Moreover, it should also be remembered that
German society was in a chaotic state of near collapse, so the
leading political figures at the time had little room to manoeuvre
when they had to make hasty and difficult decisions.

On 9 November 1918 Ebert created a provisional coalition
government:

Key question
What were the main
problems faced by
Ebert?

- 'Provisional' in the sense that it was short term until a national
  election was held to vote for a National Constituent Assembly
  (parliament).
- 'Coalition' in the sense that it was a combination of parties, the
  SPD and the USPD.

Key profile: Rosa Luxemburg ('Red Rosa') 1871–1919

1870	– Born in Poland of Jewish origins. Badly disabled and walked with a limp, endured continual pain
1905	– Took part in the revolutionary troubles in Russia
	– Joined with Karl Liebknecht in Germany to establish the revolutionary group that founded the Spartacist League
1914–18	– Imprisoned for the duration of the war
	– Campaigned secretly for a revolutionary end to the war
1917	– Welcomed the Bolshevik revolution in Russia (but soon came to criticise Lenin's repressive methods)
1918	– Freed from prison
1919	– Supported the creation of KPD (German Communist Party) from the Spartacist League
	– Opposed the Spartacus uprising in January 1919
	– Murdered in police custody in Berlin

After her death, Luxemburg was described as 'arguably one of the finest political theorists of the twentieth century' who famously said, 'Freedom is always for the person who thinks differently'. In 1905, she was one of the founders of the Spartacist League and continued to champion the cause of armed revolution that would sweep the capitalist system away. Ironically, she spoke against the uprising in January 1919 (see page 13) because she felt that Germany was not ready for communism. Although she died a committed revolutionary, she had a humane and optimistic view of communism at odds with the brutality of the Bolsheviks in Russia.

Ebert himself was a moderate and was frightened that the political situation in Germany could easily run out of control. In Table 1.2, the nature of Ebert's major problems can be seen.

Ebert's main worry was that the extreme left would gain the upper hand. He recognised the growing number of workers' councils and feared that they might threaten his policy of gradual change. He was determined to maintain law and order to prevent the country collapsing into civil war. He also feared that the return of millions of troops after the Armistice agreement, which was eventually signed on 11 November, would create enormous social and political problems (see Table 1.2). These were the main concerns in the minds of Ebert and the SPD leadership in the months that followed and were the main reasons why they made agreements with the army and industrialists.

Key date

Armistice signed between Germany and the Allies at Compiègne in northern France: 11 November 1918

Ebert-Groener agreement

On 10 November, the day after the declaration of the Republic, General Wilhelm Groener, Ludendorff's successor, telephoned Chancellor Ebert. Their conversation was very significant. The

Table 1.2: Ebert's main problems

Socio-economic	Left-wing opposition	Right-wing opposition	Military
1. Inflation Wages were falling behind prices, which was increasing social discontent	**1. Strikes** From the autumn of 1918 the number of strikes and lock-outs increased markedly	**1. *Freikorps*** A growing number of right-wing, nationalist soldiers were forming paramilitary units	**1. Demobilisation** About 1.5 million soldiers had to be returned home to Germany
2. Shortages From the winter of 1916–17 fuel and food shortages were causing real hardship in the cities	**2. German communists** Inspired by the events of 1917–18 in Russia, communists aimed to bring about a revolution in Germany	**2. The army** The army was generally conservative, but also deeply embittered by the military defeat	**2. Allied blockade** The Allies maintained the naval blockade even after the Armistice. Social distress was not relieved until June 1919
3. Flu epidemic The 'Spanish flu' killed thousands. It was the most serious flu epidemic of the twentieth century	**3. Workers' and soldiers' councils** Hundred of councils were created and many wanted changes to the army and industries	**3. Nationalists** Nationalist-conservatives were deeply against the abdication of the Kaiser and did not support the creation of a democratic republic	**3. Peace terms** The Armistice was when they agreed to stop fighting, but there was great public concern about the actual effects of the peace treaty

Supreme Army Command agreed to support the new government and to use troops to maintain the stability and security of the new republic. In return, Ebert promised to oppose the spread of revolutionary socialism and to preserve the authority of the army officers. The deal has become known simply as the Ebert-Groener agreement.

Stinnes-Legien agreement

A few days later, on 15 November, Karl Legien, leader of the trade unions, and Hugo Stinnes, leader of the industrial employers, held another significant discussion. The Stinnes-Legien agreement was, in effect, a deal where the trade unions made a commitment not to interfere with private ownership and the free market, in return for workers' committees, an eight-hour working day and full legal recognition. Ebert's provisional government endorsed this because the German trade unions were a powerful movement and traditionally closely tied with the SPD.

So, on one level, the agreement to bring about some key, long-desired reforms was a real success. However, these two

Key profile: Friedrich Ebert 1871–1925

1871   – Born in Heidelberg of humble background
1885–8 – Trained as a saddler
1889   – Became a trade union organiser and SPD member
1912   – Elected as a member of the *Reichstag*
1916   – Chosen as leader of the Party
1918   – 9 November – became chancellor of the provisional
           government when Imperial Germany collapsed
        – 10 November – Ebert-Groener agreement (see pages 9–10)
1919   – 11 February – chosen as the country's first president, a
           position he held until his death
1925   – Died at the age of 54 of a heart attack

Ebert rose from a humble background as a saddler to become the first president of Germany. His character and achievements significantly shaped the development of Weimar democracy.

The political activist
During his apprenticeship he became quickly involved in trade union work and the socialist movement. His written and spoken skills were soon recognised by the SPD leadership and he advanced through the party covering a range of full-time political jobs such as journalist and secretary. He entered the *Reichstag* in 1912 and just a year later he became chairman of the SPD as he was seen capable of conciliating the developing differences in the Party.

Leader of the SPD
The First World War divided the SPD fundamentally. Ebert worked really hard to keep it together and in 1916 he was chosen as leader. However, it proved impossible to overcome the differences and a year later the Party split and the USPD was created.

The German Revolution
When Germany collapsed in autumn 1918, Ebert wanted a democratic parliamentary government with a constitutional monarchy – along English lines – but when events got out of hand in November 1918, the monarchy collapsed and he accepted the chancellorship. It was a major success to manage to hold the first truly democratic German elections, which led to the National Constituent Assembly and the creation of the Weimar Constitution. However, Ebert has been criticised for endorsing the use of the army, the *Freikorps* (see page 37) and other conservative forces to brutally suppress the more radical elements of the left.

President
He was chosen to be the country's first president by the National Constituent Assembly in February 1919, a position he held until his death. He oversaw the years of crisis and applied the emergency decrees of Article 48 (see page 21) with success. However, he became the focus of scurrilous criticism from the extreme right – which almost certainly contributed to his early death. He was a man of great integrity and decency and, despite the critics, he was a patriot and served his office with distinction and correctness.

Key term

Freikorps
Means 'free corps' who acted as paramilitaries. They were right-wing, nationalist soldiers who were only too willing to use force to suppress communist activity.

agreements have been severely criticised over the years, particularly by the left wing. Critics have accused Ebert of having supported compromises with the forces of conservatism. The army was not reformed at all and it was not really committed to democracy. Employers resented the concessions and were unsympathetic to the Weimar system. Nevertheless, there is a counter-argument that Ebert and the SPD leadership were motivated by the simple desire to guarantee stability and a peaceful transition.

Left-wing divisions

By the last days of 1918 it was clear that the SPD had become distanced from its political 'allies' on the left and their conflicting aims resulted in fundamental differences over strategy and policies.

> **Key question**
> Why did the left-wing movement split?

USPD

In late December 1918, the USPD members of Ebert's government resigned over the shooting of some Spartacists by soldiers. However, the split had really emerged over the USPD's desire to introduce fundamental social and economic changes that the SPD did not want to adopt.

Aim
To create a socialist republic governed by workers' and soldiers' councils in conjunction with a parliament.

Strategy
To introduce radical social and economic changes.

Policies
To reform the army fundamentally.
To nationalise key industries.
To introduce welfare benefits.

SPD

The SPD government became increasingly isolated. It moved further to the political right and grew dependent on the civil service and the army to maintain effective government.

Aim
To establish a socialist republic by the creation of parliamentary democracy.

Strategy
To make arrangements for a democratic *Reichstag* election leading to a National Constituent Assembly.
To introduce moderate changes, but to prevent the spread of communist revolution.

Policies
To maintain law and order by running the country with the existing legal and police systems.
To retain the army.
To introduce welfare benefits.

Spartacists

On 1 January 1919, the Spartacists formally founded the *Kommunistische Partei Deutschlands*, the KPD – German Communist Party. It refused to participate in the parliamentary elections, preferring instead to place its faith in the workers' councils, as expressed in the Spartacist manifesto:

> German Communist Party founded:
> 1 January 1919

Key date

The question today is not democracy or dictatorship. The question that history has put on the agenda reads: bourgeois democracy or socialist democracy? For the dictatorship of the proletariat is democracy in the socialist sense of the word. Dictatorship of the proletariat does not mean bombs, *putsches*, riots and anarchy, as the agents of capitalist profits deliberately and falsely claim. Rather, it means using all instruments of political power to achieve socialism, to expropriate [dispossess of property] the capitalist class, through and in accordance with the will of the revolutionary majority of the proletariat.

Aim
To create a soviet republic based on the rule of the workers' and soldiers' councils.

Strategy
To oppose the creation of a National Constituent Assembly and to take power by strikes, demonstrations and revolts leading to fundamental social and economic changes.

Policies
To replace the army by local militias of workers.
To carry out extensive nationalisation of industries and land.
To introduce welfare benefits.

The Spartacist revolt

Key question
Why did the Spartacist revolt fail?

Key date
Start of Spartacist uprising in Berlin: 5 January 1919

In January 1919 the Spartacists decided that the time was ripe to launch an armed rising in Berlin with the aim of overthrowing the provisional government and creating a soviet republic.

On 5 January, they occupied public buildings, called for a general strike and formed a revolutionary committee. They denounced Ebert's provisional government and the coming elections. However, they had little chance of success. There were three days of savage street fighting and over 100 were killed. The Spartacist *coup* was easily defeated and afterwards, most notoriously, Liebknecht and Luxemburg were brutally murdered whilst in police custody.

The events of January 1919 showed that the Spartacists were strong on policies, but detached from political realities. They had no real strategy and their 'revolutionaries' were mainly just workers with rifles. By contrast, the government had not only the backing of the army's troops, but also 5000 'irregular' military-style groups, *Freikorps*.

This event created a very troubled atmosphere for the next few months. The elections for the National Constituent Assembly duly took place in February 1919 (see page 17), although the continuation of strikes and street disorders in Berlin meant that, for reasons of security, the Assembly's first meeting was switched to the town of **Weimar**. More serious disturbances in Bavaria in April resulted in a short-lived soviet-type republic being established there. The *Freikorps* brought the disturbances under control though, in each case, at the cost of several hundred lives. The infant republic had survived the traumas of its birth.

Weimar Republic
Took its name from the first meeting of the National Constituent Assembly in Weimar. The Assembly had moved there because there were still many disturbances in Berlin. Weimar was chosen because it was a town with a great historical and cultural tradition.

Key term

Prost Noske! — — das Proletariat ist entwaffnet!

'Cheers Noske! The Young Revolution is Dead!' A cartoon drawn in 1919 by the German Georg Grosz. Grosz was a communist artist and his images can be stark and disturbing. In this cartoon he satirises the savagery of the *Freikorps*.

Summary diagram: The German Revolution

The birth of the Republic

Mutiny and revolts

↓

Abdication of the Kaiser

↓

Why did October reform fail?

The left-wing movement

- SPD
- USPD
- Spartacists

Ebert's leadership

- The coalition government
- Ebert-Groener and Stinnes-Legien agreements

Early problems

- Socio-economic factors
- Left-wing opposition
- Right-wing opposition
- Military consequences

The Spartacist uprising
Why did it fail?

Key question
Was the election a success for democracy?

Key date
National Constituent Assembly met at Weimar: 6 February 1919

3 | The National Constituent Assembly

Despite the disturbances across Germany, in the months after the collapse of Imperial Germany, the new republic was still able to hold its first elections for a National Constituent Assembly on 19 January 1919. Most political parties took the opportunity to retitle themselves, but new names did not disguise the fact that there was considerable continuity in the structure of the party system (see Table 1.3, page 16).

The election results (see Figure 1.1, page 17) quickly led to the creation of the National Constituent Assembly on 6 February. In many respects the results represented a major success for the forces of parliamentary democracy:

- The high turnout of 83 per cent in the election suggested faith in the idea of democracy.
- 76.1 per cent of the electorate voted for pro-democratic parties.
- The solid vote for the three main democratic parties, the SPD, the DDP and the ZP, made it straightforward to form a coalition government, which became known as the 'Weimar Coalition'.

Table 1.3: The major political parties in the Weimar Republic

BVP Bayerische Volkspartei (Bavarian People's Party)	Leader: Heinrich Held	The BVP was a regional party formed from elements of the ZP in 1919 in order to uphold Bavaria's local interests. It was conservative, but generally supported the Republic.
DDP Deutsche Demokratische Partei (German Democratic Party)	Leaders: Walther Rathenau and Hugo Preuss	Formed from the National Liberals party in the old *Reichstag*, it attracted support from the professional middle classes, especially the intellectuals and some of the businessmen. The party supported the democratic republic and was committed to constitutional reform.
DNVP Deutschnationale Volkspartei (German National People's Party)	Leaders: Karl Helfferich and Alfred Hugenberg (see page 67)	The DNVP was a right-wing party formed from the old conservative parties and some of the racist, anti-Semitic groups, such as the Pan-German League. It was monarchist and anti-republican. Generally, it was closely tied to the interests of heavy industry and agriculture, including landowners and small farmers.
DVP Deutsche Volkspartei (German People's Party)	Leader: Gustav Stresemann (see pages 74–5)	A new party founded by Gustav Stresemann, who was a conservative and monarchist and at first suspicious of the Weimar Republic and voted against the new constitution (see page 21). From 1921, under Stresemann's influence, the DVP became a strong supporter of parliamentary democracy. It attracted support from the protestant middle and upper classes.
KPD Kommunistische Partei Deutschlands (German Communist Party)	Leader: Ernst Thälmann	The KPD was formed in January 1919 by the extreme left wing, e.g. Spartacists. It was anti-republican in the sense that it opposed Weimar-style democracy and supported a revolutionary overthrow of society. Most of its supporters were from the working class and strengthened by the defection of many USPD members in 1920.
NSDAP Nationalsozialistische Partei Deutschlands (National Socialist German Workers' Party – Nazi Party)	Leader: Adolf Hitler (see pages 127–8)	Extreme right-wing party formed in 1919. It was anti-republican, anti-Semitic and strongly nationalist. Until 1930 it remained a fringe party with support from the lower middle classes.
SPD Sozialdemokratische Partei Deutschlands (German Social Democratic Party)	Leaders: Friedrich Ebert (see page 11) and Philipp Scheidemann	The moderate wing of the socialist movement, it was very much the party of the working class and the trade unions. It strongly supported parliamentary democracy and was opposed to the revolutionary demands of the more left-wing socialists.
USPD Unabhängige Sozialdemokratische Partei Deutschlands (Independent German Social Democratic Party)	Leaders: Karl Kautsky and Hugo Haase	The USPD broke away from the SPD in April 1917. It included many of the more radical elements of German socialism and, therefore, sought social and political change. About half its members joined the KPD during 1919–20 whilst by 1922 most of the others had returned to the ranks of the SPD.
ZP Zentrumspartei (Centre Party)	Leaders: Matthias Erzberger and Heinrich Brüning (see page 112)	The ZP had been created in the nineteenth century to defend the interests of the Roman Catholic Church. It continued to be the major political voice of Catholicism and enjoyed a broad range of supporters from aristocratic landowners to Christian trade unionists. Most of the ZP was committed to the Republic. From the late 1920s it became more sympathetic to the right wing.

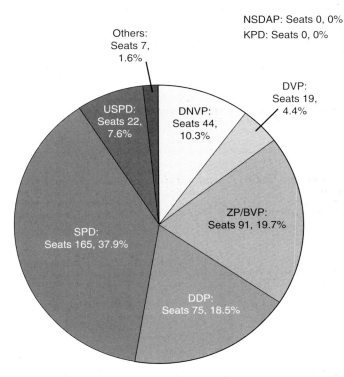

Figure 1.1: *Reichstag* election result January 1919
Turnout 83 per cent
Total number of seats 423

However, it should be borne in mind that:

- Although the DNVP gained only 10.3 per cent, it had backing from important conservative supporters, e.g. the landowners, the army officers, industrialists.
- The DVP and its leader, Stresemann, did not support the Weimar Republic in 1919 because they wanted Germany to have a constitutional monarchy.

Key question
How fundamental were the changes brought about by the German Revolution?

What kind of revolution?

By May 1919 a degree of stability had returned to Germany. The revolution had run its course and the Weimar Republic had been established. However, serious doubts remain about the nature and real extent of these revolutionary changes.

Undoubtedly, there existed the possibility of revolution in Germany as the war came to an end. The effects of war and the shock of defeat shook the faith of large numbers of the people in the old order. Imperial Germany could not survive, so Wilhelm II and the other princes were deposed and parliamentary democracy was introduced. These were important changes.

However, in the end, the German Revolution did not go much further than the October reforms and was strictly limited in scope. Society was left almost untouched by these events, for there was no attempt to reform the key institutions.

- The civil service, judiciary and army all remained essentially intact.
- Similarly, the power and influence of Germany's industrial and commercial leaders remained unchanged.
- There were no changes in the structure of big business and land ownership.

Certainly, plans for the improvement of working conditions and the beginnings of a welfare state were outlined by the government, but the SPD leadership hoped that all the changes would follow in the wake of constitutional reform. With hindsight, it seems that more thoroughgoing social and economic changes might well have been a better basis on which to establish democracy. As it was, the divisions on the left played into the hands of the conservative forces. As one historian, M. Hughes, has claim, 'it is more accurate to talk of a potential revolution which ran away into the sand rather than the genuine article'. Indeed, during the first half of 1919 the increasing reliance of the moderate left on the conservative forces of Imperial Germany became a major factor in German politics. These conservative forces were soon to put into doubt the very survival of Weimar democracy.

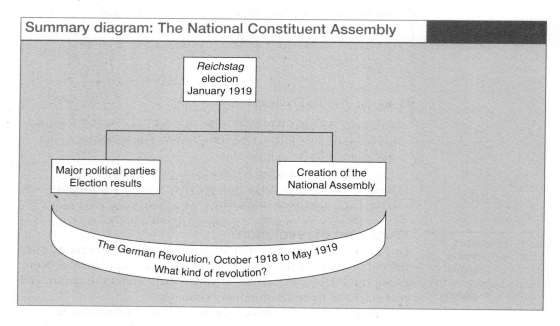

Summary diagram: The National Constituent Assembly

Reichstag election January 1919

Major political parties Election results

Creation of the National Assembly

The German Revolution, October 1918 to May 1919 What kind of revolution?

Study Guide: AS Question

In the style of Edexcel

How far did the political changes in Germany between October 1918 and May 1919 amount to a revolution? (30 marks)

Exam tips

The cross-references are intended to take you straight to the material that will help you to answer the question.

This question asks you to evaluate the extent of political change that took place in Germany in the eight months from October 1918 when it became increasingly clear that Germany had lost the war.

To assess change, you need a clear idea of what was different and what remained the same, and whether this amounted to a 'revolution'.

A good answer will be organised so that different themes – such as institutions, society, government – are evaluated in turn by comparing the extent and limitations of change in each one.

Some examples of change are:

- The effects of defeat in the First World War leading to reform and the creation of a constitutional monarchy (page 5).
- The abdication of the Kaiser and the princes (page 7).
- The creation of the National Constituent Assembly and the commitment to the creation of a parliamentary democracy (pages 15–18).
- The promise to create a welfare state and improved working conditions (pages 12–13).

Some of the ways in which the German Revolution was limited are:

- Ebert's government's over-reliance on the army and the *Freikorps* to crush revolutionary groups (pages 13–14).
- The failure to change the ownership of land and industry (pages 15–18).

Now you will need to reach a conclusion: do you see the things which remained the same as significant? Have the same groups retained the same amount of power? Or do the changes go deeper than that? Can the changes be defined as a 'revolution' as you initially defined it?

2 Weimar's Political Crisis

POINTS TO CONSIDER

In the summer of 1919 two crucial documents were drawn up that influenced the history of the Weimar Republic: the Weimar Constitution that was agreed by the German *Reichstag*, and the Treaty of Versailles which was imposed by the Allies. The importance of each document is examined in three ways:

- The key terms of the documents
- The issues of controversy
- Their significance in the history of Weimar Germany

Although the forces of democracy had successfully established the Weimar Republic, Germany remained in turmoil in the years 1919–23. This chapter concentrates on the extent of Weimar's political problems and the range of political threats it faced. It examines:

- The threats from the extreme left and the extreme right
- Uprisings of the extreme right
- Elections and governments – 'a republic without republicans'

The country also faced fundamental economic problems and these will be the focus of the next chapter.

Key dates

1919	February 6	National Assembly first meeting at Weimar
	June 28	Treaty of Versailles signed
	July 31	Weimar Constitution adopted by the National Constituent Assembly
	August 11	Weimar Constitution signed by President Ebert
1920	March	Kapp *putsch*
1921	August 26	Murder of Erzberger
1922	June 24	Murder of Rathenau
1923	Summer	The 'German October' in Saxony
	November	Munich Beer Hall *putsch*

Key question
What were the significant terms of the Weimar Constitution?

Key dates

National Assembly first meeting at Weimar: 6 February 1919

The Weimar Constitution was adopted by the National Assembly: 31 July 1919

Weimar Constitution signed by President Ebert: 11 August 1919

1 | The Weimar Constitution

The key terms of the Constitution

Back in November 1918, Ebert invited the liberal lawyer Hugo Preuss to draw up a new **constitution** for Germany and a draft was outlined by the time the National Assembly was established in February 1919. Preuss worked closely with a constitutional committee of 28 members over the next six months, though their discussions were deeply overshadowed by the dispute about the Treaty of Versailles (see pages 26–33).

The proposals for the new constitution were influenced by the long-established democratic ideas of Britain and the USA. Nevertheless, Germany's particular circumstances and traditions were not ignored as, for example, in the introduction of **proportional representation** and the creation of a **federal structure**. Eventually, on 31 July 1919, the *Reichstag* voted strongly in favour of the constitution (for: 262; against: 75) and on 11 August the president ratified it. The main features of the constitution are outlined below and in Figure 2.1 on page 22.

Key terms

Constitution
The principles and rules that govern a state. The Weimar Constitution is a good example. (Britain is often described as having an unwritten constitution. It is not drawn up in *one* document, but built on statutes, conventions and case law.)

Proportional representation
A system that allocates parliamentary seats in proportion to the total number of votes.

Federal structure
Where power and responsibilities are shared between central and regional governments, for example, the USA.

Definition
Germany was declared a 'democratic state', although it retained the title of 'Reich' (empire). It was a republic (all monarchies were ended). It had a federal structure with 17 *Länder* (regional states), e.g. Prussia, Bavaria, Saxony.

President
The people elected the president every seven years. He enjoyed considerable powers, such as:

- The right to dissolve the *Reichstag*.
- The appointment of the chancellor. (Although the president was not obliged, he tended to choose the chancellor as the leader of the largest party in the *Reichstag*. In order to form a workable coalition government, it was necessary to negotiate with the leaders of other political parties.)
- The Supreme Commander of the Armed Forces.
- The capacity to rule by decree at a time of national emergency (**Article 48**) and to oversee the *Reichstag*.

But this created a very complex relationship between the powers of the president and the *Reichstag*/chancellor.

Parliament
There were two houses in the German parliament:

- The *Reichstag* was the main representative assembly and law-making body of the parliament. It consisted of deputies elected every four years on the basis of a system of proportional representation. The PR system allocated members to parliament from the official list of political party candidates. They were distributed on the basis of one member for every 60,000 votes in an electoral district.

- The *Reichsrat* was the less important house in the parliament. It was made up of representatives from all of the 17 state regional governments (*Länder*), which all held local responsibilities such as education, police, etc. But the *Reichsrat* could only initiate or delay proposals, and the *Reichstag* could always overrule it.

Bill of Rights

The constitution also drew up a range of individual rights. It outlined broad freedoms, for example:

- personal liberty
- the right to free speech
- censorship was forbidden
- equality before the law of all Germans
- religious freedom and conscience (and no State Church was allowed).

In addition to this, the Bill of Rights provided a range of social rights, for example:

- welfare provision, e.g. for housing, the disabled, orphans
- protection of labour.

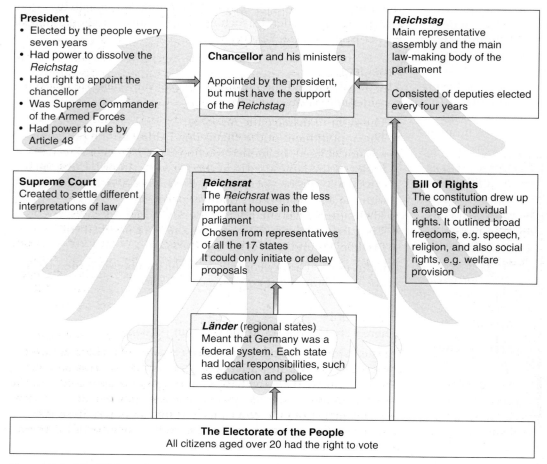

President
- Elected by the people every seven years
- Had power to dissolve the *Reichstag*
- Had right to appoint the chancellor
- Was Supreme Commander of the Armed Forces
- Had power to rule by Article 48

Chancellor and his ministers

Appointed by the president, but must have the support of the *Reichstag*

Reichstag
Main representative assembly and the main law-making body of the parliament

Consisted of deputies elected every four years

Supreme Court
Created to settle different interpretations of law

Reichsrat
The *Reichsrat* was the less important house in the parliament
Chosen from representatives of all the 17 states
It could only initiate or delay proposals

Bill of Rights
The constitution drew up a range of individual rights. It outlined broad freedoms, e.g. speech, religion, and also social rights, e.g. welfare provision

Länder (regional states)
Meant that Germany was a federal system. Each state had local responsibilities, such as education and police

The Electorate of the People
All citizens aged over 20 had the right to vote

Figure 2.1: The Weimar Constitution

Supreme Court

In order to settle different interpretations of law, a Supreme Court was created.

Key question
What were the arguments for and against the terms of Weimar Constitution?

The issues of controversy

Since the Weimar Republic lasted only 14 crisis-ridden years, it is hardly surprising that its written constitution has been the focus of considerable attention. Some historians have gone so far as to argue that the real causes of the collapse of the Republic and the success of Hitler and National Socialists can be found in its clauses. Such claims are based on three aspects of the constitution. These are:

- The introduction of proportional representation.
- The relationship between the president and the *Reichstag* and, in particular, the emergency powers available to the president under Article 48.
- The fact that the traditional institutions of Imperial Germany were allowed to continue.

Proportional representation

The introduction of proportional representation became the focus of criticism after 1945 because, it was argued, it had encouraged the formation of many new, small splinter parties, e.g. the Nazis. This made it more difficult to form and maintain governments.

In Weimar Germany it was virtually impossible for one party to form a majority government, and so coalitions were required – sometimes of three and even four parties. Furthermore, it was argued that all the negotiations and compromises involved in forming governments contributed to the political instability of Weimar. It is for these reasons that many critics of Weimar felt that a voting political system based upon two major parties, like in Britain (or the USA), which favoured the so-called **'first past the post'** model, would have created more political stability.

However, it is difficult to see how an alternative voting system, without proportional representation, could have made for a more effective parliamentary democracy in early twentieth century Germany. The main problem was the difficulty of creating coalitions amongst the main parties, which had been well established in the nineteenth century. The parties were meant to reflect the different political, religious and geographical views and so a system of PR was the only fair way. By comparison, the existence of all the splinter parties was a relatively minor issue.

There is also the view that, after the economic and political crisis of 1929–33 (see pages 101–4), proportional representation encouraged the emergence of political extremism. However, it now seems clear that the changes in the way people voted and the way they changed their allegiance from one party to another were just too volatile to be kept in check. It may also have been the case that a 'first past the post' system would have actually helped the rise of Nazism and communism.

Key term
'First past the post' An electoral system that simply requires the winner to gain one vote more than the second placed candidate. It is also referred to as the plurality system and does not require 50 per cent plus one votes. In a national election it tends to give the most successful party disproportionately more seats than its total vote merits.

The relationship between the president and the *Reichstag*

The relationship created between the *Reichstag* and the president in the Weimar Constitution was meant to have a fair system of checks and balances, but this was very complex.

It was intended to lessen the fears that an unrestricted parliament would become too powerful. Fear of an over-powerful parliament was strong on the right wing, and within liberal circles. It therefore aimed to create a presidency that could provide leadership 'above the parties' and limit the powers of the *Reichstag* (see page 21 and Figure 2.1 on page 22). The president's powers were seen as amounting to those of an *Ersatzkaiser*, a substitute emperor. When the power of the president is compared with the authority of the *Reichstag*, it seems that the attempt to prevent too much power being placed in the hands of one institution resulted in massive power being granted to another. As a result, there was uncertainty in constitutional matters from the start.

The framers of the constitution struggled to keep a balance of power between the president and the *Reichstag*. Was the ultimate source of authority in the democratic republic vested in the representative assembly of the people – the *Reichstag* – or in the popularly elected head of state – the president?

Matters were made more difficult by the powers conferred upon the president by Article 48. This Article provided the head of state with the authority to suspend civil rights in an emergency and restore law and order by the issue of presidential decrees. The intention was to create the means by which government could continue to function in a crisis. However, the effect was to create what the historian Gordon Craig referred to as 'a constitutional anomaly'. Such fears, which were actively expressed by some deputies in the constitutional debate of 1919, later assumed a particular importance during the crisis that brought

Table 2.1: Weimar *Reichstag* election results for 1919–32

	1919	1920	1924	1924	1928	1930	1932	1932
Total on register (in millions)	36.8	35.9	38.4	39.0	41.2	43.0	44.2	44.4
Size of poll (%)	83.0	79.2	74.4	78.8	75.6	82.0	84.1	80.6
Total No. of seats in *Reichstag*	423	459	472	493	491	577	608	584
NSDAP	–	–	32	14	12	107	230	196
DNVP	44	71	95	103	73	41	37	52
DVP	19	65	45	51	45	30	7	11
ZP/BVP	91	85	81	88	78	87	97	90
DDP	75	39	28	32	25	20	4	2
SPD	165	102	100	131	153	143	133	121
USPD	22	84						
KPD	–	4	62	45	54	77	89	100
Others	7	9	29	29	51	72	11	12

Hitler to power in 1933. However, it should be remembered that in the crisis of 1923 the presidential powers were used as intended and to very good effect.

The continuity of traditional institutions

Although the Weimar Constitution introduced a wide range of democratic rights and civil liberties, it made no provision to reform the old traditional institutions of Imperial Germany, such as:

- The civil service was well educated and professional, but tended to conform to the old-fashioned conservative values of Imperial Germany.
- The judiciary continued to enjoy its traditional independence under the Weimar Constitution, but the hearts of many judges did not lie with the Weimar Republic. Bluntly, they were biased and tended to favour the extreme right and condemn the extreme left. Only 28 out of 354 right-wing assassins were found guilty and punished, but 10 of the 22 left-wing assassins were sentenced to death.
- The army enjoyed great status and many of the generals were socially linked with the Prussian landowners. It sought to maintain its influence after 1918 and was generally not sympathetic to democratic Germany. It was the only real authority that had military capacity.
- Universities were very proud of their traditional status and generally more sympathetic to the old political ideas and rules.

In Weimar's difficult early years effective use was made of the established professional skills and educated institutions of the state. However, the result was that powerful conservative forces were able to exert great influence in the daily life of the Weimar Republic. This was at odds with the left wing's wishes to extend civil rights and to create a modern, democratic society. So, whilst the spirit of the Weimar Constitution was democratic and progressive, many of the institutions remained dedicated to the values of Imperial Germany.

Key question
Was the Weimar Constitution fatally flawed?

The significance of the Weimar Constitution

With hindsight, it is easy to highlight those parts of the Weimar Constitution that contributed to the ultimate collapse of the Republic. However, it should be remembered that the new constitution was a great improvement upon the previous undemocratic constitution of Imperial Germany and a very large majority voted in favour of it. Indeed, Weimar was initially seen as 'the most advanced democracy in the world'. What the Constitution could not control were the conditions and circumstances in which it had to operate. And the Weimar Republic had other more serious problems than just the Constitution, such as the Treaty of Versailles and its socio-economic problems. As Theodor Heuss, the first president of the German Federal Republic in 1949, said: 'Germany never conquered democracy for herself. Democracy came to Germany … in the wake of defeat.'

Therefore, it seems unrealistic to imagine that any piece of paper could have resolved all Germany's problems after 1918. The Weimar Constitution had weaknesses, but it was not fatally flawed – there were many more serious and fundamental problems within the Weimar Republic.

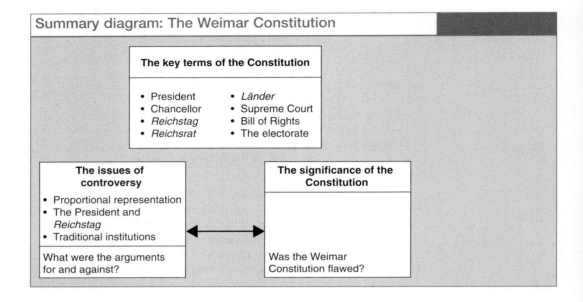

Summary diagram: The Weimar Constitution

The key terms of the Constitution

- President
- Chancellor
- *Reichstag*
- *Reichsrat*
- *Länder*
- Supreme Court
- Bill of Rights
- The electorate

The issues of controversy

- Proportional representation
- The President and *Reichstag*
- Traditional institutions

What were the arguments for and against?

The significance of the Constitution

Was the Weimar Constitution flawed?

2 | The Treaty of Versailles

For most Germans the Paris peace settlement of 1919 was a far more controversial issue than the new constitution. It had been generally assumed among German public opinion that the treaty would result in a fair peace. This was partly because defeat had never really been expected, even as late as the summer of 1918, and partly because it was generally assumed that President Wilson's Fourteen Points would lay the basis of the terms.

However, it soon became clear that the peace treaty would not be open for discussion with Germany's representatives. When the draft terms were presented in May 1919 there was national shock and outrage in Germany. In desperation, the first Weimar government led by Scheidemann resigned. The Allies were not prepared to negotiate, which obliged an embittered *Reichstag* finally to accept the Treaty of Versailles by 237 votes to 138 in June. This was because Germany simply did not have the military capacity to resist. And so, on 28 June 1919, the German representatives, led by Hermann Müller, signed the treaty in the Hall of Mirrors at Versailles near Paris.

The Treaty of Versailles was a compromise, but only in the sense that it was a compromise *between* the Allied powers. So the really decisive negotiations were between the so-called 'Big Three':

Key question
In what ways did the Allies differ over war aims?

Key date

The German government signed the Treaty of Versailles: 28 June 1919

Self-determination
The right of people of the same nation to decide their own form of government. In effect, it is the principle of each nation ruling itself. Wilson believed that the application of self-determination was integral to the Peace Settlement and it would lead to long-term peace.

League of Nations
The international body initiated by President Wilson to encourage disarmament and to prevent war.

Buffer state
The general idea of separating two rival countries by leaving a space between them. Clemenceau believed that the long-established Franco-German military aggression could be brought to an end by establishing an independent Rhineland state (though this was not implemented because Wilson saw it as against the principle of self-determination).

Key question
What were the significant terms of the Treaty of Versailles?

- Woodrow Wilson, President of the USA
- Georges Clemenceau, Prime Minister of France
- David Lloyd George, Prime Minister of Great Britain.

Woodrow Wilson

He has traditionally been portrayed as an idealist, as he had a strong religious framework. Initially, he had been an academic, but he was drawn into politics when he had campaigned against corruption. At first he had opposed American entry into the war. Once he declared war against Germany in April 1917 he drew up the Fourteen Points in the hope of creating a more just world. His main aims were:

- to bring about international disarmament
- to apply the principle of **self-determination**
- to create a **League of Nations** in order to maintain international peace.

Georges Clemenceau

He was an uncompromising French nationalist. He had been in his country twice when Germany had invaded and he was deeply influenced by the devastation from the war in northern France. He was motivated by revenge and he was determined to gain financial compensation and to satisfy France's security concerns. His main aims were:

- to annex the Rhineland and to create a '**buffer state**'
- to impose the major disarmament of Germany
- to impose heavy reparations in order to weaken Germany
- to get recompense from the damage of the war in order to finance re-building.

David Lloyd George

He may be seen as a pragmatist. He was keen to uphold British national interests and initially he played on the idea of revenge. However, he recognised that there would have to be compromise. In particular, he saw the need to restrain Clemenceau's revenge. His main aims were:

- to guarantee British military security – especially, to secure naval supremacy
- to keep communism at bay
- to limit French demands because he feared that excessively weakening Germany would have serious economic consequences for the European economy.

The terms of the Treaty of Versailles

The key terms of the Treaty of Versailles can be listed under the following headings: territorial arrangements, war guilt, reparations, disarmament and maintaining peace.

a) Territorial arrangements

- Eupen-Malmedy. Subject to **plebiscite**, the districts of Eupen and Malmedy to be handed over to Belgium.
- Alsace-Lorraine. Germany to return these provinces to France.
- North Schleswig. Subject to plebiscite, Germany to hand over the North Schleswig.
- West Prussia and Posen. Germany to surrender West Prussia and Posen, thus separating East Prussia from the main part of Germany (creating 'the Polish Corridor').
- Upper Silesia. A plebiscite was to be held in the province of Upper Silesia and as a result it was divided between Poland and Germany.
- Danzig. The German city and port of Danzig (Gdansk in Polish) was made an international 'free city' under the control of the League of Nations.
- Memel. The German port of Memel was also made an international 'free city' under the League.
- Austria. The reunification (*Anschluss*) of Germany with Austria was forbidden.
- Kiel Canal and rivers. All major rivers to be open for all nations and to be run by an international commission.
- Saar area (see 'Reparations' below).
- Rhineland (see 'Disarmament' below).
- Germany's colonies. All German colonies were distributed as '**mandates**', under control of countries supervised by the League, for example Britain took responsibility for German East Africa.

b) War guilt

Germany was forced to sign the War Guilt clause (Article 231) accepting blame for causing the war and therefore responsibility for all losses and damage:

> Germany accepts the responsibility of Germany and her allies for causing all the loss and damage to which the Allied governments and their peoples have been subjected as a result of the war.

c) Reparations

- Reparations sum to be fixed later by the IARC (Inter-Allied Reparations Commission). In 1921 the sum was fixed at £6600 million.
- Germany to make substantial payments in kind, e.g. coal.
- The Saar to be under the control of the League until 1935, when there was to be a plebiscite. Until then all coal production was to be given to France.

d) Disarmament

- Germany to abolish conscription and to reduce its army to 100,000. No tanks or big guns were allowed.
- Rhineland was to be demilitarised from the French frontier to a line 32 miles east of the Rhine. (The Rhineland remained part of Germany.)

Key terms

Plebiscite
A vote by the people on one specific issue – like a referendum.

Anschluss
Usually translated as 'union'. In the years 1919–38, it referred to the paragraph in the Treaty of Versailles that outlawed any political union between Germany and Austria, although the population was wholly German.

Mandates
The name given by the Allies to the system created in the Peace Settlement for the supervision of all the colonies of Germany (and Turkey) by the League of Nations.

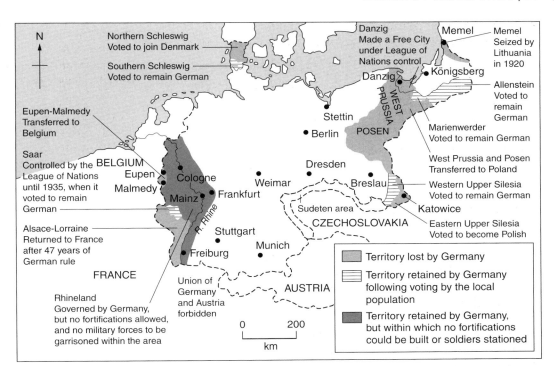

Figure 2.2: The terms of the Treaty of Versailles 1919

- Germany allowed no military aircraft.
- German navy limited to:
  - six battleships, six cruisers, 12 destroyers, 12 torpedo boats
  - no submarines were allowed.
  (The German fleet surrendered to Britain in 1918, but sank its own ships at Scapa Flow on 28 June 1919.)

e) Maintaining peace
The Treaty also set out the Covenant of the League of Nations, which included the aims and organisation of the League. Germany had to accept the League, but it was initially not allowed to join.

Table 2.2: German losses resulting from the Treaty of Versailles

Type of loss	Percentage of loss
Territory	13 per cent
Population	12 per cent (6.5 million)
Agricultural production	15 per cent
Iron-ore	48 per cent
Coal	15 per cent

The 'Diktat'

No other political issue produced such total agreement within Weimar Germany as the rejection and condemnation of the Treaty of Versailles. The Treaty's terms were seen as unfair and

Key question
Why did the Germans view the Treaty as unfair?

were simply described as a '*Diktat*'. Germany's main complaints were as follows:

- The Treaty was considered to be very different from President Wilson's Fourteen Points. Most obviously, many Germans found it impossible to understand how and why the guiding principle of self-determination was *not* applied in a number of cases. They viewed the following areas as 'German', but excluded from the new German state and placed under foreign rule:

    Austria
    Danzig
    Posen and West Prussia
    Memel
    Upper Silesia
    Sudetenland
    Saar.

    Similarly, the loss of Germany's colonies was not in line with the fifth of Wilson's Fourteen Points, which had called for 'an impartial adjustment of all colonial claims'. Instead, they were passed on to the care of the Allies as mandates.

- Germany found it impossible to accept the War Guilt clause (Article 231), which was the Allies' justification for demanding the payment of reparations. Most Germans argued that Germany could not be held solely responsible for the outbreak of the war. They were convinced that the war of 1914 had been fought for defensive reasons because their country had been threatened by 'encirclement' from the Allies in 1914.

- Germans considered the Allied demand for extensive reparations as totally unreasonable. Worryingly, the actual size of the reparations payment was not stated in the Treaty of Versailles – it was left to be decided at a later date by the IARC. From a German viewpoint this amounted to their being forced to sign a 'blank cheque'.

- The imposition of the disarmament clauses was seen as grossly unfair as Britain and France remained highly armed and made no future commitments to disarm. It seemed as if Germany had been **unilaterally disarmed**, whereas Wilson had spoken in favour of universal disarmament.

- Germany's treatment by the Allies was viewed as undignified and unworthy of a great power. For example, Germany was excluded from the League of Nations but, as part of the Treaty, was forced to accept the rules of its Covenant. This simply hardened the views of those Germans who saw the League as a tool of the Allies rather than as a genuine international organisation.

Altogether, the treaty was seen as a *Diktat*. The Allies maintained a military blockade on Germany until the Treaty was signed. This had significant human consequences such as increasing food shortages. Furthermore, the Allies threatened to take further military action if Germany did not co-operate.

Key terms

Diktat
A dictated peace. The Germans felt that the Treaty of Versailles was imposed without negotiation.

Unilateral disarmament
The disarmament of one party. Wilson pushed for general (universal) disarmament after the war, but France and Britain were more suspicious. As a result only Germany had to disarm.

A cartoon drawn in July 1919 from the German newspaper *Kladderatsch*. It portrays Georges Clemenceau (the French Prime Minister) as a vampire sucking the blood and life from the innocent German maiden.

Key question
To what extent was the Treaty of Versailles motivated by anti-German feeling?

Versailles: a more balanced view

In the years 1919–45, most Germans regarded the Treaty of Versailles as a *Diktat*. In Britain, too, there developed a growing sympathy for Germany's position. However, this was not the case in France, where the Treaty was generally condemned as being too lenient. It was only after the Second World War that a more balanced view of the Treaty of Versailles emerged in Europe. As a result, recent historians have tended to look upon the peacemakers of 1919 in a more sympathetic light. Earlier German criticisms of the Treaty are no longer as readily accepted as they once were.

Of course, at the Paris peace conferences Allied statesmen were motivated by their own national self-interests, and the representatives of France and Britain were keen to achieve these at the expense of Germany. However, it is now recognised that it was the situation created by the war that shaped the terms of the Treaty and not just anti-German feeling. The aims and objectives of the various Allies differed and achieving agreement was made more difficult by the complicated circumstances of the time. It should be remembered that the Paris peace settlement was not solely concerned with Germany, so Austria-Hungary, Bulgaria and Turkey were forced to sign separate treaties. In addition, numerous other problems had to be dealt with. For example, Britain had national interests to look after in the Middle East as a result of the collapse of the Turkish Empire. At the same time the Allies were concerned by the threat of Soviet Russia and were motivated by a common desire to contain the Bolshevik menace.

In the end, the Treaty of Versailles was a compromise. It was not based on Wilson's Fourteen Points as most Germans thought it would be, but equally it was not nearly so severe as certain sections of Allied opinion had demanded. It should be borne in mind that:

- Clemenceau, the French representative, was forced to give way over most of his country's more extreme demands, such as the creation of an independent Rhineland and the **annexation** of the Saar.
- The application of self-determination was not nearly so unfair as many Germans believed:
  - Alsace-Lorraine would have voted to return to France anyway, as it had been French before 1871.
  - Plebiscites were held in Schleswig, Silesia and parts of Prussia to decide their future.
  - Danzig's status under the League was the result of Woodrow Wilson's promise to provide 'Poland with access to the sea'.
  - The eastern frontier provinces of Posen and West Prussia were rather more mixed in ethnic make-up than Germans were prepared to admit (in these provinces Germans predominated in the towns, whereas the Poles did so in the countryside – which made it very difficult to draw a clear frontier line).
  - Austria and Sudetenland had never been part of Germany before 1918, anyway.
- Germany was not physically occupied during the war and, as a result, the real damage was suffered on foreign soil, e.g. France and Belgium.
- In comparison the Treaty of Versailles appeared relatively moderate to the severity of the terms imposed by the Germans on the Russians at the Treaty of Brest-Litovsk in 1918, which annexed large areas of Poland and the Baltic states.

Annexation
Taking over of another country against its will.

Key term

The significance of the Treaty of Versailles

The historical significance of the Treaty of Versailles goes well beyond the debate over its fairness. It raises the important issue of its impact upon the Weimar Republic and whether it acted as a serious handicap to the establishment of long-term political stability in Germany.

The economic consequences of reparations were undoubtedly a genuine concern. The English economist, Keynes, feared in 1919 that the reparations would fundamentally weaken the economy of Germany with consequences for the whole of Europe. However, Germany's economic potential was still considerable. It had potentially by far the strongest economy in Europe and still had extensive industry and resources. As will be seen later (pages 48–51), the Republic's economic problems cannot be blamed on the burden of reparations alone. And it should also be remembered that by 1932 Germany actually received more in loans under the Dawes Plan (see pages 71–2) than it paid in reparations.

It is not really possible to maintain that the Treaty had weakened Germany politically. In some respects, Germany in

Key question
Did the Treaty of Versailles fundamentally weaken Weimar Germany?

1919 was in a stronger position than in 1914. The great empires of Russia, Austria-Hungary and Turkey had gone, creating a power vacuum in central and eastern Europe that could not be filled at least in the short term by a weak and isolated Soviet Russia or by any other state. In such a situation, cautious diplomacy might have led to the establishment of German power and influence at the heart of Europe.

However, on another level, the Treaty might be considered more to blame because, in the minds of many Germans, it was regarded as the real cause of the country's problems and they really believed that it was totally unfair. In the war German public opinion had been strongly shaped by nationalist propaganda and then deeply shocked by the defeat. Both the Armistice and Versailles were closely linked to the 'stab in the back' myth that the German Army had not really lost the First World War in 1918 (see page 5). It may have been a myth, but it was a very powerful one.

As a result, although the war had been pursued by Imperial Germany, it was the new democracy of Weimar that was forced to take the responsibility and the blame for the First World War. Therefore, Weimar democracy was deeply weakened by Versailles, which fuelled the propaganda of the Republic's opponents over the years. Even for sympathetic democrats like Hugo Preuss, Versailles only served to disillusion many into thinking that the gains of the revolution were being undone: '... the German Republic was born out of its terrible defeat ... The criminal madness of the Versailles *Diktat* was a shameless blow in the face to such hopes based on international law and political common sense'. In this way the Treaty of Versailles contributed to the internal political and economic difficulties that evolved in Germany after 1919.

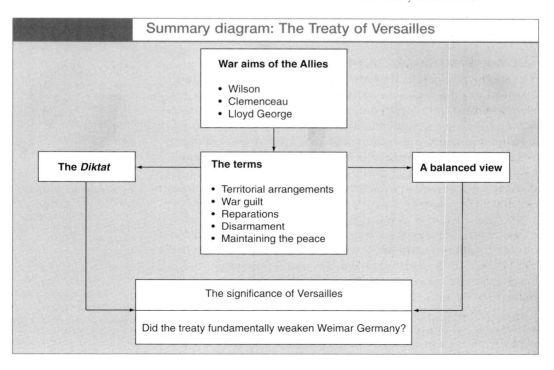

Summary diagram: The Treaty of Versailles

War aims of the Allies

- Wilson
- Clemenceau
- Lloyd George

The Diktat

The terms

- Territorial arrangements
- War guilt
- Reparations
- Disarmament
- Maintaining the peace

A balanced view

The significance of Versailles

Did the treaty fundamentally weaken Weimar Germany?

3 | The Threat from the Extreme Left

After the German revolution of 1918–19 the left-wing movement (see pages 6–14) at first remained in a state of confusion:

- The moderate socialists of the SPD were committed to parliamentary democracy.
- The Communists (the KPD) pressed for a workers' revolution.
- The USPD stood for the creation of a radical socialist society, but within a democratic framework.

This situation became clearer when, in 1920, the USPD disbanded and its members joined either the KPD or the SPD. So, from that time there were two left-wing alternative parties, but with fundamental differences.

The KPD believed that the establishment of parliamentary democracy fell a long way short of its real aims. It wanted the revolution to proceed on **Marxist** lines with the creation of a one-party communist state and the major restructuring of Germany both socially and economically. As a result of the 1917 Russian Revolution, many German communists were encouraged by the political unrest to believe that international revolution would spread throughout Europe.

The KPD's opposition to the Republic was nothing less than a complete rejection of the Weimar system. It was not prepared to be part of the democratic opposition or to work within the parliamentary system to bring about desired changes. The differences between the moderate and extreme left were so basic that there was no chance of political co-operation between them, let alone a coming together into one socialist movement. The extreme left was totally committed to a very different vision of German politics and society, whereas the moderate left was one of the pillars of Weimar democracy.

KPD opposition

The KPD was indeed a reasonable political force in the years 1919–23. It enjoyed the support of 10–15 per cent of the electorate and there were continuous revolutionary disturbances – protests, strikes and uprisings (see Table 2.3, page 35). However, all these actions by the extreme left gave the impression that Germany was really facing a Bolshevik-inspired '**Red Threat**'. Consequently, as a result of right-wing propaganda, many Germans began to have exaggerated fears about the possibility of impending revolution.

Looking back, it is clear that the extreme left posed much less of a threat to Weimar than was believed at the time. So, despite all the disturbances, the revolutionary left was never really likely to be able to seize political power. The main reasons lie in a combination of their own weaknesses and the effective resistance of the Weimar governments:

- Bad co-ordination. Even during the chaos and uncertainty of 1923, the activities of the extreme left proved incapable of mounting a unified attack on Weimar democracy.

Key question
How serious was the opposition of the extreme left to the Weimar Republic?

Key terms

Marxism
The political ideology of Karl Marx. His two major books, *Communist Manifesto* and *Capital*, outline his beliefs that the working classes will overthrow the industrial classes by revolution and create a classless society.

Red Threat
A 'Red' was a loose term used to describe anyone sympathetic to the left and it originated from the Bolshevik use of the red flag in Russia.

Key date

The revolutionary uprising in Germany in 1923 is often referred to as the German October, but it is a confusing term. Mass protests started before this, in the summer of 1923, though the uprising did not actually come to a head until October 1923 (which was also emotionally associated with the Bolshevik Revolution in Russia in October 1917)

- Poor leadership. The repression it suffered at the hands of the *Freikorps* removed some of its ablest and most spirited leaders, e.g. Liebknecht and Luxemburg (see page 9). The later leadership suffered from internal divisions and disagreements on tactics.
- Concessions. The Weimar governments played on the differences within the extreme left by making concessions which split it, e.g. over the Kapp *putsch* in March 1920 (see pages 39–40).
- Repression. The authorities systematically repressed the rebels with considerable brutality.

In the end, the extreme left was just not powerful enough to lead a revolution against the Weimar Republic.

Table 2.3: Major communist uprisings 1919–23

Date	Place	Action	Response
January 1919	Berlin	Spartacist uprising to seize power	Crushed by German army and *Freikorps*
March 1919	Bavaria	Creation of soviet republic	Crushed by the *Freikorps*
March 1920	Ruhr	Formation of the Ruhr Army by 50,000 workers to oppose the Kapp *putsch* (pages 39–41)	Crushed by German Army and *Freikorps*
March 1921	Merseburg and Halle	'March Operation'. Uprising of strikes organised by KPD	Put down by police
Summer 1923	Saxony	'German October' A wave of strikes and the creation of an SPD/KPD state government	Overthrown by German army

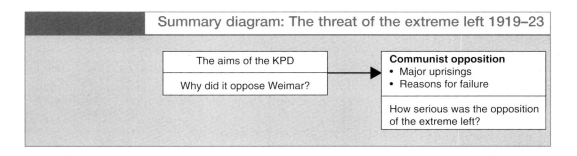

Summary diagram: The threat of the extreme left 1919–23

The aims of the KPD

Why did it oppose Weimar?

Communist opposition
- Major uprisings
- Reasons for failure

How serious was the opposition of the extreme left?

Key question
What did the extreme right stand for?

4 | The Threat from the Extreme Right

Opposition from the extreme right was very different both in its form and in its extent to that of the extreme left. On the right wing there was a very mixed collection of opponents to the Republic and their resistance found expression in different ways.

The extreme right in theory

In contrast to Marxist socialism, the extreme right did not really have an alternative organised ideology. It was simply drawn together by a growing belief in the following:

- Anti-democracy: it was united by its rejection of the Weimar system and its principles. It aimed to destroy the democratic constitution because it was seen as weak, which it believed had contributed to Germany's problems.
- **Anti-Marxism**: even more despised than democracy was the fear of communism. It was seen as a real threat to traditional values and the ownership of property and wealth – and when Russian communism was established, it reinforced the idea that communism was anti-German.
- **Authoritarianism**: the extreme right favoured the restoration of some authoritarian, dictatorial regime – though in the early 1920s there was no real consensus on what kind of strong government and leadership would be established.
- **Nationalism**: nationalism was at the core of the extreme right, but Germany's national pride had been deeply hurt by the events of 1918–19. Not surprisingly, from the time of the Treaty of Versailles, this conservative-nationalist response reinforced the ideas of the 'stab in the back' myth and the '**November criminals**'. The war, it was argued, had been lost not because of any military defeat suffered by the army, but as a result of the betrayal by unpatriotic forces within Germany. These were said to include pacifists, socialists, democrats and Jews. Right-wing politicians found a whole range of scapegoats to take the blame for German acceptance of the Armistice.

Worse still, these 'November criminals' had been prepared to overthrow the monarchy and establish a republic. Then, to add insult to injury, they had accepted the 'shameful peace' of Versailles. The extreme right accepted such interpretations, distorted as they were. They not only served to remove any responsibility from Imperial Germany, but also acted as a powerful stick with which to beat the new leaders of Weimar Germany.

Organisations of the extreme right

The extreme right appeared in various forms. It included a number of political parties and was also the driving force behind the activities of various paramilitary organisations.

DNVP

The DNVP (German National People's Party) was a coalition of nationalist-minded old imperial conservative parties and included such groups as the Fatherland Party and the Pan-German League. From the very start, it contained extremist and racist elements. Although it was still the party of landowners and industrialists, it had a broad appeal amongst some of the middle classes. It was by

Anti-Marxism
Opposition to the ideology of Karl Marx.

Authoritarianism
A broad term meaning government by strong non-democratic leadership.

Nationalism
Grew from the national spirit to unify Germany in the nineteenth century. Supported a strong policy to embrace all German-speakers in eastern Europe.

November criminals
Those who signed the November Armistice and a term of abuse to vilify all those who supported the democratic republic.

Key question
How did the extreme right manifest itself in different ways?

far the largest party in the *Reichstag* on the extreme right and was able to poll 15.1 per cent in the 1920 election.

Racist nationalism

The emergence of racist nationalism, or *völkisch* nationalism, was clearly apparent before 1914, but the effects of the war and its aftermath increased its attraction for many on the right. By the early 1920s there were probably about 70 relatively small splinter nationalist parties, which were also racist and anti-Semitic, e.g. the Nazi Party.

Bavaria became a particular haven for such groups, since the regional state government was sufficiently **reactionary** to tolerate them. One such group was the German Workers' Party, originally founded by Anton Drexler. Adolf Hitler joined the party in 1919 and within two years had become its leader. However, during the years 1919–24, regional and policy differences divided such groups and attempts to unify the nationalist right ended in failure. When, in 1923, Hitler and the Nazis attempted to organise an uprising with the Munich Beer Hall *putsch*, it ended in fiasco (see pages 41–3). It was not until the mid-1920s, when Hitler began to bring the different groups together under the leadership of the NSDAP, that a powerful political force was created.

Freikorps

The *Freikorps* that flourished in the post-war environment attracted the more brutal and ugly elements of German militarism. As a result of the demobilisation of the armed forces there were nearly 200 **paramilitary units** around Germany by 1919.

The *Freikorps* became a law unto themselves and they were employed by the government in a crucial role to suppress the threats from the extreme left. However, as the *Freikorps* was anti-republican and committed to the restoration of authoritarian rule, they had no respect for the Weimar governments. Their bloody actions became known as the '**White Terror**' and showed they were quite prepared to use acts of violence and murder to intimidate others.

Consul Organisation

From 1920 the Weimar governments tried to control the actions of the *Freikorps*, but a new threat emerged from the right wing in the form of political assassination. In the years 1919–22 there were 376 political murders – 22 by the left and 354 by the right. The most notorious terrorist gang was known as the 'Consul Organisation' because it was responsible for the assassination of a number of key republican politicians:

- Matthias Erzberger, Finance Minister 1919–21. Murdered because he was a Catholic and a member of the ZP and had signed the Armistice.

Key terms

Reactionary
Opposing change and supporting a return to traditional ways.

Paramilitary units
Informal non-legal military squads.

White Terror
The 'Whites' were seen as the opponents (in contrast to the Reds). The 'White Terror' refers to the suppression of the soviet republic in Bavaria in March 1919.

Key dates

The murder of Matthias Erzberger: 26 August 1921

The murder of Walter Rathenau: 24 June 1922

A cartoon drawn in 1919 by the German artist Grosz. He caricatures the stereotyped right-wing officer. The title, *The White General*, relates to the 'White Terror' in opposition to the Reds of the left-wing movement.

- Walther Rathenau, Foreign Minister, 1921–2 (who drew up the Rapallo treaty with USSR). Murdered because he was Jewish and was committed to democracy.
- Karl Gareis, leader of the USPD. Murdered on 9 June 1921 because he was a committed socialist.

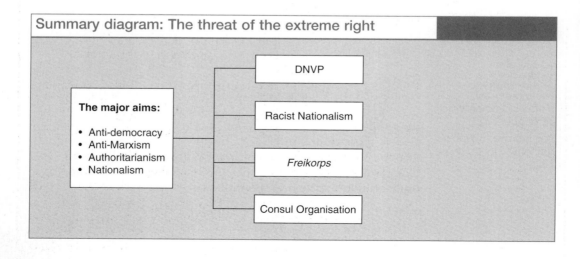

Summary diagram: The threat of the extreme right

The major aims:

- Anti-democracy
- Anti-Marxism
- Authoritarianism
- Nationalism

- DNVP
- Racist Nationalism
- *Freikorps*
- Consul Organisation

Key question
How significant was the Kapp *putsch*?

Key date

The Kapp *putsch*: March 1920

5 | Extreme Right Uprisings

The Kapp *putsch*

The *Freikorps* played a central role in the first attempt by the extreme right wing to seize power from the constitutional government. This was because by early 1920 there was considerable unease within the ranks of the *Freikorps* at the demands to reduce the size of the German army according to the terms of the Versailles Treaty.

When it was proposed to disband two brigades of the army, the Ehrhardt Marine Brigade and the Baltikum that were stationed in the Berlin area, Wolfgang Kapp (see profile below) and General Lüttwitz decided to exploit the situation. They encouraged 12,000 troops to march on Berlin and seize the main buildings of the capital virtually unopposed, where they installed a new government.

Significantly, the German army did not provide any resistance to this *putsch*. In spite of requests from Ebert and the Chancellor to put down the rebellious forces, the army was not prepared to become involved with either side. Although it did not join those involved in the *putsch*, it failed to support the legitimate government. General von Seeckt, the senior officer in the Defence Ministry, spoke for many colleagues when he declared:

> Troops do not fire on troops. So, you perhaps intend, Herr Minister, that a battle be fought before the Brandenburger Tor between troops that have fought side by side against a common enemy? When *Reichswehr* fires on *Reichswehr* all comradeship within the officers' corps will have vanished.

Profile: Wolfgang Kapp 1868–1922

1868	– Born in New York
1870	– Returned to Germany with his family
1886–1920	– Qualified as a doctor of law and then appointed as a Prussian civil servant in various posts
1917	– Helped to found the right-wing German Fatherland Party
1918	– Elected to the *Reichstag*
	– Opposed the abdication of Wilhelm II and remained committed to the restoration of the monarchy
1920	– Collaborated with Ehrhardt and Lüttwitz to launch the *putsch*. Briefly appointed chancellor by the leaders of the *putsch*. Fled to Sweden
1922	– Returned to Germany but died whilst awaiting trial

Really, only a few points stand out about Kapp. He has been described as 'a neurotic with delusions' or simply a 'crank' who represented the extreme nationalist-conservative views. He did not play any major part in politics of Imperial Germany until the war, when he was one of the founders of the German Fatherland Party. After the war he campaigned for the restoration of Kaiser Wilhelm, but his *putsch* was a fiasco. Interestingly, some of the men involved in his *putsch* had swastika symbols on their helmets.

The army's decision to put its own interests before its obligation to defend the government forced the latter to flee the capital and move to Stuttgart. However, the *putsch* collapsed. Before leaving Berlin, the SPD members of the government had called for a general strike, which soon paralysed the capital and quickly spread to the rest of the country. After four days, it was clear that Kapp and his government exerted no real authority and they fled the city.

The aftermath of the Kapp *putsch*

At first sight the collapse of the Kapp *putsch* could be viewed as a major success for the Weimar Republic. In the six days of crisis, it had retained the backing of the people of Berlin and had effectively withstood a major threat from the extreme right. However, what is significant is that the Kapp *putsch* had taken place at all. In this sense, the Kapp *putsch* highlights clearly the weakness of the Weimar Republic. The army's behaviour at the time of the *putsch* was typical of its right-wing attitudes and its lack of sympathy for the Republic. During the months after the *coup*, the government failed to confront this problem.

The army leadership had revealed its unreliability. Yet, amazingly, at the end of that very month Seeckt was appointed Chief of the Army Command (1920–6). He was appointed because he enjoyed the confidence of his fellow officers and ignored the fact that his support for the Republic was at best lukewarm. Under Seeckt's influence, the organisation of the army was remodelled and its status redefined:

- He imposed very strict military discipline and recruited new troops, increasingly at the expense of the *Freikorps*.
- However, he was determined to uphold the independence of the army. He believed it held a privileged position that placed it beyond direct government control. For example, he turned a blind eye to the Versailles disarmament clauses in order to increase the size of the army with more modern weapons.

Many within its ranks believed that the army served some higher purpose to the nation as a whole. It had the right to intervene as it saw fit without regard to its obligations to the Republic. All this suggests that the aftermath of the Kapp *putsch*, the Ebert-Groener Pact (see pages 9–10) and the Constitution's failure to reform the structures of army had made it a '**state within a state**'.

The judiciary also continued with the old political values that had not changed since imperial times. It enjoyed the advantage of maintaining its independence from the Weimar Constitution, but it questioned the legal rights of the new republic and reached some dubious and obviously biased decisions. Those involved in the *putsch* of 1920 never felt the full rigour of the law:

- Kapp died awaiting trial.
- Lüttwitz was granted early retirement.
- Only one of the 705 prosecuted was actually found guilty and sentenced to five years' imprisonment.

State within a state
A situation where the authority and government of the state are threatened by a rival power base.

Key term

Over the years 1919–22 it was clear that the judges were biased and their hearts did not lie with the Weimar Republic:

- Out of the 354 right-wing assassins only 28 were found guilty and punished (but no-one was executed).
- Of the 22 left-wing assassins 10 were sentenced to death.

The Munich Beer Hall *putsch*

Key question
Who were the plotters and why did they fail?

Key date

The Munich Beer Hall *putsch*:
8–9 November 1923

Although the Munich Beer Hall *putsch* was one of the threats faced by the young republic in the year 1923, the event is also a crucial part of the rise of Hitler and the Nazis. So the details of the events also relate to Chapter 5 on pages 89–91.

In the short term it should be noted that the government of the State of Bavaria was under the control of the ultra-conservative Gustav von Kahr, who blamed most of Germany's problems on the national government in Berlin. Like Hitler, he wished to destroy the republican regime, although his long-term aim was the creation of an independent Bavaria. By October 1923 General von Lossow, the Army's commander in Bavaria, had fallen under von Kahr's spell and had even begun to disobey orders from the Defence Minister from Berlin. And so it was both of these ultra-conservatives who plotted with Hitler and the Nazis to 'March on Berlin'.

A cartoon of 1924 derides the judiciary after the trial of Hitler and Ludendorff. The judge simply says 'High treason? Rubbish! The worst we can charge them with is breaking by-laws about entertaining in public.'

Table 2.4: The plotters in the Munich Beer Hall *putsch*

Name	Position	Background/attitude	Involvement
Erich von Ludendorff	Retired general	Took part in Kapp *putsch*. Opposed to democracy (see also pages 39–41)	Collaborated with Hitler and supported the *putsch* on 8–9 November
Gustav von Kahr	Leader of the Bavarian state government	Deeply anti-democratic and sympathetic to many of the right-wing extremists. Committed to the restoration of the monarchy in an independent Bavaria	Planned with Hitler and Lossow to seize power, but became wary. Forced to co-operate with his rally on 8 November, though did not support the *putsch* on 9 November
Otto von Lossow	Commander of the Bavarian section of the German army	Despised Weimar democracy and supported authoritarian rule. Very conservative	Planned with Hitler and Kahr to seize power, but became wary. Forced to co-operate in the rally on 8 November, though did not support the *putsch* on 9 November
Adolf Hitler	Leader of the Nazi Party	Extremist: anti-Semitic, anti-democratic and anti-communist. Backed by the Nazi SA	Planned and wholly committed to seize power. Forced the hands of Kahr and Lossow and carried on with the *putsch* on 9 November
Hans von Seeckt	General. Chief of the Army Command, 1920–6	Unsympathetic to democracy and keen to preserve the interests of the army, but suspicious of Hitler and the Nazis (see page 43)	Initially ambiguous attitude in early November. But in the crisis he used his powers to command the armed forces to resist the *putsch*

By the first week of November 1923, Kahr and Lossow, fearing failure, decided to abandon the plan. However, Hitler was not so cautious and preferred to press on rather than lose the opportunity. On 8 November Hitler, together with his Nazi supporters, stormed into and took control of a large rally, which von Kahr was addressing in one of Munich's beer halls, and declared a 'national revolution'. Under pressure, Kahr and Lossow co-operated and agreed to proceed with the uprising, but in reality they had lost their nerve when Seeckt used his powers to command the armed forces to resist the *putsch*. So when, on the next day, the Nazis attempted to take Munich they had insufficient support and the Bavarian police easily crushed the *putsch*. Fourteen Nazis were killed and Hitler himself was arrested on a charge of treason.

Key question
How significant was the Munich Beer Hall *putsch*?

The aftermath of the Munich Beer Hall *putsch*

On one level the inglorious result of the Nazi *putsch* was encouraging for Weimar democracy. It withstood a dangerous threat in what was a difficult year. Most significantly, Seeckt and the army did not throw in their lot with the Nazis – which upset Hitler so much that he described him as a 'lackey of the Weimar Republic'. However, once again it was the dealings of the judiciary that raised so much concern:

- Hitler was sentenced to a mere five years (the minimum stipulation for treason). His imprisonment at Landsberg provided quite reasonable conditions and he was released after less than 10 months.
- Ludendorff was acquitted on the grounds that although he had been present at the time of the *putsch*, he was there 'by accident'!

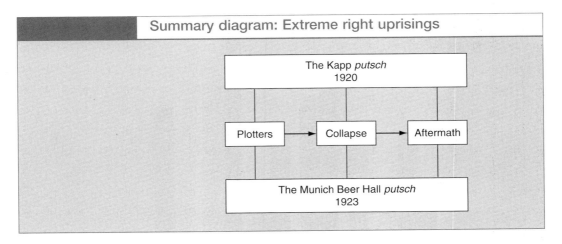

Summary diagram: Extreme right uprisings

The Kapp *putsch* 1920

Plotters → Collapse → Aftermath

The Munich Beer Hall *putsch* 1923

6 | Weimar Democracy: A Republic Without Republicans

Key question
What was the greatest threat to Weimar democracy?

The optimism of the first election of the Republic (see pages 17–18) gave way to concerns in the election of June 1920. The results can be seen in Figure 2.3 and they raise several key points:

- The combined support for the three main democratic parties declined dramatically:
  - 1919: 76.1 per cent
  - 1920: 48.0 per cent

  (The figures do not include the DVP under the leadership of Stresemann which voted against the Weimar Constitution at first, but became committed to the Republic from 1921.)
- The performance for each of the pro-democratic parties was as follows:
  - the SPD declined sharply from 37.9 to 21.7 per cent
  - the DDP declined catastrophically from 18.5 to 8.3 per cent
  - the ZP dropped down slightly from 19.75 to 18.0 per cent.
- The support for the extreme left and right increased, especially the DNVP:
  - the DNVP increased from 10.3 to 15.1 per cent
  - the KPD/USPD increased from 7.6 to 20.0 per cent.

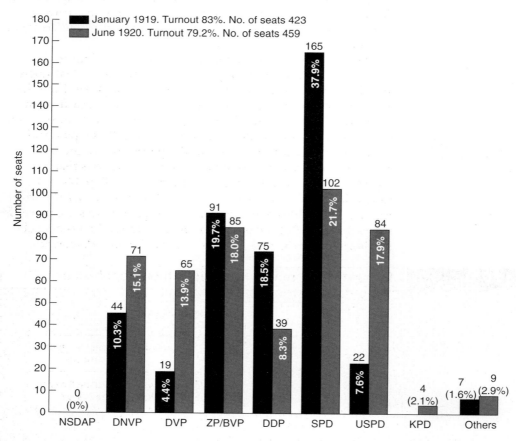

Figure 2.3: *Reichstag* election results 1919–20. (See major political parties on page 16.)

Weimar governments

The Weimar Republic not only faced overt opposition from both the extremes but also its democratic supporters struggled with the practical problem of creating and maintaining workable government coalitions. In the four years 1919–23 Weimar had six governments – the longest of which lasted just 18 months (see Table 2.5).

Table 2.5: Governments of the Weimar Republic 1919–23

Period in office	Chancellor	Make-up of the coalition
1919	Philipp Scheidemann	SPD, ZP, DDP
1919–20	Gustav Bauer	SPD, ZP, DDP
1920	Hermann Müller	SPD, Centre, DDP
1920–1	Konstantin Fehrenbach	ZP, DDP, DVP
1921–2	Joseph Wirth	SPD, DDP, ZP
1922–3	Wilhelm Cuno	ZP, DDP, DVP

Conclusion

The success of the democratic parties in the *Reichstag* elections of January 1919 at first disguised some of Weimar's fundamental problems in its political structure. But opposition to the Republic ranged from indifference to brutal violence and, as early as 1920, democratic support for Weimar began to switch to the extremes. This is shown by the results of the first election after the Treaty of Versailles.

The extent of the opposition from the extreme right to democracy was not always appreciated. Instead, President Ebert and the Weimar governments overestimated the threat from the extreme left and they came to rely on the forces of reaction for justice and law and order. This was partly because the conservative forces successfully exploited the image of the left as a powerful threat. So, in many respects, it was the persistence of the old attitudes in the major traditional national institutions that represented the greatest long-term threat to the Republic. The violent forces of counter-revolution, as shown by the *putsches* of Kapp and Hitler, were too weak and disorganised to seize power in the early years. But the danger of the extreme right was actually insidious; it was the real growing threat to Weimar democracy.

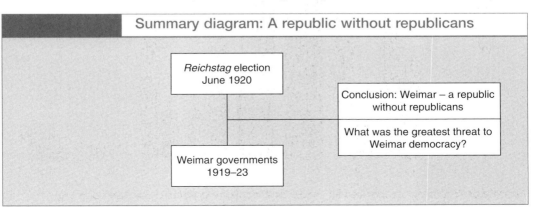

Summary diagram: A republic without republicans

Study Guide: AS Question

In the style of Edexcel

Which was the greater threat to the Weimar Republic in the years 1919–23 – the extreme left or the extreme right?   (30 marks)

Exam tips

The cross-references are intended to take you straight to the material that will help you to answer the question.

You should adopt an evaluative (comparative) approach to this question. High marks depend on your addressing and answering the question actually set. So, the real skill is to bear in mind the key phrase 'the greater threat' all the time. In order to do this, you should show:

- Some of the strengths of the extreme left that threatened Weimar – not only its direct opposition (e.g. the Spartacist uprising), but also its influence (e.g. the Party membership). Bear in mind the extent of its limitations as well (pages 34–5).
- Some of the strengths of the extreme right that threatened Weimar – not only its direct opposition (e.g. the Kapp uprising), but also its influence (e.g. influence of vested interests). Bear in mind the extent of its limitations as well (pages 35–6).
- A thoughtful conclusion is essential. It would be useful to point out that the position of the 'threats' was not constant, as they changed over time in the years 1919–23, and that the left and right threats were played out within an atmosphere which also weakened the Republic. For example, the political controversy of the Treaty of Versailles and of the Weimar constitution; and also the effects of the deteriorating economic situation (see Chapter 3). You need to justify your choice between the two threats in this context.

---

3 The Great Inflation

Key dates

1921	May	IARC (Inter-Allied Reparations Commission) fixed reparations at £6600 million (132 billion gold marks)
1923	January	Franco-Belgian occupation of the Ruhr Passive resistance proclaimed
	Jan–Nov	Period of hyper-inflation
	August	Stresemann made chancellor of Germany
	Aug–Nov	Stresemann's 100 days
	December	Introduction of *Rentenmark*
1924	April	Dawes Plan proposed and accepted

1 | The Economic Background

Key question
How did the First World War weaken the German economy?

In the 20 years before the First World War the German economy grew immensely. By 1914 it had become arguably the most powerful economy on the continent and it was in a position to compete with Britain's supremacy. These strengths were based upon:

- extensive natural resources, e.g. coal, iron-ore
- an advanced and well-developed industrial base, e.g. engineering, chemicals, electrics
- a well-educated population, with special technical skills
- an advanced banking system.

Total war
Involves the whole population in war – economically and militarily.

However, the result of four years of **total war** seriously dislocated the German economy. So, although the economy still had many

natural strengths and great potential, by 1919 it faced
fundamental economic problems. The most notable of these were:

- The loss of resources from such territories as the Saar, Alsace-
  Lorraine and Silesia which, for example, resulted in a 16 per
  cent decline in coal production, 13 per cent decline in arable
  agricultural land and 48 per cent loss of iron-ore.
- The cost of paying reparations (set at £6600 million in 1921).
- The growing increase in prices. Between 1914 and 1918 the real
  value of the mark fell, dropping from 4.2 to 8.9 against the US
  dollar, while the prices of basic goods increased nearly four-fold.
- The increase in national debt to 144,000 million marks by 1919
  compared with 5000 million marks in 1914.

Significantly, Germany had always depended on its ability to export
to achieve economic growth. However, between 1914 and 1918 world
trade had collapsed and even after 1919 it remained very sluggish.

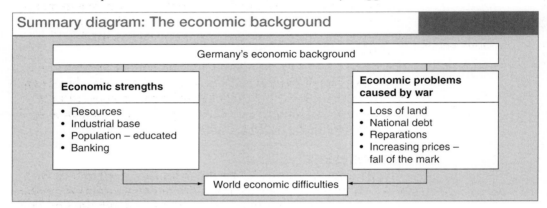

Summary diagram: The economic background

2 | The Causes of the German Inflation

Germany's growing economic problems came to a head in 1923
when prices soared and money values spiralled down. This is
often referred to as **hyper-inflation**. However, the crises of that
year blinded many to the fact that prices had been rising since
the early months of the war. Many Germans glibly assumed it was
a result of the Treaty of Versailles and particularly the reparations.
Still more unthinking explanations simply blamed it on the
financial greed and corruption of the Jews.

However, with hindsight it is clear that the fundamental cause of
the inflation was the huge increase in the amount of paper money
in circulation, resulting from the government's printing more and
more notes to pay off the interest on its massive debts. The causes
of the Great Inflation can be divided into three phases:

- long term – the military demands of the First World War
  (1914–18) led to an enormous increase in financial costs
- medium term – the costs of introducing social reforms and
  welfare and the pressure to satisfy the demands for reparation
  payments from 1921
- short term – the French occupation of the Ruhr in 1923
  resulted in crisis and the government of Cuno encouraged a
  policy of '**passive resistance**'.

Key question
Why did Germany
suffer hyper-inflation?

Hyper-inflation
Hyper-inflation is
unusual. In
Germany in 1923, it
meant that prices
spiralled out of
control because the
government
increased the
amount of money
being printed. As a
result, it displaced
the whole economy.

Passive resistance
Refusal to work with
occupying forces.

Key terms

War bonds
In order to raise more money to pay for the war, Imperial Germany encouraged people to invest into government funds in the belief they were helping to finance the war and their savings would be secure.

Balanced budget
A financial programme in which a government does not spend more than it raises in revenue.

Long term

Not surprisingly, Germany had made no financial provision for a long drawn-out war. However, despite the increasing cost of the war, the Kaiser's government had decided, for political reasons, against increases in taxation. Instead, it had borrowed massive sums by selling '**war bonds**' to the public. When this proved insufficient from 1916, it simply allowed the national debt to grow bigger and bigger.

The result of Imperial Germany's financial policies was that by the end of 1918 only 16 per cent of war expenditure had been raised from taxation – 84 per cent had been borrowed.

Another factor was that the war years had seen almost full employment. This was because the economy had concentrated on the supply of military weapons. But, since production was necessarily military based, it did not satisfy the requirements of the civilian consumers. Consequently, the high demand for, and the shortage of consumer goods began to push prices up.

Victory would doubtless have allowed Imperial Germany to settle its debts by claiming reparations from the Allies, but defeat meant the reverse. The Weimar Republic had to cope with the massive costs of war. By 1919, Germany's finances were described by Volker Berghahn as 'an unholy mess'.

Medium term

The government of the Weimar Republic (like any government with a large deficit) could control inflation only by narrowing the gap between the government's income and expenditure through:

- increasing taxation in order to raises its income
- cutting government spending in order to reduce its expenditure.

However, in view of Germany's domestic situation neither of these options was particularly attractive, as both would alienate the people and cause political and social difficulties, such as increased unemployment and industrial decline.

Consequently, from 1919 the Weimar government guided by Erzberger, the Finance Minister (see page 37), extensively increased taxation on profits, wealth and income. However, it decided not to go so far as aiming to **balance the budget**. It decided to adopt a policy of deficit financing in the belief that it would:

- maintain the demand for goods and, thereby, create work
- overcome the problems of demobilising millions of returning troops
- cover the cost of public spending on an extensive welfare state, e.g. health insurance, housing and benefits for the disabled and orphans
- reduce the real value of the national debt.

Deficit financing means planning to increase the nation's debt by reducing taxation in order to give the people more money to spend and so increase the demand for goods and thereby create work. The government believed that this would enable Germany to overcome the problems of demobilisation – a booming economy would ensure there were plenty of jobs for the returning soldiers and sailors – and also reduce the real value of the national debt. Unfortunately, an essential part of this policy was to allow inflation to continue.

The reparations issue should be seen as only a contributory factor to the inflation. It was certainly not the primary cause. Nevertheless, the sum drawn up by the Reparations Commission added to the economic burden facing the Weimar government because the reparation payments had to be in **hard currency**, like dollars and gold (not inflated German marks). In order to pay their reparations, the Weimar governments proceeded to print larger quantities of marks and sell them to obtain the stronger currencies of other countries. This was not a solution. It was merely a short-term measure that had serious consequences. The mark went into sharp decline and inflation climbed even higher (see Table 3.1).

Hard currency

Key term

A currency that the market considers to be strong because its value does not depreciate. In the 1920s the hardest currency was the US dollar.

The IARC (Inter-Allied Reparations Commission) fixed the sum for reparations at £6600 million (132 billion gold marks): May 1921

Key date

Table 3.1: The Great Inflation: exchange rate and wholesale prices

The Great Inflation	Exchange rate of German marks against the dollar	Wholesale price index. The index is created from a scale of prices starting with 1 for 1914
1914 July	4.2	1
1919 January	8.9	2
1920 January	14.0	4
1920 July	39.5	N/A
1921 January	64.9	14
1921 July	76.7	N/A
1922 January	191.8	37
1922 July	493.2	100
1923 January	17,792	2,785
1923 July	353,412	74,787
1923 September	98,860,000	23,949,000
1923 November	200,000,000,000	750,000,000,000

Short term

Germany had already been allowed to postpone several instalments of her reparations payments in early 1922, but an attempt to resolve the crisis on an international level by calling the Genoa Economic Conference was ill fated. When, in July 1922, the German government made another request for a 'holiday' from making reparations payments, the final stage of the country's inflationary crisis set in.

The French government, at this time led by Raymond Poincaré, suspected German intentions and was determined to secure what was seen as France's rightful claims. Therefore, when in December 1922 the Reparations Commission declared Germany to be in default, Poincaré ordered French and Belgian troops to occupy the Ruhr, the industrial heartland of Germany. In the next few months the inflationary spiral ran out of control – hyper-inflation.

Key dates

'Passive resistance' in Ruhr against French and Belgian soldiers: 13 January 1923

Period of hyper-inflation: January–November 1923

The government, led by Wilhelm Cuno, embarked on a policy of 'passive resistance' and in a way the invasion did help to unite the German people. It urged the workers to go on strike and refuse to co-operate with the French authorities, although it also promised to carry on paying their wages. At the same time, the government was unable to collect taxes from the Ruhr area and the French prevented the delivery of coal to the rest of Germany, thus forcing the necessary stocks of fuel to be imported.

In this situation, the government's finances collapsed and the mark fell to worthless levels. By autumn 1923, it cost more to print a bank note than the note was worth and the *Reichsbank* was forced to use newspaper presses to produce sufficient money. The German currency ceased to have any real value and the German people had to resort to barter (see Table 3.2).

Table 3.2: Prices in the Great Inflation (in German marks)

Items for sale in	1913	Summer 1923	November 1923
1 kg of bread	0.29	1,200	428,000,000,000
1 egg	0.08	5,000	80,000,000,000
1 kg of butter	2.70	26,000	6,000,000,000,000
1 kg of beef	1.75	18,800	5,600,000,000,000
1 pair of shoes	12.00	1,000,000	32,000,000,000,000

Conclusion

The fundamental cause of the German Inflation is to be found in the mismanagement of Germany's finances from 1914 onwards. Certainly, the inflationary spiral did not increase at an even rate and there were short periods, as in the spring of 1920 and the winter of 1920–1, when it did actually slacken. However, at no time was there willingness by the various German governments to bring spending and borrowing back within reasonable limits.

Until the end of 1918 the cost of waging war was the excuse, but in the immediate post-war period the high levels of debt were allowed to continue. It has been argued by some that the inflation remained quite modest in the years 1914–22 and perhaps acceptable in view of all the various difficulties facing the new government. However, the payment of reparations from 1921 simply added to an already desperate situation and the government found it more convenient to print money than to tackle the basic problems facing the economy.

By the end of 1922 hyper-inflation had set in. Cuno's government made no effort to deal with the situation. Indeed, it could be said that Cuno deliberately exacerbated the economic crisis and played on the nationalist fervour brought by the popular decision to encourage 'passive resistance'. It was only in August 1923 when the German economy was on the verge of complete collapse that a new coalition government was formed under Gustav Stresemann. He found the will to introduce an economic policy, which was aimed at controlling the amount of money in circulation.

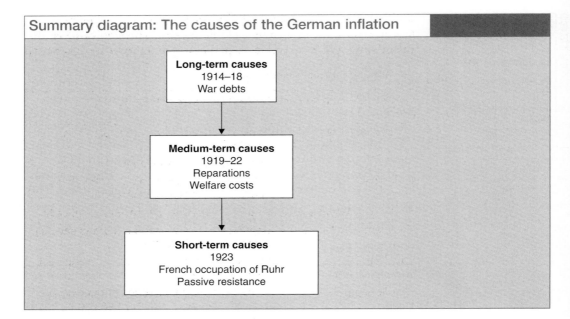

Summary diagram: The causes of the German inflation

Long-term causes
1914–18
War debts

Medium-term causes
1919–22
Reparations
Welfare costs

Short-term causes
1923
French occupation of Ruhr
Passive resistance

3 | The Consequences of the Great Inflation

Key question
Why did some
Germans lose and
some win?

It has been claimed that the worst consequence of the inflation
was the damage done to the German middle class. Stresemann
himself said as much in 1927. Later on in the 1930s it was
generally assumed that the reason a large proportion of the
middle class voted for the Nazis was because of their economic
sufferings in 1923. In the light of recent historical research, such
assumptions have come to be questioned and a much more
complex interpretation has emerged about the impact of the
inflation on the whole of society.

The key to understanding who gained and who lost during the
period of the hyper-inflation lies in considering each individual's
savings and their amount of debt. However, it was not always clearly
linked to class differences. So what did this mean in practice?

The real winners were those sections of the community who
were able to pay off their debts, mortgages and loans with inflated
and worthless money. This obviously worked to the advantage of
such groups as businessmen and homeowners, which included
members of the middle class. Those who recognised the situation
for what it was exploited it by making massive gains from buying
up property from those financially desperate. Some businessmen
profited from the situation by borrowing cheaply and investing in
new industrial enterprises. Amongst these, one of the most
notorious examples was Hugo Stinnes who, by the end of 1923,
controlled 20 per cent of German industry.

At the other extreme, were those who depended on their
savings. Any German who had money invested in bank accounts
with interest rates found their real value had eroded. Most
famously, millions who had bought and invested in war bonds
now could not get their money back. The bonds were worth

nothing. Those living on fixed incomes, such as pensioners, found themselves in a similar plight. Their savings quickly lost value, since any increase was wiped out by inflation (see Table 3.3).

Table 3.3: Financial winners and losers

Financial winners and losers	Explanation of gains or losses
Mortgage holders	Borrowed money was easily paid off in valueless money
Savers	Money invested was eroded
Exporters	Sales to foreign countries was attractive because of the rate of exchange
Those on fixed incomes	Income declined in real terms dramatically
Recipients of welfare	Depended on charity or state. Payments fell behind the inflation rate
Long-term renters/landlords	Income was fixed in the long term and so it declined in real terms
The German State	Large parts of the government debt were paid off in valueless money (but not reparations)

Key question
Who were the winners and the losers?

The human consequences

The material impact of the hyper-inflation has recently been the subject of considerable historical research in Germany and, as a result, our understanding of this period has been greatly increased and many previous conclusions have been revised. However, you should remember that the following discussion of the effects of the hyper-inflation on whole classes deals with broad categories, e.g. region and age, rather than individual examples. Two people from the same social class could be affected in very different ways depending on their individual circumstances.

Peasants

In the countryside the peasants coped reasonably well as food remained in demand. They depended less on money for the provision of the necessities of life because they were more self-sufficient.

Key term

Mittelstand
Can be translated as 'the middle class', but in German society it tends to represent the lower middle classes, e.g. shopkeepers, craft workers and clerks. Traditionally independent and self-reliant but increasingly felt squeezed out between the power and influence of big business and industrial labour.

Mittelstand

Shopkeepers and craftsmen also seem to have done reasonably good business, especially if they were prepared to exploit the demands of the market.

Industrial workers

Workers' real wages and standard of living improved until 1922. It was in the chaos of 1923 that, when the trade unions were unable to negotiate wage settlements for their members, wages could not keep pace with the rate of inflation and a very real decline took place. However, as they had fewer savings, they lost proportionally less than those living on saved income. Unemployment did go up to 4.1 per cent in 1923, but it was still at a relatively low level.

Children playing with blocks of worthless banknotes in 1923.

Civil servants

The fate of public employees is probably the most difficult to analyse. Their income fell sharply in the years 1914–20, but they made real gains in 1921–2. They suffered again in the chaos of 1923 because they depended on fixed salaries, which fell in value before the end of each month. They tended to gain – if they were buying a property on a mortgage – but many had been attracted to buy the war bonds and so lost out.

Retired

The old generally suffered badly because they depended on fixed pensions and savings.

Businessmen

Generally, they did well because they bought up property with worthless money and they paid off mortgages. They also benefited if they made sales to foreign countries, as the rate of exchange was very attractive.

Key question
In what other ways did the Great Inflation affect people's lives?

Other social effects

By merely listing the financial statistics of the Great Inflation, there is a danger of overlooking the very real human dimension. As early as February 1923 the health minister delivered a speech to the *Reichstag*:

> … It is understandable that under such unhygienic circumstances, health levels are deteriorating ever more seriously. While the figures for the Reich as a whole are not yet available, we do have a preliminary mortality rate for towns with 100,000 or more inhabitants. After having fallen in 1920–1, it has climbed again for the year 1921–2, rising from 12.6 to 13.4 per thousand inhabitants … thus, oedema [an unpleasant medical condition which occurs when water accumulates in parts of the body] is reappearing, this so-called war dropsy, which is a consequence of a bad and overly watery diet. There are increases in stomach disorders and food poisoning, which are the result of eating spoiled foods. There are complaints of the appearance of scurvy, which is a consequence of an unbalanced and improper diet. From various parts of the Reich, reports are coming in about an increase in suicides … More and more often one finds 'old age' and 'weakness' listed in the official records as the cause of death; these are equivalent to death through hunger.

Even more telling than the health minister's description about Germany's declining health were the possible effects on behaviour, as people began to resort to desperate solutions:

- a decline in law and order
- an increase in crime
- a decline in 'morality', for example, more prostitution
- a growth in suicides
- an increase in prejudice and a tendency to find scapegoats, e.g. Jews.

It has often been suggested that such social problems contributed to people's lack of faith in the republican system. The connection is difficult to prove, as it is not easy to assess the importance of morality and religious codes in past societies. However, it would be foolish to dismiss out of hand their effects upon German society and its traditional set of values. At the very least, the loss of some old values led to increased tensions. Even more significantly, when another crisis developed at the end of the decade, the people's confidence in the ability of Weimar to maintain social stability was eventually lost. In that sense the inflation of 1923 was not the reason for the Weimar Republic's decline, but it caused psychological damage that continued to affect the Republic in future years.

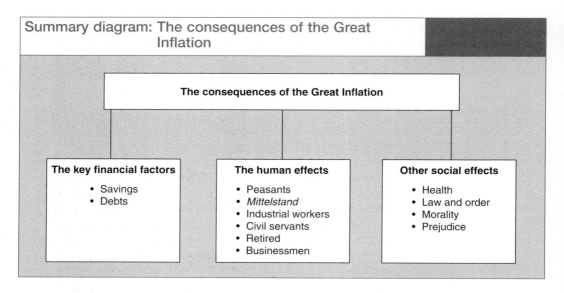

4 | Stresemann's 100 Days

In the summer of 1923 the problems facing the Weimar Republic came to a head and it seemed close to collapse:

- the German currency had collapsed and hyper-inflation had set in
- French and Belgian troops were occupying the Ruhr
- the German government had no clear policy on the occupation, except for 'passive resistance'
- there were various left-wing political disturbances across the country – in Saxony the creation of an SPD/KPD regional state government resulted in an attempted Communist uprising (pages 34–5)
- the ultra-conservative state government in Bavaria was defying the national government. This finally resulted in the Munich Beer Hall *putsch* (see pages 41–3).

Yet, only a few months later a semblance of calm and normality returned. The Weimar Republic's remarkable survival illustrates the telling comment of the historian Peukert that even 1923 shows 'there are no entirely hopeless situations in history'.

Stresemann's achievements

It is important to recognise that, during the summer of 1923, things had just been allowed to slide under the chancellor, Cuno. Nevertheless, the appointment of Gustav Stresemann as chancellor in August 1923 resulted in the emergence of a politician who was actually prepared to take difficult political decisions. Stresemann led a broad coalition of DVP, DDP, ZP and SPD and aimed to resolve Germany's economic plight and also tackle the problem of her weakness internationally.

Key question
How did the Weimar Republic survive the crisis of 1923?

Stresemann appointed chancellor: 12 August 1923

Stresemann's 100 days of leadership: August–November 1923

Key dates

Within a few weeks Stresemann made a series of crucial initiatives:

- First, in September, he called off the 'passive resistance' in the Ruhr and promised to resume the payment of reparations. He needed to conciliate the French in order to evoke some sympathy for Germany's economic and international position.
- Under the guidance of Finance Minister, Hans Luther, the government's expenditure was sharply cut in order to reduce the deficit. Over 700,000 public employees were sacked.
- He appointed the leading financial expert Hjalmar Schacht to oversee the introduction of a new German currency. In December 1923 the trillions of old German marks were replaced and a new stable currency, the *Rentenmark*, was established.
- He evoked some sympathy from the Allies for Germany by the 'miracle of the *Rentenmark*' and his conciliatory policy. He therefore asked the Allies to hold an international conference to consider Germany's economic plight and, as a result, the Dawes Committee was established. Its report, the Dawes Plan, was published in April 1924. It did not reduce the overall reparations bill, but for the first five years it fixed the payments in accordance with Germany's ability to pay (see pages 71–2).
- The extremists of the left and the right were defeated (pages 35 and 41–3).

Key dates

Introduction of the *Rentenmark*: December 1923

Dawes Plan proposed and accepted: April 1924

The survival of Weimar

Although Stresemann's resolute action in tackling the problems might help to explain why the years of crisis came to an end, on its own it does not help us to understand why the Weimar Republic was able to come through. The Republic's survival in 1923 was in marked contrast to its collapse 10 years later when challenged by the Nazis.

Why, then, did the Republic not collapse during the crisis-ridden months before Stresemann's emergence on the political scene? This is a difficult question to answer, though the following factors provide clues:

- Popular anger was directed more towards the French and the Allies than towards the Weimar Republic itself.
- Despite the effects of inflation, workers did not suffer to the same extent as they did during the mass unemployment of the 1930s.
- Similarly, employers tended to show less hostility to the Republic in its early years than they did in the early 1930s at the start of the depression.
- Some businessmen did very well out of the inflation, which made them tolerant of the Republic.

If these suggestions about public attitudes towards the Republic are correct, then it seems that, although there was distress and disillusionment in 1923, hostility to the Weimar Republic had not yet reached unbearable levels – as it was to do 10 years later.

Moreover, in 1923 there was no obvious political alternative to Weimar. The extreme left had not really recovered from its divisions and suppression in the years 1918–21 and, in its isolated position, it did not enjoy enough support to overthrow Weimar.

The extreme right, too, was not yet strong enough. It was similarly divided and had no clear plans. The failure of the Kapp *putsch* served as a clear warning of the dangers of taking hasty action and was possibly the reason why the army made no move in 1923.

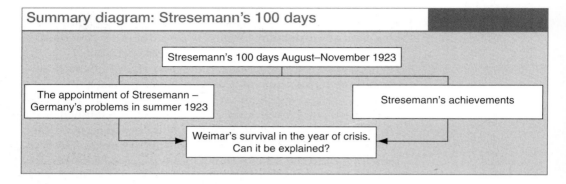

Summary diagram: Stresemann's 100 days

Stresemann's 100 days August–November 1923

The appointment of Stresemann – Germany's problems in summer 1923

Stresemann's achievements

Weimar's survival in the year of crisis. Can it be explained?

Study Guide: AS Question

In the style of Edexcel

How far were the consequences of the German inflation disastrous for Germany in 1923?   (30 marks)

> **Exam tips**
>
> *The cross-references are intended to take you straight to the material that will help you to answer the question.*
>
> In this question you should evaluate the extent to which the Great Inflation was a disaster for Germany by:
>
> - assessing the financial factors, supported with some examples as evidence (pages 52–3)
> - assessing the effects on the different social classes and how some won and some lost, supported with some examples as evidence (pages 53–5)
> - distinguishing between the mild inflation of 1919–22 and the hyper-inflation of 1923 (pages 48–51)
> - setting the economic situation faced by Germany within the context of political threats from both the left and right, and assessing the extent of damage caused by these threats (Chapter 2, pages 34–6).
>
> Finally, round off your answer by offering an opinion on how far you agree or disagree with the view that the German inflation was disastrous for Germany in 1923.

4 Weimar: The Years of Stability 1924–9

POINTS TO CONSIDER
It is generally held that after the turmoil of the early 1920s, the years 1924–9 were a time of recovery and stability in German history. Indeed, it is quite common to refer to the period as the 'golden twenties'. The purpose of this chapter is to consider the accuracy of this picture by examining the following themes:

- The extent of Germany's economic recovery
- The political stability of the Weimar Republic
- The achievements of Gustav Stresemann
- The developments in German foreign policy
- The development of Weimar culture

Key dates

1922		Treaty of Rapallo
1923–9		Stresemann as Foreign Minister
1924	April	Dawes Plan
1925		Hindenburg elected president
	October	Locarno Conference
1928	May	Müller's Grand Coalition
		Hugenberg leader of DNVP
	August	Kellogg-Briand Pact
1929		Young Plan
	October	Death of Stresemann
	October	Wall Street Crash

1 | The Economic Recovery

It is often claimed that after the hyper-inflation, the introduction of the new currency – the *Rentenmark* – and the measures brought about by the Dawes Plan ushered in five years of economic growth and affluence. Certainly the period stands out between the economic chaos of 1922–3 and the **Great Depression** of 1929–33. So, for many Germans looking back from the end of the 1920s, it seemed as if Germany had made a remarkable recovery.

The strengths of the German economy

In spite of the loss of resources as a result of the Treaty of Versailles, heavy industry was able to recover reasonably quickly and, by 1928, production levels reached those of 1913. This was

Key term

Great Depression
The severe economic crisis of 1929–33 that was marked by mass unemployment, falling prices and a lack of spending.

Key question
What were the strengths of the German economy?

the result of the use of more efficient methods of production, particularly in coal-mining and steel manufacture, and also because of increased investment. Foreign bankers were particularly attracted by Germany's high interest rates.

At the same time, German industry had the advantage of being able to lower costs because of the growing number of **cartels**, which had better purchasing power than smaller industries. For example, *IG Farben*, the chemicals giant, became the largest manufacturing enterprise in Europe, whilst *Vereinigte Stahlwerke* combined the coal, iron and steel interests of Germany's great industrial companies and grew to control nearly half of all production.

Between 1925 and 1929, German exports rose by 40 per cent. Such economic progress brought social benefits as well. Hourly wage rates rose every year from 1924 to 1930 and by as much as 5–10 per cent in 1927 and 1928.

The benefits of social welfare

There were striking improvements in the provision of social welfare. The principles of a welfare state were written into the new Weimar Constitution and in the early 1920s generous pensions and sickness benefits were introduced. In 1927, a compulsory unemployment insurance covering 17 million workers was created, which was the largest scheme of its kind in the world. In addition, state subsidies were provided for the construction of local amenities such as parks, schools, sports facilities and especially council housing. All these developments, alongside the more obvious signs of wealth, such as the increasing number of cars and the growth of the cinema industry, supported the view that the Weimar Republic's economy was enjoying boom conditions. However, it should be borne in mind that the social costs had economic implications (see page 62).

The weaknesses in the German economy

From the statistics for 1924–9 it is easy to get an impression of the 'golden twenties'. However, the actual rate of German recovery was unclear:

- There was economic growth, but it was uneven, and in 1926 production actually declined. In overseas trade, the value of **imports** always exceeded that of **exports**.
- Unemployment never fell below 1.3 million in this period. And even before the effects of America's financial crisis began to be felt (see pages 101–2), the number of unemployed workers averaged 1.9 million in 1929.
- In agriculture, grain production was still only three-quarters of its 1913 figure and farmers, many of whom were in debt, faced falling incomes. By the late 1920s, income per head in agriculture was 44 per cent below the national average.

Fundamental economic problems

The economic indicators listed above suggest that the German economy had fundamental problems in this period and it is

Key terms

Cartel
An arrangement between businesses to control the market by exercising a joint monopoly.

Imports
Goods purchased from foreign countries.

Exports
Goods sold to foreign countries.

Key question
Was the Weimar economy fundamentally weak?

therefore important to appreciate the broader view by looking at the following points.

- World economic conditions did not favour Germany. Traditionally, Germany had relied on its ability to export to achieve economic growth, but world trade did not return to pre-war levels. German exports were hindered by protective **tariffs** in many parts of the world. By the Treaty of Versailles, they were also handicapped by the loss of valuable resources in territories, such as Alsace-Lorraine and Silesia (see page 28). German agriculture also found itself in difficulties because of world economic conditions. The fall in world prices from the mid-1920s placed a great strain on farmers, who made up one-third of the German population. Support in the form of government financial aid and tariffs could only partially help to reduce the problems. Most significantly, this decline in income reduced the spending power of a large section of the population and this led to a fall in demand within the economy as a whole.

- The changing balance of the population. From the mid-1920s, there were more school leavers because of the high pre-war birth rate. The available workforce increased from 32.4 million in 1925 to 33.4 million in 1931. This meant that, even without a recession, there was always likely to be an increase in unemployment in Germany.

- Savings and investment discouraged. Savers had lost a great deal of money in the Great Inflation and, after 1924, there was less enthusiasm to invest money again. As a result, the German economy came to rely on investors from abroad, for example the USA, who were attracted by the prospect of higher interest rates than those in their own countries. Germany's economic well-being became ever more dependent on foreign investment.

- Government finances raised concern. Although the government succeeded in balancing the budget in 1924, from 1925 it continually ran into debt. It continued to spend increasing sums of money and by 1928 public expenditure had reached 26 per cent of **GNP**, which was double the pre-war figure. The government found it difficult to encourage domestic savings and was forced to rely more and more on international loans. Such a situation did not provide the basis for solid future economic growth.

Key terms

Tariffs
Taxes levied by an importing nation on foreign goods coming in, and paid by the importers.

GNP
Gross national product is the total value of all goods and services in a nation's economy (including income derived from assets abroad).

Depression
An economic downturn marked by mass unemployment, falling prices and a lack of spending. The world depression lasted from 1929 to 1933. In the USA it was called the Great Depression.

Key question
Was the Weimar economy a fundamentally sick economy?

Conclusion
It has been suggested that the problems faced by the German economy before the world **depression** of 1929 were disguised by the flood of foreign capital and exacerbated by the development of an extensive social welfare system. The German economy could be seen to be in a poor state because:

- The foreign loans made it liable to suffer from any problems that arose in the world economy.
- The investment was too low to encourage growth.

- The cost of the welfare state could only be met by the government taking on increasing debts.
- The agricultural sector faced serious problems from mid-1920s and various sectors of the German economy had actually started to slow down from 1927.

Whether this amounts to the view of Weimar Germany as 'an abnormal, in fact a sick economy' (Borchardt) remains controversial, and it is hard to assess what might have happened without a world economic crisis. However, it is interesting that Stresemann wrote in 1928, 'Germany is dancing on a volcano. If the short-term credits are called in, a large section of our economy would collapse.' So, on balance, the evidence suggests that by 1929 the Weimar Republic was facing serious difficulties and was already heading for a major economic downturn of its own making.

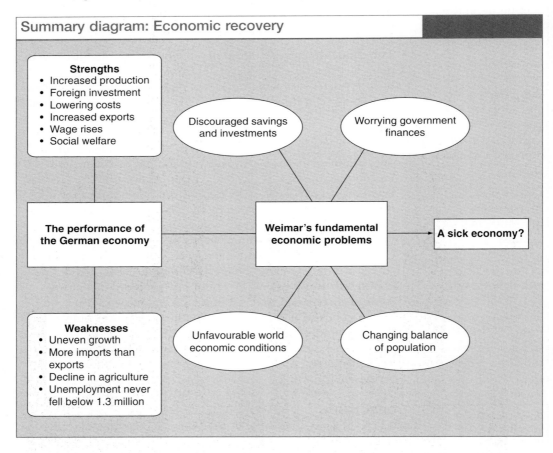

Summary diagram: Economic recovery

Strengths
- Increased production
- Foreign investment
- Lowering costs
- Increased exports
- Wage rises
- Social welfare

Discouraged savings and investments

Worrying government finances

The performance of the German economy

Weimar's fundamental economic problems

A sick economy?

Weaknesses
- Uneven growth
- More imports than exports
- Decline in agriculture
- Unemployment never fell below 1.3 million

Unfavourable world economic conditions

Changing balance of population

Key question
Did the general election results of 1924–8 reflect optimism about the Weimar Republic among German voters?

2 | Political Stability

The election results during the middle years of the Weimar Republic gave grounds for cautious optimism about its survival (see Figure 4.1). The extremist parties of both left and right lost ground and altogether they polled less than 30 per cent of the votes cast. The DNVP peaked in December 1924 with 103 seats (20.5 per cent of the vote) and fell back to 73 (14.2 per cent) in May 1928. The Nazis lost ground in both elections and were

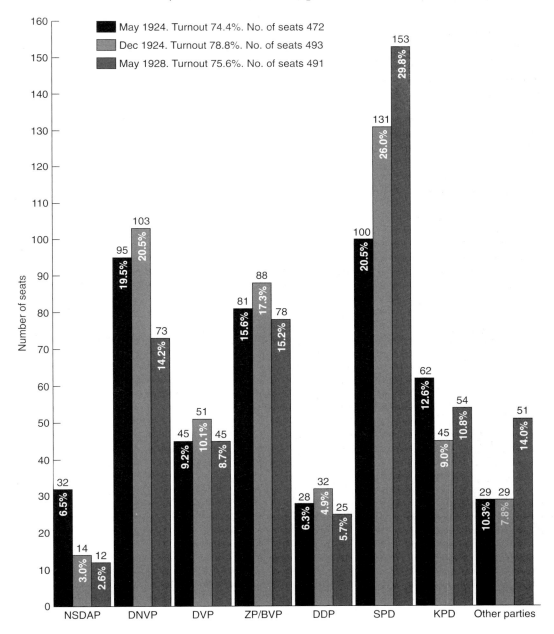

Figure 4.1: Weimar *Reichstag* election results 1924 and 1928. (See major political parties on page 16.)

reduced to only 12 seats (2.6 per cent) by 1928. The KPD, although recovering slightly by 1928 with 54 seats (10.6 per cent), remained below their performance of May 1924 and well below the combined votes gained by the KPD and USPD in June 1920 (see page 51).

In comparison, the parties sympathetic to the Republic maintained their share of the vote and the SPD made substantial gains, winning 153 seats (29.8 per cent) in 1928. As a result, following the 1928 election, a 'Grand Coalition' of the SPD, DDP, DVP and Centre was formed under Hermann Müller, the leader of the SPD. It enjoyed the support of over 60 per cent of the *Reichstag* and it seemed as if democracy was at last beginning to emerge in Weimar politics.

Müller's 'Grand Coalition' formed: May 1928

Coalition politics

The election of 1928 must not be regarded as typical in Weimar history, and it should not hide the continuing basic weaknesses of the German parliamentary system. These included not only the problems created by proportional representation (see page 23), but also the ongoing difficulty of creating and maintaining coalitions from the various parties. In such a situation each party tended to put its own self-interests before those of the government.

Key question
Why did the political parties find it so difficult to co-operate?

The parties tended to reflect their traditional interests; in particular, religion and class. So attempts to widen their appeal made little progress. As a result, the differences between the main parties meant that opportunities to form workable coalitions were very limited.

- There was never any possibility of a coalition including both the SPD and the DNVP because the former believed in parliamentary democracy whereas the latter fundamentally rejected the Weimar political system.
- The Communists, KPD, remained totally isolated.
- A right–centre coalition of Centre, DVP and DNVP created a situation in which the parties tended to agree on domestic issues, but disagree on foreign affairs.
- On the other hand, a broad coalition of SPD, DDP, DVP and Centre meant that these parties agreed on foreign policy, but differed on domestic issues.
- A minority government of the political centre, including the DDP, DVP and Centre, could only exist by seeking support from either the left or right. It was impossible to create a coalition with a parliamentary majority that could also consistently agree on both domestic and foreign policy.

In this situation, there was very little chance of democratic government being able to establish any lasting political stability. Of the seven governments between 1923 and 1930 (see Table 4.1), only two had majorities and the longest survived for just 21 months. In fact, the only reason governments lasted as long as they did was that the opposition parties were also unable or unwilling to unite. More often than not, it was conflicts within the parties that formed the coalition governments that led them to collapse.

Table 4.1: Governments of the Weimar Republic, 1923–30

Period in office	Chancellor	Make-up of the coalition
1923–4	Wilhelm Marx	Centre, DDP, DVP
1924–5	Wilhelm Marx	Centre, DDP, DVP
1925	Hans Luther	Centre, DVP, DNVP
1926	Hans Luther	Centre, DDP, DVP
1926	Wilhelm Marx	Centre, DDP, DVP
1927–8	Wilhelm Marx	Centre, DDP, DNVP
1928–30	Hermann Müller	SPD, DDP, Centre, DVP

The responsibility of the parties

The attitude of the Weimar Republic's political parties towards parliamentary government was irresponsible. This may well have been a legacy from the imperial years. In that time the parties had expressed their own narrow interests in the knowledge that it was the Kaiser who ultimately decided policy. However, in the 1920s, parliamentary democracy needed the political parties to show a more responsible attitude towards government. The evidence suggests that no such attitude existed, even in the most stable period of the Republic's history.

The SPD

Until 1932 the SPD remained the largest party in the *Reichstag*. However, although firm in its support of the Republic, the Party was divided between its desire to uphold the interests of the working class and its commitment to democracy. Some members, and especially those connected with the trade unions, feared that joining coalitions with other parties would lead to a weakening of their principles. Others, the more moderate, wanted to participate in government in order to influence it. At the same time, the Party was hindered by the old argument between those committed to a more extreme left-wing socialist programme and those who favoured moderate, gradual reform.

As a result, during the middle years of the Republic the SPD did not join any of the fragile government coalitions. This obviously weakened the power base of those democratic coalitions from 1924 to 1928. The SPD remained the strongest party during those years: although it was committed to democracy, it was not prepared to take on the responsibility of government until 1928.

The Centre Party

It therefore fell to the Centre Party to provide real political leadership in Weimar politics. The ZP electoral support was solid and the party participated in all the coalition governments from 1919 to 1932 by taking ministerial posts. However, its support did not increase because its appeal was restricted to traditional Catholic areas. Further, its social and economic policies which aimed at bridging the gaps between the classes led to internal quarrels.

Key question
In what ways was the SPD divided?

Key question
What were the limitations of the Centre Party?

In the early years, such differences had been put to one side under the strong left-wing leadership of Matthias Erzberger and Josef Wirth. However, during the 1920s, the Party moved decisively to the right and the divisions within the Party widened. In 1928, the leadership eventually passed to Ludwig Kaas and Heinrich Brüning, who appealed more to the conservative partners of the coalition than to the liberal or social democratic elements. This was a worrying sign both for the future of the Centre Party and for Germany herself.

The liberal parties

The position of the German liberals was not a really strong one. The DDP and DVP joined in all the coalition governments of this period and in Gustav Stresemann, the leader of the DVP, they possessed the Republic's only really capable statesman. However, this hid some worrying trends. Their share of the vote, though constant in the mid-1920s, had nearly halved since 1919–20, when it had been between 22 and 23 per cent.

The reasons for the liberals' eventual collapse after 1930 were already established beforehand. This decline was largely a result of the divisions within both parties. The DDP lacked clear leadership and its membership was involved in internal bickering over policy. The DVP was also divided and, despite Stresemann's efforts to bring unity to the Party, this remained a source of conflict. It is not really surprising that moves to bring about some kind of united liberal party came to nothing. As a result, German liberalism failed to gain popular support; and after 1929 its position declined dramatically.

Key question
What were the weaknesses of the German liberal parties?

The DNVP

One promising feature of German party politics came unexpectedly from the conservative DNVP. Since 1919, the DNVP had been totally opposed to the Republic and it had refused to take part in government. In electoral terms, it had enjoyed considerable success, and in December 1924, gained 103 seats (20.5 per cent). However, as the Republic began to recover after the 1923 crisis (see pages 56–8), it became increasingly clear that the DNVP's hopes of restoring a more right-wing government were diminishing. The continuous opposition policy meant that the Party had no real power and achieved nothing. Some influential groups within the DNVP realised that if they were to have any influence on government policy, then the Party had to be prepared to participate in government. As a result, in 1925 and 1927, the DNVP joined government coalitions. This more sympathetic attitude towards the Weimar Republic was an encouraging development.

However, that more conciliatory policy was not popular with all groups within the Party. When, in the 1928 election, the DNVP vote fell by a quarter, the more extreme right wing asserted its influence. Significantly, it elected Alfred Hugenberg, an extreme nationalist, as the new leader (see profile, page 67). Hugenberg was Germany's greatest media tycoon: and he owned 150

Key question
How did the DNVP change over time?

Hugenberg leader of DNVP: October 1928

Key date

newspapers, a publishing house; and had interests in the film industry. He utterly rejected the idea of a republic based on parliamentary democracy. He now used all his resources to promote his political message. The DNVP reverted to a programme of total opposition to the Republic and refused to be involved in government. A year later, his party was working closely with the Nazis against the Young Plan (see pages 75 and 105).

President Hindenburg

Key question
Was the appointment of Hindenburg as president a good or a bad sign for Weimar democracy?

Key date
Hindenburg elected president: 1925

A presidential election was due in 1925. It was assumed that President Friedrich Ebert would be re-elected. So his unexpected death in February 1925 created political problems. There was no clear successor in the first round of the election and so a second round was held. It did result in the choice of Hindenburg as president, but the figures clearly underlined the divisions in German society (see Table 4.2).

Table 4.2: Presidential election, second round, 26 April 1925

Candidate (party)	Votes (millions)	Percentage
Paul von Hindenburg (DNVP)	14.6	48
Wilhelm Marx (ZP)	13.7	45
Ernst Thälmann (KPD)	1.9	6

Profile: Alfred Hugenberg 1865–1951

1865 – Born in Hanover
1894 – Founder of Pan-German League
1920 – *Reichstag* DNVP deputy
1927 – Leader of UFA, Germany's largest film company
1928 – Leader of DNVP until 1933
1929 – Campaigned against the Young Plan
1931 – Joined the Harzburg Front against Brüning (see page 111)
1933 – Member of Hitler's coalition, but replaced in June
1945 – Survived (his fortune intact) and was not prosecuted by the Allies
1951 – Death

Hugenburg was a civil servant, banker, industrialist and 'press baron' who was strongly against the Weimar Republic from the outset. He played a crucial role in forming the DNVP in 1919 from various established conservative-nationalist parties and he became a member of the *Reichstag* in 1920. Most significantly, he used his massive fortune to finance the DNVP and several other campaigns against reparations and the Treaties of Versailles and Locarno. Once he became leader of the Party he began to fund Hitler and the Nazis and in 1931–3 his political and financial power were instrumental in Hitler's rise to power. However, although he remained a member of the *Reichstag*, he lost his political power and influence when Hitler established the Nazi dictatorship from mid-1933.

Profile: Paul von Hindenburg 1847–1934

1847	– Born in Posen, East Prussia
1859	– Joined the Prussian army
1870	– Fought in the Franco-Prussian war
1911	– Retired with the rank of General
1914	– Recalled at start of First World War
	– Won the victory of the Battle of Tannenberg on Eastern Front
1916	– Promoted to Field Marshal and war supremo
1918	– Accepted the defeat of Germany and retired again
1925	– Elected president of Germany
1930–2	– Appointed Brüning, Papen and Schleicher as chancellors, who ruled by presidential decree
1932	– Re-elected president
1933	– Persuaded to appoint Hitler as chancellor
1934	– Death. Granted a national funeral

Background and military career

Hindenburg was born into a Prussian noble family that could trace its military tradition back over many centuries. Described as 'steady rather than exceptional', he was regularly promoted.

In 1914, he was recalled from retirement. His management of the campaign against the Russians on the Eastern Front earned him distinction. However, Hindenburg, who was distinguished in appearance and 'looked the part', did not have great military skills and was outshone by his chief-of-staff, Ludendorff.

After 1916, his partnership with Ludendorff was less successful against the British and French on the Western Front. During the years 1917 and 1918, the two men were effectively the military dictators of Germany.

Appointment as president of Weimar Republic

After the war, Hindenburg briefly retired but in 1925 he was elected president of Germany, a position he held until 1934. He was not a democrat and looked forward to the return of the monarchy and in many respects he only accepted the post reluctantly. Nevertheless, he took up the responsibility of his office and performed his duties correctly.

Rise of Hitler

From 1930 Hindenburg's political significance increased when Weimar faced growing political and economic crisis. As president, he was responsible for the appointment of all the chancellors from 1930–4, though he became a crucial player in the political intrigue of the competing forces. Given his authority, he must be held ultimately responsible for the events that ended with the appointment of Hitler, but he was very old and easily influenced by Papen and Schleicher. He had no respect for Hitler, but he did not have the will and determination to make a stand against Nazism.

The appointment of President Hindenburg has remained controversial. On the one hand, on Hindenburg's coming to power there was no immediate swing to the right. The new president proved totally loyal to the constitution and carried out his presidential duties with correctness. Those nationalists who had hoped that his election might lead to the restoration of the monarchy, or the creation of a military-type regime, were disappointed. Indeed, it has been argued that Hindenburg as president acted as a true substitute kaiser or **Ersatzkaiser** (so although Wilhelm II had abdicated and Germany had lost its monarchy, Hindenburg was seen by monarchists as, in effect, fulfilling the role of sovereign). In that sense, the status of Hindenburg as president at last gave Weimar some respectability in conservative circles.

On the other hand, it is difficult to ignore the pitfalls resulting from the appointment of an old man. In his heart, Hindenburg had no real sympathy for the Republic or its values. Those around him were mainly made up of anti-republican figures, many of them from the military. He preferred to include the DNVP in government and, if possible, to exclude the SPD. From the start, Hindenburg's view was that the government should move towards the right, although it was really only after 1929 that the serious implications of his outlook became fully apparent for Weimar democracy. As the historian A.J. Nicholls put it: 'he refused to betray the republic, but he did not rally the people to its banner'.

The limitations of the political system

During this period the parliamentary and party political system in Germany failed to make any real progress. It just coped as best it could. Government carried out its work but with only limited success. There was no *putsch* from left or right and the anti-republican extremists were contained. Law and order were restored and the activities of the various paramilitary groups were limited.

However, these were only minor and very negative successes and, despite the good intentions of certain individuals and groups, there were no signs of any real strengthening of the political structure. Stable government had not been established. This is not surprising when it is noted that one coalition government collapsed in 1926 over a minor issue about the use of the national flag and the old imperial flag. Another government fell over the creation of religious schools.

Even more significant for the future was the growing contempt and cynicism shown by the people towards party politics. This was particularly connected with the negotiating and bargaining involved in the creation of most coalitions. The turn-out of the elections declined in the mid-1920s compared to 1919 and 1920. There was also an increasing growth of small fringe parties. The apparent stability of these years was really a deception, a mirage. It misled some people into believing that a genuine basis for lasting stable government had been achieved. It had not.

Key term

Ersatzkaiser
Means 'substitute emperor'. After Marshal Hindenburg was elected president, he provided the *ersatzkaiser* figure required by the respectable right wing – he was a conservative, a nationalist and a military hero.

Key question
Was Weimar's political recovery a 'false stability'?

Summary diagram: Political recovery

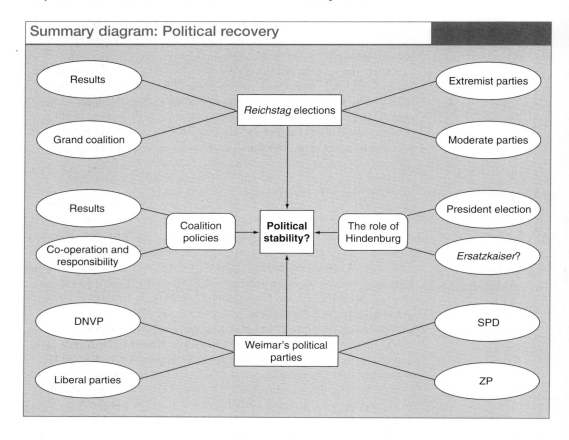

3 | Gustav Stresemann's Achievements

Before 1921–2, there was little to suggest that Stresemann was to become the mainstay of Weimar democracy. In the years before 1914 his nationalism found expression in his support of the Kaiser's **Weltpolitik** and from the start of the First World War, Stresemann was an ardent supporter of the **Siegfriede**. He campaigned for 'unrestricted submarine warfare' and opposed supporters of peace in 1917 (page 2).

By 1918 his support for the military regime and the Treaty of Brest-Litovsk had earned him the title of 'Ludendorff's young man' (see pages 4–5). And when the war came to an end in defeat, Stresemann was deliberately excluded from the newly created DDP and, so, was left no real option but to form his own party, the DVP. At first, his party was hostile to the revolution of 1918 and the Republic and campaigned for the restoration of the monarchy.

Turning point

Indeed, it was only after the failed Kapp *putsch* and the murders of Erzberger and Rathenau (pages 39–41) that Stresemann led his party into adopting a more sympathetic approach towards the Weimar Republic. His sudden change of heart has provided plenty of evidence for those critics who have regarded his support of the Weimar Republic as sham. This charge is not entirely fair.

Key question
How did Stresemann's career change and develop?

Key terms

Weltpolitik
'World policy' – the imperial policy of Kaiser Wilhem II to make Germany a great power by overseas expansion.

Siegfriede
'A peace through victory' – referring to Germany fighting the First World War to victory and making major land gains.

Despite the conservatism of his early years, Stresemann's subsequent career shows that he was a committed supporter of constitutional government.

Stresemann's ideal was a constitutional monarchy. But that was not to be. By 1922 he had become convinced that the Republic and its constitution provided Germany with its only chance of preventing the dictatorship of either left or right. This was his realistic assessment of the situation and why he was referred to as a *Vernunftrepublikaner*, a rational republican, rather than a convinced one.

Key question
What were Stresemann's aims and objectives?

Key term

Vernunftrepublikaner
'A rational republican' – used in the 1920s to define those people who really wanted Germany to have a constitutional monarchy but who, out of necessity, came to support the democratic Weimar Republic.

Stresemann's aims

From the time he became responsible for foreign affairs at the height of the 1923 crisis, Stresemann's foreign policy was shaped by his deep understanding of the domestic and international situations. He recognised, unlike many nationalists, that Germany had been militarily defeated and not simply 'stabbed in the back'. He also rejected the solutions of those hardliners who failed to understand the circumstances that had brought Germany to its knees in 1923.

Stresemann's main aims were to free Germany from the limitations of Versailles and to restore his country to the status of a great power, the equal of Britain and France. Offensive action was ruled out by Stresemann and so his only choice therefore was diplomacy. As he himself once remarked, he was backed up only by the power of German cultural traditions and the German economy. So, at first, he worked towards his main aims in the 1920s by pursuing the following objectives:

- To recognise that France did rightly have security concerns and that France also controlled the balance of power on the continent. He regarded Franco-German friendship as essential to solving outstanding problems.
- To play on Germany's vital importance to world trade in order to earn the goodwill and co-operation of Britain and the USA. The sympathy of the USA was also vital so as to attract American investment into the German economy.
- To maintain the Rapallo-based friendship with the USSR. He rejected out of hand those 'hardliners' who desired an alliance with Soviet Russia and described them as the 'maddest of foreign policy makers'. Stresemann's strategy was in the tradition of Wirth's fulfilment.
- To encourage co-operation and peace, particularly with the Western powers. This was in the best interests of Germany to make it the leading power in Europe once again.

Key question
What were the strengths and weaknesses of the Dawes Plan?

Stresemann and foreign affairs 1923–9

The Dawes Plan

The starting point of Stresemann's foreign policy was the issue of reparations. As chancellor, he had called off 'passive resistance' and agreed to resume the payment of reparations. The result of this was the US-backed Dawes Plan (see Figure 4.2 on page 72), which has

---

THE DAWES PLAN 1924

The reorganisation of German currency
- One new *Rentenmark* was to be worth one billion of the old marks.
- The setting up of a German national bank, the *Reichsbank*, under Allied supervision.

An international loan of 800 million gold marks to aid German economic recovery
- The loan was to be financed mainly by the USA.

New arrangements for the payment of reparations
- Payment to be made annually at a fixed scale over a longer period.

The US-backed Dawes Plan was accepted by the German government: April 1924

Key date

Figure 4.2: The Dawes Plan

been described as 'a victory for financial realism'. Despite opposition from the right wing it was accepted in April 1924.

Although the Dawes Plan left the actual sum to be paid unchanged, the monthly instalments over the first five years were calculated according to Germany's capacity to pay. Furthermore, it provided for a large loan to Germany to aid economic recovery. For Stresemann, its advantages were many:

- For the first time since the First World War, Germany's economic problems received international recognition.
- Germany gained credit for the cash-starved German economy by means of the loan and subsequent investments.
- It resulted in a French promise to evacuate the Ruhr during 1925.

In the short term, the Dawes Plan was a success. The German economy was not weakened, since it received twice as much capital from abroad as it paid out in reparations. The mere fact that reparations were being paid regularly contributed to the improved relations between France and Germany during these years. However, the whole system was dangerously dependent on the continuation of American loans, as can be seen in Figure 4.3. In attempting to break out of the crisis of 1923, Stresemann had linked Germany's fortunes to powerful external forces, which had dramatic effects after 1929.

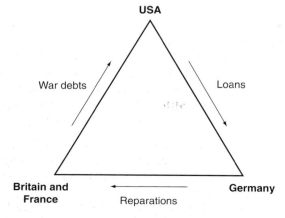

Figure 4.3: The reparations triangle in the 1920s

Key question
Why were the
Locarno treaties so
significant?

Key date

Locarno Pact: the
conference was held
in October 1925 and
the treaties were
signed in December

Key terms

Alliance
An agreement where
members promise to
support the other(s),
if one or more of
them is attacked.

**Mutual guarantee
agreement**
An agreement
between states on a
particular issue, but
not an alliance.

Demilitarisation
The removal of
military personnel,
weaponry or forts.
The Rhineland
demilitarised zone
was outlined by the
Treaty of Versailles
(pages 27–9).

Arbitration treaty
An agreement to
accept the decision
by a third party to
settle a conflict.

The Locarno Pact

The ending of the occupation of the Ruhr and the introduction of the Dawes Plan showed that the Great Powers were prepared to take Germany's interests seriously. However, Stresemann continued to fear that Anglo-French friendship could lead to a military **alliance**. In order to counter this concern, Stresemann proposed an international security pact for Germany's western frontiers. Although France was at first hesitant, Britain and the USA both backed the idea. This formed the basis for the Locarno Pact.

In October 1925 a series of treaties was signed which became known as the Locarno Pact. The main points were:

- A **mutual guarantee agreement** accepted the Franco-German and Belgian-German borders. These terms were guaranteed by Britain and Italy. All five countries renounced the use of force, except in self-defence.
- The **demilitarisation** of the Rhineland was recognised as permanent.
- The **arbitration treaties** between Germany, Poland and Czechoslovakia agreed to settle future disputes peacefully – but the existing frontiers were not accepted as final.

To see the territories affected by the Treaty of Locarno, refer to the map on page 29.

The Locarno treaties represented an important diplomatic development. Germany was freed from its isolation by the Allies and was again treated as an equal partner. Stresemann had achieved a great deal at Locarno at very little cost.

He had confirmed the existing frontiers in the west, since Germany was in no position to change the situation. In so doing he had also limited France's freedom of action since the occupation of the Ruhr or the possible annexation of the Rhineland was no longer possible. Moreover, by establishing the beginnings of a solid basis for Franco-German understanding, Stresemann had lessened France's need to find allies in eastern Europe. The Poles viewed the treaties as a major setback, since Stresemann had deliberately refused to confirm the frontiers in the east.

Further diplomatic progress

Stresemann hoped that further advances would follow Locarno, such as the restoration of full German rule over the Saar and the Rhineland, a reduction in reparations, and a revision of the eastern frontier. However, although there was further diplomatic progress in the years 1926–30 it remained limited:

- Germany had originally been excluded from the League of Nations (see page 29) but, in 1926, she was invited to join the League and was immediately recognised as a permanent member of the Council of the League.
- Two years later in 1928 Germany signed the Kellogg-Briand Pact, a declaration that outlawed 'war as an instrument of

Profile: Gustav Stresemann 1878–1929

1878	– Born in Berlin, the son of a publican and brewer
1900	– Graduated from Berlin University in Political Economy and went into business
1907	– Elected the youngest member of *Reichstag*
1914–18	– Unconditional nationalist and supporter of the war. Worked politically closely with Hindenburg and Ludendorff
1919	– Formed the DVP and became its leader, 1919–29. Initially opposed the creation of the Weimar Republic
1921	– Decided to work with the Weimar Republic and became a *Vernunftrepublikaner*, a republican by reason
1923	– Chancellor of Germany
1923–9	– Foreign Minister in all governments; major successes:
	1924 – Dawes Plan
	1925 – Locarno Pact
	1926 – Treaty of Berlin
	– Germany entry into League of Nations
	1928 – Kellogg-Briand Pact
	1929 – Young Plan
1926	– Awarded the Nobel Peace Prize
1929	– Death at the age of 51

Political background 1878–1918

Stresemann was born in Berlin, the son of a publican, and successfully entered university to study economics. He went into business and quickly earnt a reputation as a skilled trade negotiator, which laid the basis for his political outlook. His wife was the daughter of a leading Jewish family with strong social and business contacts.

Stresemann joined the old National Liberals and was elected in 1907 to the *Reichstag* at the age of just 29. He was a committed monarchist and nationalist and in the years before 1914 he supported the Kaiser's *Weltpolitik*. In the war, Stresemann was an ardent supporter of the *Siegfriede* and more expansionist policies with the result that he was forced to leave his old party.

His turning-point 1919–22

Stresemann was appalled by the defeat of Germany in the First World War and the Treaty of Versailles. In his heart, he remained a monarchist and hoped to create a constitutional monarchy. So, in the years 1919–21, he formed the DVP and opposed the Weimar Republic. However, by 1921 he came to recognise the political reality and finally committed himself and his party to the Republic.

Chancellor 1923

In the year of crisis Stresemann was made chancellor, and it is generally recognised by historians that it marked the climax of his career. All the problems were confronted: the occupation of the Ruhr, the hyper-inflation and the opposition from left and right wing extremists. So, although his term in office lasted for just three months it laid the basis for the recovery 1924–9.

Foreign Minister 1923–9

Stresemann was Foreign Minister in all the Weimar governments and was the 'main architect of republican foreign policy' (Kolb). Most significantly, he showed a strength of character and a realism which allowed him to negotiate with the Allies. Stresemann achieved a great deal in securing Germany's international position. Nevertheless, it should be remembered that that he failed to generate real domestic support for Weimar. So, it is questionable whether he could have saved the Weimar Republic from Nazism.

Key dates

Treaty of Rapallo: 1922

Stresemann as Foreign Minister: 1923–9

Kellogg-Briand Pact: August 1928

Young Plan: 1929

national policy'. Although of no real practical effect it showed that Germany was working with 68 nations.

- In 1929 the Allies agreed to evacuate the Rhineland earlier than intended, in return for a final settlement of the reparations issue. The result was the Young Plan, which further revised the scheme of payments. Germany now agreed to continue to pay reparations until 1988, although the total sum was reduced to £1850 million, only one-quarter of the figure demanded in 1921 (see page 28).

Key question
How was Stresemann able to reach agreements with both the USSR and the West?

The Treaty of Berlin

Although Stresemann viewed friendship with the West as his priority, he was not prepared to drop the **Rapallo treaty**. He was still determined to stay on good terms with the USSR. As a result, the two countries signed the Treaty of Berlin in April 1926 in order to continue the basis of a good Russo-German relationship. This was not double-dealing by Stresemann, but was simply a recognition that Germany's defence needs in the heart of Europe meant that she had to have understanding with both the East and the West. The treaty with the Soviet Union therefore reduced strategic fears on Germany's Eastern Front and placed even more pressure on Poland to give way to German demands for frontier changes. It also opened up the possibility of a large commercial market and increased military co-operation.

Key term

Rapallo treaty
This was not an alliance, but a treaty of friendship between Germany and the USSR.

Key question
Did Stresemann fail or succeed?

Assessment of Stresemann

In 1926 Stresemann was awarded the Nobel Peace Prize (along with his British and French counterparts Aristide Briand and Austen Chamberlain). Only three years later, at the early age of 51, he died suddenly of a heart attack. However, Stresemann has always been the focus of debate. He has been regarded by some as a fanatical nationalist and by others as a 'great European' working for international reconciliation. He has been praised for his staunch support of parliamentary government, but condemned for pretending to be a democrat. He has also been portrayed as an idealist on the one hand and an opportunist on the other.

Stresemann achieved a great deal in a short time to change both Germany's domestic and international positions. Moreover, the improvement had been achieved by peaceful methods. When one also considers the dire situation he inherited in 1923 with forces, both internal and external, stacked against him, it is perhaps not surprising that his policy has been described as 'astonishingly successful' (Kolb) and he has been referred to as 'Weimar's greatest statesman' (Wright).

However, it should be borne in mind that the circumstances in the years 1924–9 were working strongly in Stresemann's favour. Also, in terms of foreign policy, he failed to achieve his aims to revise Versailles fundamentally. By 1929 it seems that these limited changes had come to a dead end – and there was no hint of any revision of the Polish frontier.

Also, Stresemann's policies failed to generate real domestic support for Weimar. The right wing was always totally against 'fulfilment' and, although a minority, they became increasingly loud and influential, so by the time of Stresemann's death, the nationalist opposition was already mobilising itself against the Young Plan (see page 75). Even more significantly, it seems that the silent majority had not really been won over by Stresemann's policy of conciliation. Consequently, by 1929 his policy had not had time to establish itself and generate sufficient support to survive the difficult circumstances of the 1930s.

Key date

Death of Gustav Stresemann in the same month as the Wall Street Crash: October 1929

'He looks to the right, he looks to the left – he will save me.' A German cartoon drawn in 1923 portrays Stresemann as the guardian angel of the young Republic. However, it is worth noting that the little boy is the German Michael – a stereotype for the naïve German.

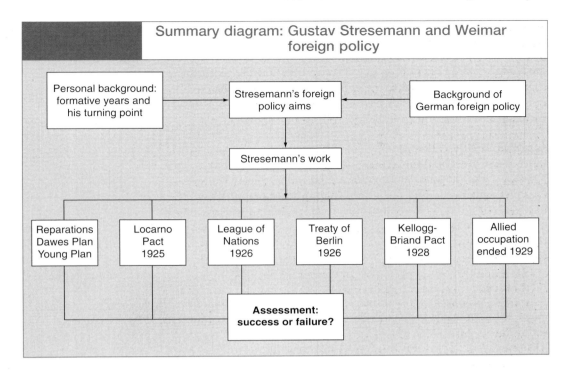

Summary diagram: Gustav Stresemann and Weimar foreign policy

4 | Weimar Culture

Key question
Why were the 1920s a culturally rich period?

The Weimar years witnessed a radical cultural reaction to the turmoil that followed the war and defeat. Whereas the Germany of the Second Reich had been conservative, authoritarian and conformist, in contrast, the Weimar Republic was a liberal society that upheld **toleration** and reduced censorship. These factors contributed to the label of the 'golden years', as described by William Shirer, the European correspondent of the American newspaper, the *Chicago Tribune*:

Key terms

Toleration
Acceptance of alternative political, religious and cultural views.

New functionalism
A form of art that developed in post-war Germany which tried to express reality with a more objective view of the world.

> A wonderful ferment was working in Germany. Life seemed more free, more modern, more exciting than in any place I had ever seen. Nowhere else did the arts or the intellectual life seem so lively … In contemporary writing, painting, architecture, in music and drama, there were new currents and fine talents.

More broadly, the period was also one of dramatic changes in communication and the media, for this decade saw the emergence of film, radio and the car.

The new cultural ferment

Key question
What was *Neue Sachlichkeit* and how did it express itself?

The term generally used to reflect the cultural developments in Weimar Germany was *Neue Sachlichkeit*. It can be translated as 'new practicality' or '**new functionalism**', which means essentially a desire to show reality and objectivity. These words are best explained by looking at some of the major examples of different art forms.

Art

Artists in favour of the 'new objectivity' broke away from the traditional nostalgia of the nineteenth century. They wanted to understand ordinary people in everyday life – and by their art they aimed to comment on the state of society. This approach was epitomised by Georg Grosz and Otto Dix whose paintings and caricatures had strong political and social messages.

Architecture and design

One of the most striking artistic developments in Weimar Germany was the Bauhaus school led by the architect Walter Gropius, which was established in 1919 in the town of Weimar itself. The Bauhaus movement was a new style that influenced all aspects of design. Its approach was functional and it emphasised the close relationship between art and technology, which is underlined by its motto 'Art and Technology – a new unity'.

Literature

It is impossible to categorise the rich range of writing which emerged in Weimar Germany. Not all writers were **expressionists** influenced by the *Neue Sachlichkeit*. For example, the celebrated Thomas Mann, who won the Nobel Prize for literature, was not part of that movement. In fact, the big sellers were the authors who wrote traditional nostalgic literature – such as Hans Grimm. In the more *avant garde* style were the works of Arnold Zweig and Peter Lampel, who explored a range of social issues growing out of the distress and misery of working people in the big cities. Two particular books to be remembered are: the pacifist *All Quiet on the Western Front*, published in 1928 by Erich Maria von Remarque, an ex-soldier critical of the First World War; and *Berlin Alexanderplatz* written by Alfred Döblin, which examined the life of a worker in Weimar society.

Key terms

Expressionism
An art form which suggests that the artist transforms reality to express a personal outlook.

Avant garde
A general term suggesting new ideas and styles in art.

A painting from 1927 by the German artist Otto Dix. Dix's war service deeply influenced his experiences and this piece underlines the contrast between the good-life of the affluent and the seedier side of the poor and disabled.

Pillars of Society: a painting from 1926 by the German artist Georg
Grosz. Grosz was wounded in the war and in 1918 he joined the KPD.
The title is an ironic comment on the dominant social forces in Germany,
as he mocks the image of the soldier, the priest, the banker.

The *Weißenhofsiedlung* was built on the Killesberg in Stuttgart in 1927. It is one of the best examples of the 'new architecture' in Germany and formed part of the exhibition *Die Wohnung* ('The flat') organised by the German *Werkbund*.

Theatre

In drama, *Neue Sachlichkeit* developed into what was called *Zeittheater* (theatre of the time) that introduced new dramatic methods often with an explicit left-wing sympathies – and were most evident in the plays of Bertolt Brecht and Erwin Piscator. They used innovative techniques such as banners, slogans, film and slides, and adopted controversial methods to portray characters' behaviour in their everyday lives.

Mass culture

The 1920s were a time of dramatic changes that saw the emergence of a modern mass culture. Germany was no exception. It saw the development of mass communication methods and international influences, especially from USA, such as jazz music and consumerism.

> **Key question**
> In what ways did Weimar culture reach out to ordinary people?

Film

During the 1920s, the German film industry became the most advanced in Europe. German film-makers were well respected for their high-quality work; most notable of the films of the time were:

- *Metropolis* (1926) by Fritz Lang
- *Fridericus Rex* (*King Frederick the Great*) (1922)
- *Blue Angel* (1930), with the young actress Marlene Dietrich.

However, although the German film market was very much dominated by the organisation, UFA, run by Alfred Hugenberg (see page 67), from the mid-1920s American 'movies' quickly made an exceptional impact. The popular appeal of the comedy of Charlie Chaplin shows that Weimar culture was part an international mass culture and was not exclusively German.

Radio
Radio also emerged very rapidly as another mass medium. The German Radio Company was established in 1923 and by 1932, despite the depression, one in four Germans owned a radio.

Cabaret
Berlin had a vibrant nightlife. Cabaret clubs opened up with a permissiveness that mocked the conventions of the old Germany: satirical comedy, jazz music, and women dancers (and even wrestlers) with varying degrees of nudity.

Key question
Who reacted against *Neue Sachlichkeit* and why?

The conflict of cultures
There were some respected conservative intellectuals, like Arthur Möller and Oswald Spengler, who condemned democratic and industrial society. Moreover, many of the writers in the 1920s opposed pacifism and proudly glorified the sacrifices of the First World War. Berlin was definitely not typical of all Germany, but it left a very powerful impression – both positive and negative. Some could enjoy and appreciate the cultural experimentation, but most Germans were horrified by what they saw as the decline in established moral and cultural standards. It has also been suggested that Weimar culture never established a genuinely tolerant attitude. The *avant garde* and the conservatives were clearly at odds with each other. More significantly, both sides took advantage of the freedoms and permissiveness of Weimar liberalism to criticise it, while not being genuinely tolerant or sympathetic towards each other. Weimar society was become increasingly **polarised** before the onset of the political and economic crisis in 1929.

Key term

Polarisation
The division of society into distinctly opposite views (the comparison is to the north and south poles).

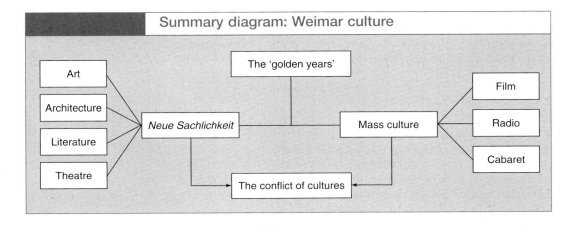

Summary diagram: Weimar culture

5 | Weimar 1924–9: An Overview

Key question
Were the years
1924–9 deceptively
stable?

The years 1924–9 marked the high point of the Weimar Republic.
By comparison with the periods before and after, these years do
appear stable. The real increase in prosperity experienced
by many, and the cultural vitality of the period, gave support
to the view that these years were indeed the 'golden years'.
However, historians have generally tended to question this
stability because it was in fact limited in scope. This is the reason
why the historian Peukert describes these years as a 'deceptive
stability'.

An unstable economy

Germany's economic recovery was built on unstable foundations
that created a false idea of prosperity. Problems persisted in the
economy and they were temporarily hidden only by an increasing
reliance on credit from abroad. In this way Germany's economy
became tied up with powerful external forces over which it had no
control. Hindsight now allows historians to see that, in the late
1920s, any disruption to the world's trade or finance markets was
bound to have a particularly damaging effect on the uncertain
German economy.

A divided society

German society was still divided by deep class differences
as well as by regional and religious differences that prevented
the development of national agreement and harmony.
The war and the years of crisis that followed had left
bitterness, fear and resentment between employers and their
workers. Following the introduction of the state scheme for
settling disputes in 1924, its procedure was used
as a matter of course, whereas the intention had been that it
would be the exception, not the rule. As a result, there was
arbitration in some 76,000 industrial disputes between 1924
and 1932.

In 1928, workers were locked out from their place of work in
the Ruhr ironworks when the employers refused to accept the
arbitration award. It was the most serious industrial confrontation
of the Weimar period. A compromise solution was achieved, but it
showed the extent of the bitterness of industrial relations even
before the start of the world depression.

Political division

Tension was also evident in the political sphere where the
parliamentary system had failed to build on the changes of 1918.
The original ideals of the Constitution had not been developed
and there was little sign that the system had produced a
stable and mature system. In particular, the main democratic
parties had still not recognised the necessity of working together
in a spirit of compromise. It was not so much the weaknesses of
the Constitution, but the failure to establish a shared political
outlook that led to its instability.

Foreign affairs

Even the successes of Stresemann in the field of foreign affairs were offset by the fact that significant numbers of his fellow countrymen rejected his policy out of hand and pressed for a more hardline approach.

In reality, the middle years of the Weimar Republic were stable only in comparison with the periods before and after. Weimar's condition suggested that the fundamental problems inherited from war and the years of crisis had not been resolved. They persisted, so that when the crisis set in during 1929–30 the Weimar Republic did not prove strong enough to withstand the storm.

Summary diagram: Weimar 1924–9: an overview

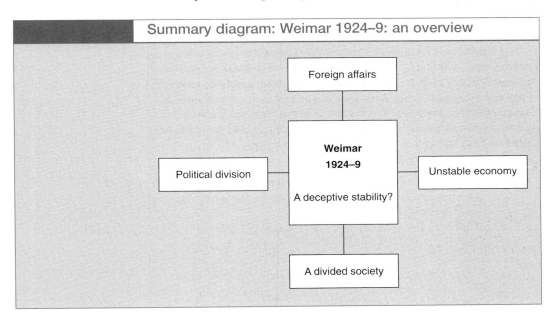

Study Guide: AS Question

In the style of Edexcel

How accurate is it to describe the years 1924–9 in Germany as a period of deceptive stability? (30 marks)

Exam tips

The cross-references are intended to take you straight to the material that will help you to answer the question.

This question is asking you to assess how stable the Weimar Republic really was during these years. You will need to show those aspects which made Germany appear more stable during these years than it had been before, and then ask whether fundamental problems remained.

You only have 40 minutes to answer the question and you will need to spend at least five minutes planning your answer, so you will need to be selective about what you focus on. Key problems for the Republic in its early years were: lack of support for it within Germany associated with resentment of the terms of the Treaty of Versailles; economic weaknesses; and the challenge to democratic government from political divisions and extremist political groups.

You could consider the following:

- In what ways did Germany experience economic recovery during these years (pages 59–60 and 72)? But did significant economic weaknesses remain (pages 60–1, 72 and 82)?
- Did political divisions continue to threaten the stability of the Weimar Republic? How much did extremist parties lose ground in general elections during 1924–8 (pages 63–4)? Do the results suggest democratic politics were strengthening? However, what evidence is there of a lack of political stability created by the problems of forming workable coalitions (pages 64–5 and 69) and the irresponsible attitude of Weimar political parties to parliamentary government (pages 65 and 82)?
- Did support for the Weimar Republic grow within Germany in the period 1924–9 (pages 70 and 71) or was it fragile and easily lost? Why had Stresemann's foreign policy of conciliation not created more domestic acceptance (pages 76 and 83)? How far did powerful figures and forces within Germany continue to oppose the republican system of government (pages 67–8)?
- Was Weimar Germany a divided society? Why was Weimar culture not admired by everyone (see page 81)? Why was there resentment between the workers and employers (see page 82)?

It could be helpful for you to organise your material and notes for each of the main themes – political, economic, social and foreign affairs – into two columns: one 'Stability' and the other 'Deceptive stability'.

Finally, you will need to decide whether the evidence in the 'Deceptive' column is strong enough for you to agree with the description in the question.

5 The Early Years of the Nazis 1919–29

POINTS TO CONSIDER

In the 1920s Hitler and the Nazi Party enjoyed a rather chequered history and they did not made any real political impact until the onset of the Great Depression. However, Nazism did take root. The purpose of this chapter is to examine the role of the Nazis in 1920s' Germany through the following themes:

- The personal background of Adolf Hitler and the creation of the Nazi Party
- The Munich Beer Hall *putsch*
- Nazi ideas
- Mixed fortunes of Nazism in the 1920s

Key dates

1919		Creation of German Workers' Party (DAP) by Anton Drexler
1920	February	Party name changed to NSDAP (National Socialist German Workers' Party)
		25-Points party programme drawn up by Drexler and Hitler
1923	November 8–9	Beer Hall *putsch* in Munich
1924		Hitler in Landsberg prison
		Mein Kampf written
1925	February	NSDAP re-founded in Munich
1926	February	Bamberg conference: Hitler's leadership of the Party re-established
1928	May	*Reichstag* election result
1929–33		The Great Depression

1 | Adolf Hitler and the Creation of the Nazi Party

Hitler's early years

Key question
How did Hitler become involved in politics?

There was little in the background of Adolf Hitler (1889–1945) to suggest that he would become a powerful political figure. Hitler was born at Braunau-am-Inn in 1889 in what was then the Austro-Hungarian Empire. He failed to impress at school, and after the death of his parents he moved to Vienna in 1907. There he applied unsuccessfully for a place as a student at the Academy of Fine Arts. For the next six years he led an aimless and unhappy existence in the poorer districts of the city. It was not until he joined the Bavarian Regiment on the outbreak of war in 1914 that he found a real purpose in life. He served bravely throughout the war and was awarded the Iron Cross First Class.

When the war ended he was in hospital recovering from a British gas attack. By the time he had returned to Bavaria in early 1919 he had already framed in his mind the core of what was to become National Socialism:

- fervent German nationalism
- support of authoritarianism and opposition to democracy and socialism
- a racially inspired view of society which exhibited itself most obviously in a rabid **anti-Semitism** and a veneration of the German *Volk* as the master race.

Such a mixture of ideas in a man whose personal life was much of a mystery – he had no close family and few real friends – has excited some historians to resort to psychological analysis leading to extraordinary speculation. Did his anti-Semitism originate from contracting syphilis from a Jewish prostitute? Could his authoritarian attitude be explained by his upbringing at the hands of an old and repressive father? Such psychological diagnoses – and there are many – may interest the student, but the supporting evidence for such explanations is at best flimsy. As a result, the conclusions reached are highly speculative and do not really help to explain the key question of how and why Hitler became such an influential political force.

The creation and emergence of the Nazi Party

It was because of his committed right-wing attitudes that Hitler was employed in the politically charged atmosphere of 1919 as a kind of spy by the political department of the Bavarian section of the German Army. One of his investigations brought him into contact with the DAP (*Deutsche Arbeiterpartei* – German Workers' Party) which was not a movement of the revolutionary left, as Hitler had assumed on hearing its name, but one committed to nationalism, anti-Semitism and **anti-capitalism**. Hitler joined the tiny party and immediately became a member of its committee. His energy, oratory and propaganda skills soon made an impact on the small group and it was Hitler who, with the Party's founder, Anton Drexler, drew up the Party's 25-points programme in February 1920 (see Figure 5.1). At the same time, it was agreed to change the Party's name to the NSDAP, the National Socialist German Workers' Party. (For analysis of Nazi ideology, see pages 91–4.)

By mid-1921 it was clear Hitler was the driving-force behind the Party. Although he still held only the post of propaganda chief, it was his powerful speeches that had impressed local audiences and had helped to increase party membership to 3300. He had encouraged the creation of the armed squads to protect

Key terms

Anti-Semitism
The hatred of Jews. It became the most significant part of Nazi racist thinking. For Hitler, the 'master-race' was the pure Aryan (the people of northern Europe) and the Germans represented the highest caste. The lowest race for Hitler was the Jews.

Volk
Often translated as 'people', although it tends to suggest a nation with the same ethnic and cultural identities and with a collective sense of belonging.

Key question
How significant was the NSDAP by 1922?

Key date
Creation of the German Workers' Party (DAP) by Anton Drexler: 1919

Key term

Anti-capitalism
Rejects the economic system based upon private property and profit. Early Nazi ideas laid stress upon preventing the exploitation of workers and suggesting social reforms.

Key dates

Name of the DAP party changed to NSDAP (National Socialist German Workers' Party): February 1920

Party's programme of 25 points drawn up by Drexler and Hitler: February 1920

1. We demand the union of all Germans in a Greater Germany on the basis of the right of national self-determination.

2. We demand equality of rights for the German People in its dealings with other nations, and the revocation of the peace treaties of Versailles and Saint Germain.

3. We demand land and territory (colonies) to feed our people and to settle our surplus population.

4. Only members of the *Volk* (nation) may be citizens of the State. Only those of German blood, whatever their creed may be members of the nation. Accordingly no Jew may be a member of the nation.

7. We demand that the State shall make it its primary duty to provide a livelihood for its citizens. If it should prove impossible to feed the entire population, non-citizens must be deported from the Reich.

10. It must be the first duty of every citizen to perform physical or mental work. The activities of the individual must not clash with the general interest, but must proceed within the framework of the community and be for the general good.

14. We demand profit sharing in large industrial enterprises.

15. We demand the extensive development of insurance for old age.

18. We demand the ruthless prosecution of those whose activities are injurious to the common interest. Common criminals, usurers, profiteers must be punished with death, whatever their creed or race.

22. We demand the abolition of the mercenary army and the formation of a people's army.

23. We demand legal warfare on deliberate political mendacity and its dissemination in the press.

25. We demand the creation of a strong central power of the Reich.

Figure 5.1: Extracts from the 25 points of the programme of the German Workers' Party

Party meetings and to intimidate the opposition, especially the communists. It was his development of early propaganda techniques – the Nazi salute, the swastika, the uniform – that had done so much to give the Party a clear and easily recognisable identity.

Alarmed by Hitler's increasing domination of the Party, Drexler and some other members of the committee tried to limit his influence. However, it was here, for the first time, that Hitler showed his political ability to manoeuvre and to gamble. He was by far the most influential speaker and the Party knew it, so, shrewdly, he offered to resign. In the ensuing power struggle he was quickly able to mobilise support at two meetings in July 1921. He was invited back in glory. Embarrassed, Drexler resigned and Hitler became chairman and Führer (leader) of the Party.

Having gained supreme control over the Party in Munich, Hitler aimed to subordinate all the other right-wing groups under his Party's leadership and certainly, in the years 1921–3, the Party was strengthened by a number of significant developments:

- The armed squads were organised and set up as the **SA** in 1921 as a paramilitary unit led by Ernst Röhm (see page 149). It was now used to organise planned thuggery and violence. Most notoriously, the conflict in the town of Coburg degenerated into a pitched battle between the Communists and the SA, but it showed how politically vital it was to win to control of the streets.
- The Party established its first newspaper in 1921, the *Völkischer Beobachter* (the *People's Observer*).
- In 1922 Hitler won the backing of Julius Streicher, who previously had run a rival right-wing party in northern Bavaria. Streicher also published his own newspaper, *Der Stürmer*, which was overtly anti-Semitic with a range of seedy articles devoted to sex and violence.
- Hitler was also fortunate to win the support of the influential Hermann Göring, who joined the Party in 1922 (see page 168). He was born into a Bavarian landowning family, while his wife was a leading Swedish aristocratic. They made many very helpful social contacts in Munich, which gave Hitler and Nazism respectability.

By 1923, the Party had a membership of about 20,000. Hitler certainly enjoyed an impressive personal reputation and, as a result, Nazism successfully established an influential role on the extreme right in Bavaria. However, despite Nazi efforts, it still proved difficult to control all the radical right-wing political groups, which remained independent organisations across Germany. The Nazi Party was still very much a fringe party, limited to the region of Bavaria.

Key term

SA
Sturm Abteilung became known in English as the Stormtroopers. They were also referred to as the Brownshirts after the colour of the uniform. They supported the radical socialist aspects of Nazism.

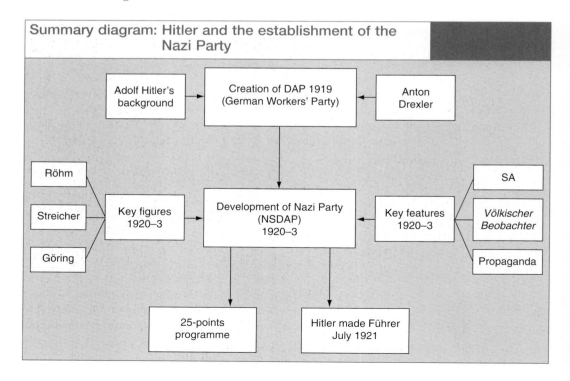

Summary diagram: Hitler and the establishment of the Nazi Party

Key question
How did Hitler manage to turn the failure of the Munich Beer Hall *putsch* to his advantage?

Key date

The Beer Hall *putsch* in Munich:
8–9 November 1923

2 | The Beer Hall *Putsch* 1923

The successful take-over of power by Mussolini in Italy in October 1922, combined with the developing internal crisis in Germany, convinced Hitler that the opportunity to seize power had arrived. Indeed, a leading Nazi introduced Hitler at one of his speeches in Munich by saying: 'Germany's Mussolini is called Adolf Hitler'. However, the Nazis were far too weak on their own to stage any kind of political take-over and Hitler himself was still seen merely as a 'drummer' who could stir up the masses for the national movement. It was the need for allies which led Hitler into negotiations with Kahr and the Bavarian State Government and the Bavarian section of the German army under Lossow (see pages 41–2).

It was with these two men that Hitler plotted to 'March on Berlin' (in the style of Mussolini's *coup* which, only the previous year, had become known as the 'March on Rome'). They aimed to mobilise all the military forces from Bavaria – including sections of the German army, the police, the SA and other paramilitaries – and then, by closing in on Berlin, to seize national power. With hindsight, Hitler's plan was unrealistic and doomed because:

- he grossly over-estimated the level of public support for a *putsch* – despite the problems faced by Weimar's democratic government in 1923
- he showed a lack of real planning
- he relied too heavily on the promise of support of Ludendorff
- most significantly, at the eleventh hour, Kahr and Lossow, fearing failure, decided to hold back.

A photograph of the main leaders of the Beer Hall *putsch* posing before the trial in February 1924. Frick (A), Ludendorff (B), Hitler (C), and Röhm (D) can be identified by the letters.

Hitler was not so cautious and preferred to press on rather than lose the opportunity. On 8 November, when Kahr was addressing a large audience in one of Munich's beer halls, Hitler and the Nazis took control of the meeting, declared a 'national revolution' and forced Kahr and Lossow to support it. The next day Hitler, Göring, Streicher, Röhm, Himmler (and Ludendorff) marched into the city of Munich with 2000 SA men, but they had no real military backing, and the attempted take-over of Munich was easily crushed by the Bavarian police. Fourteen Nazis were killed and Hitler himself was arrested on a charge of treason.

The consequences

In many respects the *putsch* was a farce. Hitler and the *putschists* were arrested and charged with treason and the NSADP itself was banned. However, Hitler gained significant political advantages from the episode:

- He turned his trial into a great propaganda success both for himself and for the Nazi cause. He played on all his rhetorical

'Hitler's entry into Berlin.' A cartoon published by the *Simplicissimus* magazine in April 1924 just after Hitler's trial. It mocks Hitler's march on Berlin and shows Ebert in chains.

Key date

Hitler imprisoned in Landsberg prison; *Mein Kampf* written: 1924

Key term

Mein Kampf
'My struggle'. The book written by Hitler in 1924, which expresses his political ideas.

skills and evoked admiration for his patriotism. For the first time he made himself a national figure.

- He won the respect of many other right-wing nationalists for having had the courage to act.
- The leniency of his sentence – five years, the minimum stipulated by the Weimar Constitution and actually reduced to 10 months – seemed like an act of encouragement on the part of the judiciary.
- He used his months in prison to write and to reassess his political strategy (see below), including dictating *Mein Kampf*.

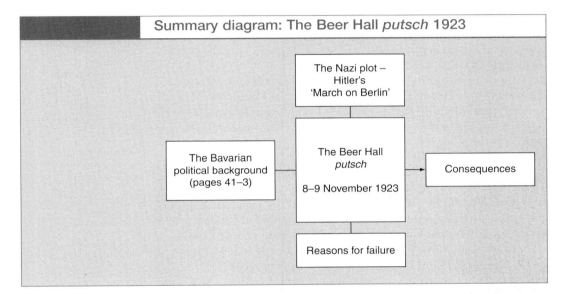

Summary diagram: The Beer Hall *putsch* 1923

The Nazi plot – Hitler's 'March on Berlin'

The Bavarian political background (pages 41–3)

The Beer Hall *putsch*

8–9 November 1923

Consequences

Reasons for failure

Key question
What were the main elements of Nazi thinking?

Key term

Social Darwinism
A philosophy that portrayed the world as a 'struggle' between people, races and nations. Hitler viewed war as the highest form of 'struggle' and was deeply influenced by the theory of evolution based upon natural selection.

3 | Nazi Ideas

Nazism always emphasised the importance of action over thought. However, whilst in Landsberg prison, Hitler dictated the first part of *Mein Kampf* which, in the following years, became the bible of National Socialism. Together with the 25-points programme of 1920, it provides the basic framework of Hitler's ideology and of Nazism itself.

Racism

Hitler's ideas were built upon his concept of race. He believed that humanity consisted of a hierarchy of races and that life was no more than 'the survival of the fittest'. He argued that **social Darwinism** necessitated a struggle between races, just as animals fought for food and territory in the wild. Furthermore, he considered it vital to maintain racial purity, so that the blood of the weak would not undermine the strong.

It was a crude philosophy, which appears even more simplistic when Hitler's analysis of the races is considered. The *Herrenvolk* (master-race) was the **Aryan** race and was exemplified by the Germans. It was the task of the Aryan to remain pure and to dominate the inferior races. In the following extract from *Mein Kampf* Hitler writes:

> The adulteration of the blood and racial deterioration conditioned thereby are the only causes that account for the decline of ancient civilisations; for it is never by war that nations are ruined, but by the loss of their powers of resistance, which are exclusively a characteristic of pure racial blood. In this world everything that is not of sound stock is like chaff. Every historical event in the world is nothing more nor less than a manifestation of the instinct of racial self-preservation, whether for weal or woe [for better or for worse].

(See also the 25-points programme, page 87: points 4 and 7.)

Anti-democracy

In Hitler's opinion there was no realistic alternative to strong dictatorial government. Ever since his years in Vienna he had viewed parliamentary democracy as weak and ineffective. It went against the German historical traditions of militarism and the power of the state. Furthermore, it encouraged the development of an even greater evil, communism.

More specifically, Hitler saw Weimar democracy as a betrayal. In his eyes, it was the democratic and socialist politicians of 1918, 'the November criminals', who had stabbed the German army in the back, by accepting the armistice and establishing the Republic (page 5). Since then Germany had lurched from crisis to crisis.

In place of democracy Hitler wanted an all-embracing one-party state that would be run on the ***Führerprinzip***, which rejected representative government and liberal values. Thus, the masses in society were to be controlled for the common good, but an individual leader was to be chosen in order to rouse the nation into action, and to take the necessary decisions. (See also the 25-points programme, page 87: point 25.)

Nationalism

A crucial element in Nazi thinking was an aggressive nationalism, which developed out of the particular circumstances of Germany's recent history. The armistice of 1918 and the subsequent Treaty of Versailles had to be overturned, and the lost territories had to be restored to Germany (see pages 26–9). But Hitler's nationalism called for more than a mere restoration of the 1914 frontiers. It meant the creation of an empire (*Reich*) to include all those members of the German *Volk* who lived beyond the frontiers of the Kaiser's Germany: the Austrian Germans; the Germans in the Sudetenland; the German communities along the Baltic coast; all were to be included within the borderlands of Germany.

Yet, Hitler's nationalist aims did not end there. He dreamed of a Greater Germany, a superpower, capable of competing with the British Empire and the United States. Such an objective could be achieved only by territorial expansion on a grand scale. This was

Key terms

Aryan
Broadly refers to all the peoples of the Indo-European family. However, the term was more specifically defined by the Nazis as the non-Jewish people of northern Europe.

Führerprinzip
'The leadership principle'. Hitler upheld the idea of a one-party state, built on an all-powerful leader.

Key terms

Lebensraum
'Living space'.
Hitler's aim to
create an empire by
establishing
German supremacy
over the eastern
lands in Europe.

Volksgemeinschaft
'A people's
community'.
Nazism stressed the
development of a
harmonious,
socially unified and
racially pure
community.

the basis of Hitler's demand for *Lebensraum* for Germany. Only by the conquest of Poland, the Ukraine and Russia could Germany obtain the raw materials, cheap labour and food supplies so necessary for continental supremacy. The creation of his 'New Order' in eastern Europe also held one other great attraction: namely, the destruction of the USSR, the centre of world communism.

In *Mein Kampf* Hitler wrote:

> The German people must be assured the territorial area which is necessary for it to exist on earth ... People of the same blood should be in the same Reich. The German people will have no right to engage in a colonial policy until they shall have brought all their children together in one state. When the territory of the Reich embraces all the Germans and finds itself unable to assure them a livelihood, only then can the moral right arise, from the need of the people, to acquire foreign territory ... Germany will either become a World Power or will not continue to exist at all. ... The future goal of our foreign policy ought to be an Eastern policy, which will have in view the acquisition of such territory as is necessary for our German people.

(See also the 25-points programme, page 87: points 1, 2 and 3.)

The socialist aspect of Nazism

A number of points in the 1920 programme demanded socialist reforms and, for a long time, there existed a faction within the Party that emphasised the anti-capitalist aspect of Nazism, for example:

- profit-sharing in large industrial enterprises
- the extensive development of insurance for old age
- the nationalisation of all businesses.

Hitler accepted these points in the early years because he recognised their popular appeal but he himself never showed any real commitment to such ideas. As a result they were the cause of important differences within the Party and were not really dropped until Hitler had fully established his dominant position by 1934. (See also the 25-points programme, page 87: points 10, 14 and 15.)

What Hitler and Goebbels later began to promote was the concept of the *Volksgemeinschaft* (people's community). This remained the vaguest element of the Nazi ideology, and is therefore difficult to define precisely. First, it was intended to overcome the old differences of class, religion and politics. But secondly, it aimed to bring about a new collective national identity by encouraging people to work together for the benefit of the nation and by promoting 'German values'. Such a system could of course only benefit those who racially belonged to the German *Volk* and who willingly accepted the loss of individual freedoms in an authoritarian system.

The ideology of National Socialism

Key question
Was Nazism an
original German
ideology?

Early historians and biographers of Hitler simply saw him as a cynical opportunist motivated by the pursuit of power. Others have now generally come to view him as a committed political leader influenced by certain key ideas that he used to lay the basis of a consistent Nazi programme.

However, to describe Hitler's thinking, or Nazism, as an ideology is really to flatter it. An 'ideology' suggests a coherent thought-through system or theory of ideas, as found, for example, in Marxism. Nazism lacked coherence and was intellectually superficial and simplistic. It was not genuinely a rational system of thought. It was merely a collection of ideas which grew out of the age of enlightenment and the spirit of German romanticism. It was not in any positive sense original – every aspect of Hitler's thinking was to be found in the nationalist and racist writings of the nineteenth century:

- His nationalism was an outgrowth of the fervour generated in the years leading up to Germany's unification of 1871.
- His idea of an all-German *Reich* was a simple repetition of the demands for the 'Greater Germany' made by those German nationalists who criticised the limits of the 1871 unification.
- Even the imperialism of *Lebensraum* had already found expression in the programme of 'Germanisation' supported by those writers who saw the German race as somehow superior.
- The growing veneration for the *Volk* had gone hand-in-hand with the development of racist ideas, and in particular of anti-Semitism.

Thus, even before Hitler and other leading Nazis were born, the core of what would become Nazism was already current in political circles. It was to be found in the cheap and vulgar pamphlets sold to the masses in the large cities; in the political programme of respectable pressure groups, such as the **Pan-German League**; within the corridors of Germany's great universities; and in the creative works of certain cultural figures, such as the composer Richard Wagner.

However, despite these links, one must avoid labelling Nazi ideology as the logical result of German intellectual thinking. It is all too easy to emphasise those elements that prove the linkage theory, whilst ignoring the host of other evidence that points to entirely different views, e.g. the strong socialist tradition in Germany. Moreover, it is well to remember that a number of countries, but especially Britain and France, also witnessed the propagation of very similar ideas at this time. In that sense nationalism and racism were an outgrowth of nineteenth-century European history. Nazi ideology may not have been original, but it should not therefore be assumed that it was an inevitable result of Germany's past.

Pan-German
League
A movement
founded at the end
of the nineteenth
century
campaigning for
the uniting of all
Germans into one
country.

Key term

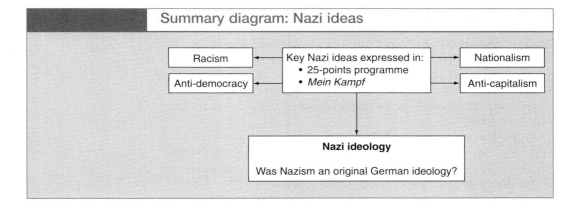

Summary diagram: Nazi ideas

Racism ← Key Nazi ideas expressed in: → Nationalism

• 25-points programme
• *Mein Kampf*

Anti-democracy ← → Anti-capitalism

Nazi ideology

Was Nazism an original German ideology?

Key question
In what ways was the Nazi Party revitalised?

Key dates

NSDAP re-founded in Munich: 27 February 1925

Bamberg conference: Hitler established his leadership of the Party: 14 February 1926

4 | Nazi Fortunes in the 1920s

When Hitler left prison in December 1924 the future for Nazism looked bleak. The Party was in disarray; its leading members were split into factions and the membership was in decline. More significantly, the atmosphere of crisis that had prevailed in the early years of the Republic had given way to a period of political and economic calm (see pages 59–62). Nevertheless, the Party was officially re-founded on 27 February 1925 and at the same time Hitler wrote a lengthy editorial for the *Völkischer Beobachter* with the heading 'A new beginning'.

Strategy and leadership

In Landsberg prison Hitler, reflecting on the failure of the 1923 *putsch*, became convinced of two vital points:

• He must establish his own absolute control over the Party.
• An armed *coup* was no longer an appropriate tactic and the only sure way to succeed was to work within the Weimar Constitution and to gain power by legal means. Such a policy of legality would necessitate the creation of a party structure geared to gaining success in the elections. As Hitler himself said in prison in 1924:

… we shall have to hold our noses and enter the *Reichstag* against the Catholic and Marxist deputies. If out-voting them takes longer than our shooting them, at least the result will be guaranteed by their own Constitution. Any lawful process is slow.

However, the Party remained deeply divided in a number of ways:

• Not everyone agreed with the new policy of legality.
• Traditional regional hostilities continued to exist, particularly between the Party's power base in Bavaria and the branches in northern Germany.
• Most importantly, policy differences had got worse between the nationalist and anti-capitalist wings of the Party (see page 93).

For over a year Hitler struggled with this internal friction. The problem was highlighted by the power and influence of Gregor Strasser and also his brother Otto. Gregor Strasser joined the NSDAP in 1920 and stood loyally next to Hitler in the Munich *putsch*, but he epitomised the opposing standpoint within the Party. He favoured the more socialist anti-capitalist policies for the workers and he was in effect the leader of the movement in northern Germany.

Eventually, in February 1926, the differences within the Party came to a head at a special party conference in Bamberg. On the one hand it was a significant victory for Hitler, as he mobilised sufficient support to re-establish his supremacy. The Nazi Party was to be run according to the *Führerprinzip* and there was to be no place for disagreements. On the other hand, the Party declared that the original 25 points of the programme with its socialist elements remained unchangeable. So, although Hitler had cleverly outmanoeuvred his greatest threat and he had re-established a degree of unity within the Party, there were still significant rivalries and differences.

Profile: Gregor Strasser 1892–1934

1892		– Born in Bavaria
1914–18		– Served in the First World War
1920		– Joined the NASDP and supported the anti-capitalist 'left-wing' socialist faction
1923	November	– Took part in the Munich *putsch*
1926	February	– Defeated by Hitler over the Party's leadership at the Bamberg Conference, but he continued to criticise Hitler's policies
1926–32		– Responsible for building the mass movement of the Party in the 1920s
		– Led the NSDAP in northern Germany
1932	December	– Offered the post of vice-chancellor by Schleicher (see page 136). Differences with Hitler came to a head in a major row and he was expelled from the Party
1934	June	– Murdered in the SA purge (see page 151)

Because Gregor Strasser was murdered in 1934 and because he played no role in the government of the Third Reich, it is easy to ignore his significance in the rise of Nazism. Yet, until the day he resigned from the Party, Strasser was, in effect, second to Hitler. He was always a supporter of the anti-capitalist 'left-wing' socialist faction, which became increasingly disillusioned when Hitler courted big business. Like Hitler, an inspiring political speaker, he also showed the administrative skills to develop a mass movement for the Party. (He also worked closely with his brother until Otto left the Party in 1930.)

The creation of the Party structure

The most significant development in the years before the Great Depression lay in the reorganisation of the Party structure. The whole of Germany was divided into regions (*Gaue*), which reflected the electoral geography of Weimar's system of proportional representation. The control of each region was placed in the hands of a ***Gauleiter***, who then had the responsibility of creating district (*Kreis*) and branch (*Ort*) groups. In this way a vertical Party structure was created throughout Germany, which did not detract from Hitler's own position of authority as leader.

Perhaps the most renowned of the *Gauleiter*s was the holder of the Berlin post, Joseph Goebbels. Goebbels had originally been a sympathiser of Gregor Strasser's socialist ideas, but from 1926 he gave his support to Hitler. He was then rewarded by being given the responsibility for winning over the capital, a traditionally left-wing stronghold of the SPD. He showed a real interest in propaganda and created the newspaper, *Der Angriff* (*The Attack*), but was not appointed chief of party propaganda until 1930 (see pages 237–8).

The Nazis also founded a number of new associated Nazi organisations that were geared to appeal to the specific interests of particular groups of Germans. Among these were:

- The Hitler Youth
- The Nazi Teachers' Association
- Union of Nazi Lawyers
- The Order of German Women.

Gregor Strasser was mainly responsible for building up an efficient Party structure and this was reflected in its increasing membership during these years (see Table 5.1).

Key terms

Gauleiter
Means 'leader of a regional area'. The Nazi Party was organised into 35 regions from 1926.

SS
Schutz Staffel (protection squad); became known as the Blackshirts, named after the uniform.

Table 5.1: NSDAP membership

Year	Membership numbers
1925	27,000
1926	49,000
1927	72,000
1928	108,000

One other significant initiative in these years was the creation of the **SS**. It was set up in 1925 as an élite body of black-shirted guards, sworn to absolute obedience to the Führer. In 1929 it had only 200 members. At first, it was just Hitler's personal bodyguard though, when it was placed under the control of Himmler later that year, it soon developed its own identity.

The *Reichstag* election of May 1928

By 1928 it can be seen clearly that the Party had made progress and was really an effective political machine, most obviously because:

- the structure was effectively organised
- the membership had increased four-fold since 1925
- Hitler's leadership was authoritative and secure (despite the ongoing challenge from the Strasser faction).

As a result, the Nazi Party had also successfully taken over many of the other right-wing racist groups in Germany.

Such advances, however, could not compensate for Nazi disappointment after the *Reichstag* election in May 1928. When the votes were counted, the Party had won only 2.6 per cent of the vote and a mere 12 seats (see page 63). It seemed as if Hitler's policy of legality had failed to bring political success, whereas in the favourable socio-economic circumstances Weimar democracy had managed to stabilise its political position. So, Nazism may have taken root, but there was no real sign that it could flourish in Germany.

If this evidence confirmed the belief of many that Hitler was nothing more than an eccentric without the personal leadership to establish a really broad national appeal, there was just one telling sign. In the election, the Party made significant gains in the northern part of Germany amongst the rural and middle and lower middle classes of areas such as Schleswig-Holstein.

This trend was reflected in the regional state elections of 1929, which suggested that the fall in agricultural prices was beginning to cause discontent – demonstrations and protests were giving way to bankruptcies and violence. Most significantly, in the province of Thuringia, in central Germany, the Nazi Party trebled its vote and broke the 10 per cent barrier for the first time, recording 11.3 per cent. Such figures suggested that the Nazis could exploit the increasingly difficult economic times of the Great Depression.

Key question
How strong was the Nazi Party by the end of the 1920s?

Key dates

Reichstag election result, very disappointing Nazi performance: May 1928

Great Depression: 1929–33

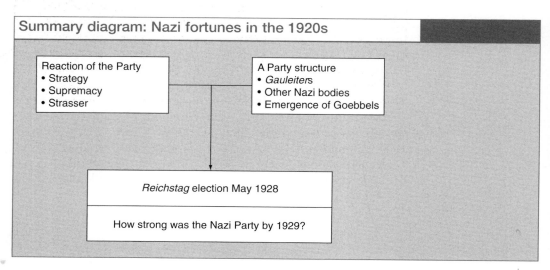

Summary diagram: Nazi fortunes in the 1920s

Reaction of the Party
- Strategy
- Supremacy
- Strasser

A Party structure
- *Gauleiters*
- Other Nazi bodies
- Emergence of Goebbels

Reichstag election May 1928

How strong was the Nazi Party by 1929?

Study Guide: AS Question

In the style of Edexcel

How accurate is it to describe the Nazi Party as weak in the years before 1929? (30 marks)

> *Exam tips*
>
> *The cross-references are intended to take you straight to the material that will help you to answer the question.*
>
> This question requires you to make an overall judgement about whether the Nazi Party can be dismissed as a political force in the 1920s. In coming to a judgement, you will need to consider the evidence of its weaknesses and limitations – and also the evidence which suggests its potential to challenge other parties within the political system.
>
> Weaknesses might include:
>
> - Limitations of the party in the early years and the failure of the *putsch* (pages 85–90).
> - Party disarray and division in 1924–5 (pages 95–6).
> - Recovery and stability in Weimar Germany making the possibility of challenge less likely (pages 59–69).
> - Lack of overall success in the *Reichstag* elections in 1928 (page 98).
>
> On the other hand, you could consider some evidence of growing strength:
>
> - The restructuring of the party to make it more effective (page 97).
> - The growth in membership (page 97).
> - By 1928 it had strong leadership and was an 'effective political machine' (page 98).
> - Electoral successes in certain areas and among certain groups (page 98).
>
> Your conclusion could emphasise both early weakness and the signs of a different position in 1928. In 1928 the evidence points in both directions and that gives you the opportunity to make a balanced case. You could point out that despite the lack of success in the 1928 election there is also evidence which suggests that the Nazi Party was gaining significant electoral support in key areas and among key groups.

6 The Decline of Weimar and the Rise of Nazism 1929–32

POINTS TO CONSIDER

Weimar already faced pressures before 1929, but the Wall Street Crash, in the very same month as the death of Gustav Stresemann, ushered in the Great Depression that precipitated a political and economic crisis in Germany. This chapter focuses on the collapse of the Weimar Republic and the emergence of the Nazis, which, although closely linked, raises two questions. The first one is why did the Weimar Republic collapse? This is the subject of this chapter. Its main themes are:

- The effects of the world economic crisis on Germany
- The breakdown of parliamentary government
- The advent of presidential government under Brüning, 1930–2
- The appointment of Papen as chancellor
- The death of the Weimar Republic

The next chapter of this book will concentrate on how and why the Nazis established a brutal dictatorship.

Key dates

1929	October	Wall Street Crash
1930	March	Resignation of Müller's government. Brüning appointed chancellor
		Young Plan approved by the *Reichstag*
	September	*Reichstag* election: Nazis emerged as second largest party in the *Reichstag*
	December	Brüning's economic measures imposed by presidential decree
1931	July	Five leading German banks failed
	October	Formation of Harzburg Front
1932	January	Unemployment peaked at 6.1 million
	April	Re-election of Hindenburg as president of Germany
	May	Brüning resigned
		Papen appointed chancellor
	July	*Reichstag* election: Nazis emerged as largest party in the *Reichstag*

Key question
Did the Wall Street Crash cause the economic crisis in Germany?

Key date

The Wall Street Crash: October 1929

1 | The Impact of the World Economic Crisis on Germany

There is no dispute amongst historians that the world economic crisis, which is known as the Great Depression, was an event of major significance. Its effects were felt throughout the world; although not in the Soviet Union.

Germany undoubtedly felt it in a particularly savage way. It suffered the consequences of the Wall Street Crash – the collapse of share prices on the New York Stock Exchange in October 1929 – more than any other country. Almost immediately the American loans and investment dried up and this was quickly followed by demands for the repayment of those short-term loans. At the same time, the crisis caused a further decline in the price of food and raw materials as the industrialised nations reduced their imports. As demand for exports collapsed, so world trade slumped. In this situation, German industry could no longer pay its way. Without overseas loans and with its export trade falling, prices and wages fell and the number of bankruptcies increased.

Table 6.1: Economic effects of the world economic crisis on Germany

Economic effects	Key features
Trade Slump in world trade. Demand for German exports fell rapidly, e.g. steel, machinery and chemicals	Exports value fell by 55 per cent 1929 = £630m 1932 = £280m
Employment Workers laid off – mass unemployment	Number of registered unemployed (annual averages) 1929 = 1.8m 1932 = 5.6m
Industry Industrial production declined sharply	Production: (1928 = 100) 1929 = 100 1932 = 58 50,000 businesses collapsed
Agriculture Wages and incomes fell sharply. Many farms sold off	Agricultural prices (1913 = 100) 1927 = 138 1932 = 77
Finance Banking sector dislocated by loss of confidence	Five major banks collapsed in 1931 50,000 businesses bankrupted

However, it is all too easy to put Germany's economic crisis down to the Wall Street Crash. It should be borne in mind that there were fundamental weaknesses in the German economy *before* the Wall Street Crash:

- The balance of trade was in the red, i.e. in debt.
- The number of unemployed averaged 1.9 million in 1929, even before the Wall Street Crash.

- Many farmers were already in debt and had been facing falling incomes since 1927.
- German government finances from 1925 were continually run in deficit.

So, although the Wall Street Crash contributed to Germany's economic problems, it is *probable* that the Germany economy faced a chance of a serious depression without it. This suggests that the world economic crisis should really be seen as simply the final push that brought the Weimar economy crashing down. In that sense, it could be said that the Wall Street Crash was merely the occasion, not the cause of Germany's economic crisis.

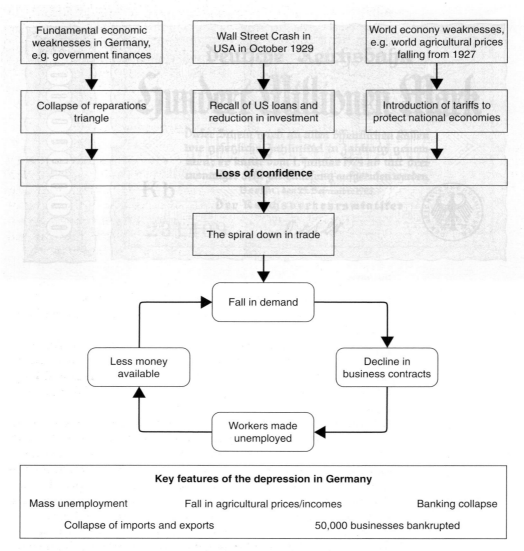

Figure 6.1: Germany in the Great Depression: causes and consequences of the world economic crisis

A camp for the unemployed and homeless in Berlin. Because there were so many poor people, large camps of tents were set up. These camps gave the impression of orderliness: numbered tents in neat rows with names, like streets.

Key question
How did the economic crisis affect the German people's lives?

Key date

Unemployment peaked at 6.1 million: January 1932

The human effects of the Great Depression

During the winter of 1929–30, unemployment rose above two million and only 12 months after the Crash, it had reached three million. By January 1932 it stood at 6.1 million, which did not substantially fall until the spring of 1933. On their own, such figures can provide only a limited understanding of the effects of the depression of this magnitude. Unemployment figures, for example, do not take into account those who did not register. Nor do they record the extent of part-time working throughout German industry.

Above all, statistics fail to convey the extent of the human suffering that was the consequence of this disaster because the depression in Germany affected virtually everyone; few families escaped its effects.

Many manual industrial workers, both skilled and unskilled, faced the prospect of long-term unemployment. For their wives, there was the impossible task of trying to feed families and keep homes warm on the money provided by limited social security benefits.

However, such problems were not to be limited to the working class. This depression dragged down the middle classes. From the small shopkeepers to the well-qualified professionals in law and medicine, people struggled to survive in a world where there was little demand for their goods and services. For such people, the decline in their economic position and the onset of poverty were made more difficult by the loss of pride and respectability.

The situation in the countryside was no better than in the towns. As world demand fell further, the agricultural depression deepened, leading to widespread rural poverty. For some tenant farmers there was even the ultimate humiliation of being evicted from their homes, which had often been in their families for generations.

In the more prosperous times we live in today, it is difficult to appreciate the scale of the suffering that struck German people in the early 1930s. The city of Cologne could not pay the interest on its debts, banks closed their doors and, in Berlin, large crowds of unemployed youngsters were kept occupied with open-air games of chess and cards. To many ordinary respectable Germans it seemed as if society itself was breaking down uncontrollably. It is not surprising that many people lost faith in the Weimar Republic, which seemed to offer no end to the misery, and began to see salvation in the solutions offered by political extremists. This was why the economic crisis in Germany quickly degenerated into a more obvious political crisis.

The political implications

The impact of the depression in Germany was certainly more severe than in either Britain or France, but it was on a par with the American experience. In Germany, one in three workers was unemployed in 1933 and by 1932 industrial production had fallen by 42 per cent of its 1929 level. In the USA, the comparable figures were one in four and 46 per cent.

Key question
Why did the economic crisis turn into a political one?

However, in Germany the economic crisis quickly became a political crisis, simply because there was a lack of confidence that weakened the Republic's position in its hour of need. Britain, France and the USA were all well-established democracies and did not face the possibility of a wholesale collapse of their political systems.

Taken together these two points suggest that the Great Depression hastened the end of the Weimar Republic, but only because its economy was already in serious trouble, and the democratic basis of its government was not sufficiently well established.

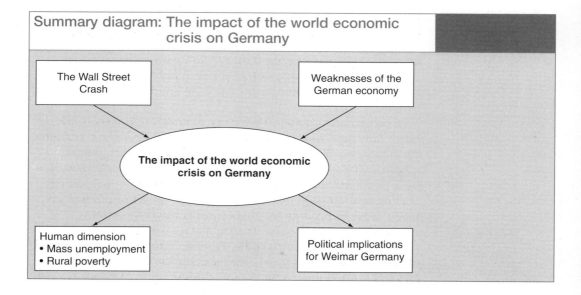

Summary diagram: The impact of the world economic crisis on Germany

The Wall Street Crash

Weaknesses of the German economy

The impact of the world economic crisis on Germany

Human dimension
• Mass unemployment
• Rural poverty

Political implications for Weimar Germany

2 | Parliamentary Government's Breakdown

Key question
How and why did the Young Plan increase political exposure for the Nazis?

Key date

Young Plan approved by *Reichstag:* March 1930

In 1929 the German government was in the hands of Hermann Müller's Grand Coalition, which had been formed after the general election of May 1928 (see pages 64–5). Yet, at the very time when unity and firm government were required to tackle the economic crisis, the Weimar Republic was being torn apart by the re-emergence of the emotive issue of reparations.

The Dawes Plan (1924) successfully overcame the reparations crisis of the early 1920s by rescheduling payments based on Germany's capacity to pay but, from the outset, it was seen as a temporary measure until Germany regained its economic strength (see pages 71–2). In early 1929 the IARC (Inter-Allied Reparations Commission) formed a committee of international financiers under the chairmanship of the American banker Owen Young. Its report in June 1929 suggested a new scheme of payments. Germany was to continue paying reparations until 1988 but the final sum was reduced to £1850 million (only one-quarter of the figure demanded in 1921). So, after some negotiation by Stresemann with the Allies, the German government accepted the Young Plan shortly before Stresemann's death.

However, in right-wing circles in Germany, Stresemann's diplomatic achievement was seen as yet another betrayal of national interests to the Allies. In the view of the right wing, any payment of reparations was based upon the 'lie' of Germany's war guilt (Article 231 of the Treaty of Versailles) and the new scheme had, therefore, to be opposed. A national committee, led by the new leader of the Nationalists, Alfred Hugenberg, was formed to fight the Young Plan (see page 74). Hugenberg was also Germany's greatest media tycoon. He owned 150 newspapers and a publishing house, as well as UFA, a world-famous film organisation. He now used all his resources to promote his message. Moreover, he generated support from a wide variety of right-wing nationalist factions:

Key term

National Opposition
A title given to various political forces that united to campaign against Weimar. It included the DNVP, the Nazis, the Pan-German League and the *Stahlhelm* – an organisation of ex-soldiers. The 'National Opposition' was forged out of the Young Plan in 1929 to oppose all reparations payments.

- DNVP
- *Stahlhelm* (the largest ex-servicemen's organisation) led by Franz Seldte
- Pan-German League
- some leading industrialists, e.g. Fritz Thyssen
- Hitler and the Nazi Party.

Together this '**National Opposition**' drafted a *Law against the Enslavement of the German People*, which denounced any payment of reparations and demanded the punishment of any minister agreeing to such a treaty. The proposal gained enough signatures for it to be made the issue of a national referendum in December 1929. In the end the National Opposition won only 5.8 million votes, a long way short of the 21 million required by the constitution for success.

However, the campaign of the National Opposition had stirred nationalist emotions, focusing opposition on the democratic government at a vital time. It had also brought together many right-wing opponents of the Republic. For Hitler, the campaign showed clear-cut benefits:

- The Party membership grew to 130,000 by end of 1929.
- Nazism really gained a national standing for the first time.
- The main Party rally at Nuremberg had been a great propaganda success on a much more grandiose scale than any before.
- Hitler made influential political contacts on the extreme right wing.
- The opportunity of having access to Hugenberg's media empire.

The collapse of Müller's Grand Coalition

Müller's coalition government successfully withstood the attack from the 'National Opposition'. However, it was not so successful in dealing with its own internal divisions. Müller, a Social Democrat, struggled to hold the coalition together but, not surprisingly, it was an issue of finance which finally brought down the government in March 1930.

The sharp increase in unemployment had created a large deficit in the new national insurance scheme, and the four major parties in the coalition could not agree on how to tackle it. The SPD, as the political supporters of the trade unions, wanted to increase the contributions and to maintain the levels of welfare payments. The DVP, on the other hand, had strong ties with big business and insisted on reducing benefits. Müller could no longer maintain a majority and he had no option but to tender the resignation of his government.

The appointment of Heinrich Brüning

President Hindenburg granted the post of chancellor to Heinrich Brüning. At first sight, this appeared an obvious choice, since he was the parliamentary leader of the ZP, the second largest party in the *Reichstag*. However, with hindsight, it seems that Brüning's appointment marked a crucial step towards the end of true parliamentary government. This was for two reasons.

First, because he was manoeuvred into office by a select circle of political intriguers, who surrounded the ageing President Hindenburg:

- Otto Meissner, the president's State Secretary
- Oskar von Hindenburg, the president's son
- Major General Kurt von Schleicher, a leading general who had held a series of government and military posts.

All three were conservative-nationalists and had no real faith in the democratic process. Instead, they looked to the president and the emergency powers of Article 48 of the constitution (see pages 21 and 24) as a means of creating a more authoritarian government. In Brüning, they saw a respectable, conservative figure, who could offer firm leadership.

Secondly, Brüning's response to the growing economic crisis led to a political constitutional crisis. His economic policy was to propose cuts in government expenditure, so as to achieve a balanced budget and prevent the risk of reviving inflation. However, the budget was rejected in the *Reichstag* by 256 votes to

Key question
Why could the Grand Coalition not agree?

Resignation of Müller's government: March 1930

Brüning appointed chancellor: March 1930

Key dates

Key question
How was parliamentary government weakened by the leadership of Heinrich Brüning?

193 in July 1930. When, despite this, Brüning put the proposals into effect by means of an emergency decree, signed by the president according to Article 48, the *Reichstag* challenged the decree's legality and voted for its withdrawal. Deadlock had been reached. Brüning, therefore, asked Hindenburg to dissolve the *Reichstag* and to call an election for September 1930.

Key question
Why was the 1930 *Reichstag* election so significant?

Nazi breakthrough

Brüning had hoped that in the developing crisis the people would be encouraged to support the parties of the centre-right from which a coalition could be formed. However, the election results proved him wrong and the real beneficiary was the Nazi Party, which increased its vote from 810,000 to a staggering 6,409,600 (see Figure 6.2).

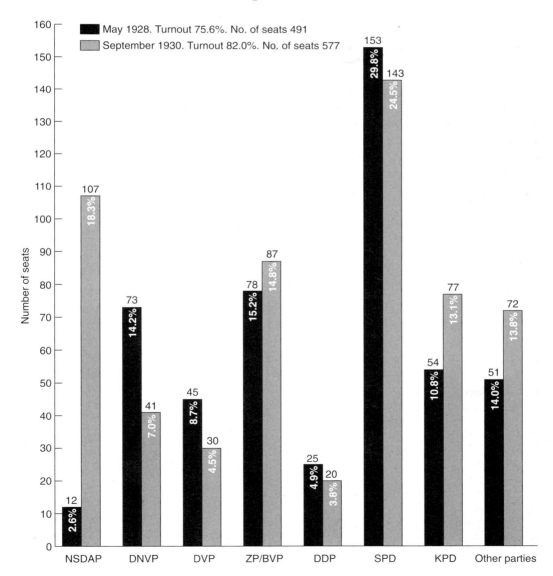

Figure 6.2: *Reichstag* election results for 1928 and 1930. (See major political parties on page 16.)

The key features about the performance of the political parties are as follows:

Reichstag election – Nazis emerged as second largest party in *Reichstag*: September 1930

Key date

- Nazis: With 107 seats and 18.3 per cent, the NSDAP became the second largest political party in Germany.
- Nationalists: The vote of the DNVP was halved from 14.2 per cent to 7 per cent, largely benefiting the Nazis.
- Middle-class democratic parties: The DDP and the DVP lost 20 seats between them.
- Left-wing parties: The vote of the SPD declined from 29.8 per cent to 24.5 per cent, though in contrast the vote of the KPD increased from 10.8 per cent to 13.1 per cent.

Because the result of the 1928 *Reichstag* election had been so disappointing, not even Hitler could have expected the dramatic gains of 1930. Nevertheless, there are several key factors to explain the Nazi breakthrough:

- Since 1928 the Nazi leaders had deliberately directed their propaganda at rural and middle-class/lower middle-class audiences. Nazi gains were at the expense of the DNVP, DVP and DDP.
- Nazi success cannot just be explained by these 'protest votes'. Nearly half of the Nazi seats were won by the Party's attracting 'new' voters:
  - The electorate had grown by 1.8 million since the previous election because a new generation of voters had been added to the roll.
  - The turn-out had increased from 75.6 per cent to 82 per cent.

It would seem that the Nazis had not only picked up a fair proportion of these young first-time voters, but also persuaded many people who had not previously participated in elections to support their cause.

The implications of the 1930 *Reichstag* election were profound. It meant that the left and right extremes had made extensive gains against the pro-democratic parties. This now made it very difficult for proper democratic parliamentary government to function.

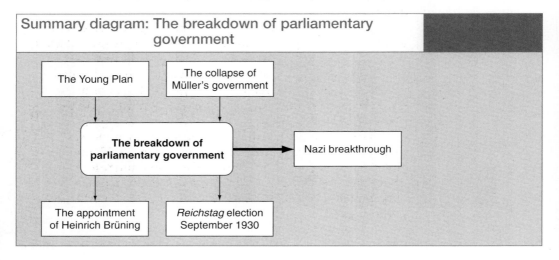

Summary diagram: The breakdown of parliamentary government

The Young Plan

The collapse of Müller's government

The breakdown of parliamentary government → Nazi breakthrough

The appointment of Heinrich Brüning

Reichstag election September 1930

Key question
Was Brüning simply a victim of the circumstances?

3 | Brüning: Presidential Government

Brüning's political position after the election was undoubtedly very difficult. His plan of reinforcing his parliamentary support from the centre–right had not succeeded. Instead, he faced the committed opposition of the more powerful extremes of left and right. However, he was not dismissed as chancellor. Brüning still enjoyed the support of Hindenburg and the SPD decided to 'tolerate' his cabinet. So, although the SPD did not join the government, given the threat now facing the Republic from the extremists it was not prepared to defeat the emergency decrees by the use of Article 48.

In this way, true parliamentary democracy gave way to 'presidential government' with some backing from the *Reichstag*. From 1930–2 Brüning remained as chancellor and he governed Germany by the use of Article 48 through President Hindenburg. He was almost a semi-dictator, as can be seen from his growing use of presidential decrees (see Table 6.2).

Table 6.2: Presidential government, 1930–2

	1930	1931	1932
Presidential decree laws (Article 48)	5	44	66
Reichstag laws	98	34	5
Sitting days of the *Reichstag*	94	42	13

Initially, many historians were sympathetic to Brüning and saw him as a sincere statesman struggling in the face of enormous difficulties to save democracy. They believed that his decision to use Article 48 was an understandable reaction to the failure of party government in the crisis. Others, however, saw him as a reactionary, opposed to democracy, who used his position to introduce emergency powers that paved the way to destroying the Republic and to building the road towards Hitler's dictatorship.

Surprisingly, original defenders of Brüning were forced to give way after the publication of his *Memoirs, 1918–34* following his death in 1970. This shows beyond any doubt that Brüning was an ultra-conservative and monarchist, who had little sympathy for the democratic Republic. His aims in government were decisively to weaken the *Reichstag* and to re-establish an authoritarian constitution that would ignore the power and influence of the left. To these ends, he was prepared to use the emergency powers of the presidency and to look for backing from the conservative vested interests. Therefore, it is now generally accepted that Brüning's appointment did mark a decisive move away from parliamentary government.

Das tote Parlament

DAS BLIEB VOM JAHRE 1848** ÜBRIG!**
So sieht der Reichstag aus, der am 13. Oktober eröffnet wird.

The Dead Parliament. A cartoon/photomontage published by the German communist John Heartfield in October 1930. It shows an empty *Reichstag* with the number 48 superimposed on it, reflecting Brüning's use of the emergency decrees. The caption below the picture reads: 'The dead parliament. It's what's left from 1848! That's what the parliament looks like which is going to open on 13 October.'

Economic policy

Brüning's economic policy was at least consistent. Throughout his two years in office his major aims were imposed by presidential decree:

- To balance the budget.
- To prevent the chance of restarting inflation.
- To get rid of the burden of German reparations.

And so, his policy's main measures were:

- To cut spending drastically.
- To raise taxes.

Key question
Was Brüning economically incompetent?

This clearly lowered demand and it led to a worsening of the slump. Most obviously, there was a large increase in the number of unemployed and a serious decline in the welfare state provision. Soon he was mocked with the title 'the Hunger Chancellor'.

Many historians have condemned Brüning's economic regime of sticking to his policy of reducing expenditure, for seriously worsening the situation and making possible the rise of the Nazis. He was criticised particularly for his failure to introduce economic measures in the summer of 1931, such as work creation schemes in the construction industry and the reduction of agricultural subsidies. These might just have been enough to lessen the worst effects of the depression during 1932.

However, it could be argued that Brüning had no real alternatives to his economic policy. This was because the German economy had *entered* the depression with such severe weaknesses from the 1920s (see pages 60–1) that economic failure was unavoidable. On these grounds, therefore, it could be argued that no Chancellor would have been in a position to expand the economy and Brüning was at the mercy of other forces.

Key dates

Brüning's economic measures imposed by presidential decree: December 1930

Five leading German banks failed: July 1931

Formation of Harzburg Front: October 1931

Key question
Why did Hindenburg force Brüning to resign?

Brüning's fall from power

In the spring of 1932, Hindenburg's first seven-year term of office as President came to an end. Brüning committed himself to securing the old man's re-election and after frenetic campaigning Hindenburg was re-elected on the second ballot. He gained 19.3 million votes (53 per cent) compared with Hitler's 13.4 million (36.8 per cent). However, it was a negative victory. Hindenburg had only been chosen because he was the only alternative between Hitler and the KPD candidate, Ernst Thälmann. Also, Hitler had doubled the Nazi vote, despite losing, and had projected an even more powerful personal image. Moreover, Hindenburg showed no real gratitude to Brüning and, at the end of May 1932, the president forced his chancellor to resign by refusing to sign any more emergency decrees. Why was this?

Banking crisis

The collapse of the major bank, the Danat, and several others in June 1931, revived fears of financial crisis. By the end of the year unemployment was approaching five million people and there were demonstrations in the streets. Moreover, in October 1931 the 'National Opposition' (see pages 105–6) was reborn as the Harzburg Front. It brought together again a range of right-wing political, military and economic forces who demanded the resignation of Brüning and a new *Reichstag* election. The Front arranged a massive rally to denounce Brüning, but in the winter 1931–2 the chancellor still enjoyed the support of Hindenburg.

Land reform

The fundamental cause of Brüning's fall from grace with Hindenburg was his aim to issue an emergency decree to turn some *Junker* estates in east Prussia into 600,000 allotments for

Profile: Heinrich Brüning 1885–1970

1885		– Born into a Catholic trading family
1904–11		– Attended the universities of Munich and Strasbourg and awarded a doctorate in economics
1915–18		– Volunteered to fight in the First World War and gained a commission in the Machine Gun Corps
1918		– Won the Iron Cross First Class
1920		– Entered politics after the war and joined the ZP
1924–33		– Elected to the *Reichstag* and rapidly rose up the ranks of the ZP
1929		– Chosen as leader of the ZP
1930	March	– Appointed chancellor by Hindenburg
	July	– Tried to pass the budget with a presidential decree, but rejected by *Reichstag*. This resulted in the *Reichstag* election of September 1930
1931	July	– Hoover Moratorium on reparations
1932	April	– Proposed the land reform of the Prussian estates
	May	– Dismissed by Hindenburg
1934		– Fled to Holland and then emigrated to America. Lectured at Harvard University
1947		– Returned to Germany and lectured at Cologne University
1970		– Died

The significance of Brüning's career is almost completely concentrated into the two years of his chancellorship, 1930–2. He was very much on the right wing of the ZP so, when he became the leader of the Party, his anti-socialism made it impossible for him to work with the left-wing parties. In his heart, he remained a monarchist and he hoped to amend the Weimar Constitution to make it a more authoritarian system. However, he was opposed to the Nazis – his real mistake was that he underestimated the extent of their threat.

His policies and decisions have been heavily criticised on various fronts:

- He called for the *Reichstag* election in September 1930 and misread the political consequences.
- He remained committed to the economic programme of balancing the budget, which resulted in enormous economic and political pressures.
- He relied on Hindenburg for the use of emergency decrees – and he failed to recognise his over-dependence on the president.

In his defence, it may be claimed that he was a man of integrity and a victim of exceptional circumstances. His historic reputation is perhaps overshadowed by the later development of the Nazi dictatorship.

unemployed workers. Landowners saw this as a threat to their property interests and dubbed it 'agrarian bolshevism'.

Intrigue

Brüning's unpopularity over the above spurred on the group of right wingers, led by Kurt von Schleicher. He managed to persuade Hindenburg to force the chancellor's resignation at the end of May 1932 and to create a right-wing government.

One might be tempted to view Brüning as an innocent sacrifice who was removed by Hindenburg without consultation with the *Reichstag*. However, it should be borne in mind that he had only survived as chancellor because he enjoyed the personal backing of the president. Brüning had agreed with the creation of presidential government based on the powers granted by Article 48 of the constitution, but he was not astute enough to recognise the precarious nature of his own position. He depended solely on retaining the confidence of the president. This makes it harder to sympathise with him when he became the victim of the intrigue of the presidential court.

Assessment of Brüning

Brüning was an honest, hard-working and honourable man who failed. He was not really a committed democrat, but neither was he sympathetic to Nazism, and it is very important to remember that last point. In many respects, Brüning was making good progress towards his aims, when he was dismissed:

- He succeeded in ending the payment of reparations.
- He sympathised with the reduction of the democratic powers of the *Reichstag*.

However:

- He was not clever enough to appreciate how dangerous and unstable the economic crisis had become in Germany by 1932.
- Neither did he realise how insecure was his own position. For as long as Brüning retained the confidence of Hindenburg, presidential government protected his position.

With no real hope of improvement in the economic crisis, it is not surprising that large sections of the population looked to the Nazis to save the situation. Brüning would have nothing to do with Hitler and the Nazis and he continued to uphold the **rule of law**. Sadly, presidential rule had accustomed Germany again to rule by decree. In this way democracy was undermined and the way was cleared for more extreme political parties to assume power. In the end, it is hard to escape the conclusion that Brüning's chancellorship was a dismal failure, and, in view of the Nazi tyranny that was soon to come, a tragic one.

Key dates

Re-election of Hindenburg as president of Germany: April 1932

Brüning resigned. Papen appointed chancellor: May 1932

Key question
Was Brüning a failure?

Key term

Rule of law
Governing a country according to its laws.

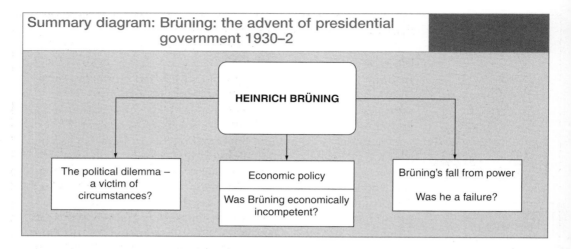

Summary diagram: Brüning: the advent of presidential government 1930–2

HEINRICH BRÜNING

The political dilemma – a victim of circumstances?

Economic policy

Was Brüning economically incompetent?

Brüning's fall from power

Was he a failure?

4 | From Brüning to Papen

Key question
What was Papen's political aim?

Schleicher had recommended the new chancellor, Franz von Papen, to Hindenburg. As an aristocrat, Papen had good connections with high society; as a Catholic he was a member of the Centre Party, although his political views mirrored those of the Nationalists. His outlook quickly formed the basis for a close friendship with Hindenburg.

Papen was also politically ambitious, but his understanding and experience of politics was limited (he did not even hold a seat in the *Reichstag*). If many greeted the choice of Papen with disbelief, it was the man's very lack of ability which appealed to Schleicher, who saw the opportunity to influence events more directly through him.

The new cabinet was called a non-party government of 'national concentration', though it was soon nicknamed the 'Cabinet of Barons'. It was a presidential government dominated by aristocratic landowners and industrialists – and many were not even members of the *Reichstag*. In order to strengthen the government, Papen and Schleicher wanted to secure political support from the Nazis – though Hitler only agreed not to oppose the new government in return for two concessions:

- The dissolution of the *Reichstag* and the calling of fresh elections.
- The ending of a government ban on the SA and SS, which had been introduced in the wake of violence during the presidential campaign.

In this way, Papen and Schleicher hoped that this agreement with the Nazis would result in the creation of a right-wing authoritarian government with a measure of popular support in the form of the Nazis. The *Reichstag* was therefore dissolved and an election was arranged to take place on 31 July 1932.

Reichstag election: July 1932

The election campaign was brutal, as street violence once again took hold in the large cities. In the month of July alone 86 people died as a result of political fights.

Key question
Why was the *Reichstag* election of July 1932 so politically significant?

Profile: Franz von Papen 1879–1969

1879		– Born into a Catholic aristocratic family
1913–18		– Having been trained as a cavalry officer, he embarked on his diplomatic career and served in the USA, Mexico and Turkey
1921		– Elected to the Prussian regional state as a member of ZP
1932	May	– Appointed as chancellor by Hindenburg to head the so-called 'Cabinet of Barons', which did not include any member of the *Reichstag*
		– Decided to call for the *Reichstag* election of July 1932, with serious consequences
	July	– Removed the state regional government of Prussia and appointed himself as Reich Commissioner of Prussia
	September	– Personally defeated by a massive vote of 'no confidence' in the *Reichstag* (512 votes to 42)
	November	– Dismissed by Hindenburg but schemed to replace Schleicher and to recover his power
1933	January	– Appointed as vice-chancellor in Hitler's Nazi–Nationalist coalition
1934	July	– Resigned after the Night of Long Knives
1934–44		– German ambassador in Austria and Turkey
1946		– Charged with war crimes in the Nuremberg trials, but found not guilty
1969		– Lived privately until his death

There have been few political careers that were so short and so disastrous as that of Franz von Papen. He had limited political experience and was out of his depth. His advance was mainly due to his connections with the aristocracy, the Catholic Church and big business (his wife was the daughter of a very rich industrialist).

He was always a monarchist and a nationalist (although he remained nominally a member of ZP). When he became chancellor, he aspired to undo the Weimar Constitution and so he was quite happy to rule by presidential decrees and to denounce the state government of Prussia. Despite his failings, he pursued his personal ambitions and was quickly outmanoeuvred by Hitler in the early months of 1933.

Yet, such bloodshed provided Schleicher and Papen with the excuse to abolish the most powerful regional state government in Germany, Prussia. This government of Prussia had long been a coalition of the SPD and the ZP and had been the focus of right-wing resentment since 1919. So, on 20 July 1932, it was simply removed by Papen who declared a state of emergency and appointed himself as Reich Commissioner of Prussia. This was of immense significance:

- It was an arbitrary and unconstitutional act.
- It replaced a parliamentary system with a presidential authoritarian government.

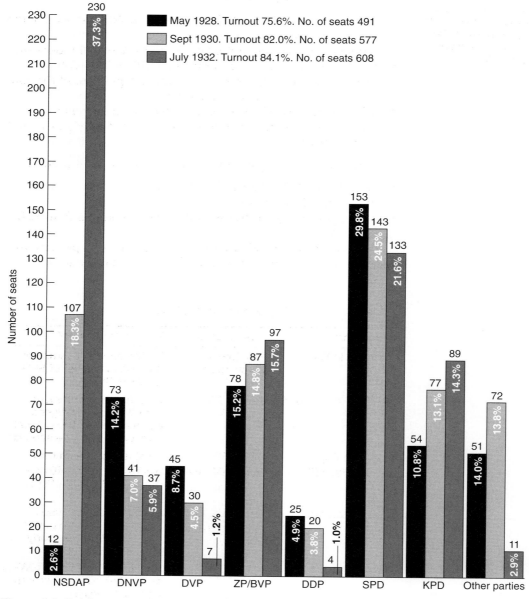

Figure 6.3: *Reichstag* election results 1928–32. (See major political parties on page 16.)

- Democrats – especially the SPD and the trade unions – gave in without any real opposition. Their passive response shows how far the forces of democracy had lost the initiative.

Many on the right wing congratulated Papen on the Prussian *coup*. However, it did not win him any additional electoral support. When the election results came in, it was again the Nazis who had cause to celebrate. They had polled 13.7 million votes and had won 230 seats. Hitler was the leader of by far the largest party in Germany and constitutionally he had every right to form a government.

It is worth bearing in mind the following key features about the performance of the political parties:

Key date

Nazis emerged as the largest party in the *Reichstag* election: July 1932

- Nazis: With 230 seats and 37.3 per cent the NSDAP became the largest political party in Germany.
- Nationalists: The vote of the DNVP fell further to 5.9 per cent.
- Middle-class democratic parties: The DDP and the DVP collapsed disastrously. They polled only 2.2 per cent of the vote and gained just 11 seats between them.
- Left-wing parties: The vote of the SPD declined further to 21.6 per cent, though in contrast the vote of the KPD increased to 14.3 per cent.

In electoral terms the gains of the Nazis could be explained by:

- the collapse of the DDP and DVP vote
- the decline of the DNVP
- a small percentage of disgruntled workers changing from SPD to NSDAP
- the support for the 'other parties' falling from 13.8 per cent to 2.9 per cent, which suggests their loyalty transferred to the Nazis

Table 6.3: Germany's governments 1928–33

Chancellors	Dates in office	Type of government
Hermann Müller (SPD)	May 1928– March 1930	Parliamentary government. A coalition cabinet of SPD, ZP, DDP, DVP
Heinrich Brüning (ZP)	March 1930– May 1932	Presidential government dependent on emergency decrees. A coalition cabinet from political centre and right
Franz von Papen (ZP, but very right wing)	May 1932– December 1932	Presidential government dependent on emergency decrees. Many non-party cabinet members
General Kurt von Schleicher (Non-party)	December 1932– January 1933	Presidential government dependent on emergency decrees. Many non-party cabinet members
Adolf Hitler (NSDAP)	1933–45	Coalition cabinet of NSDAP and DNVP, but gave way to Nazi dictatorship

- the turnout increasing to 84 per cent which indicated the same trend as September 1930 that the Party was attracting even more 'new voters'.

Two further points worth remembering about the *Reichstag* election of July 1932 are:

- Only 39.5 per cent voted for the pro-democratic parties.
- Added together, the percentage of votes for the KPD and NSDAP combined to 51.6 per cent.

These two political facts are telling indeed. The German people had voted to reject democracy.

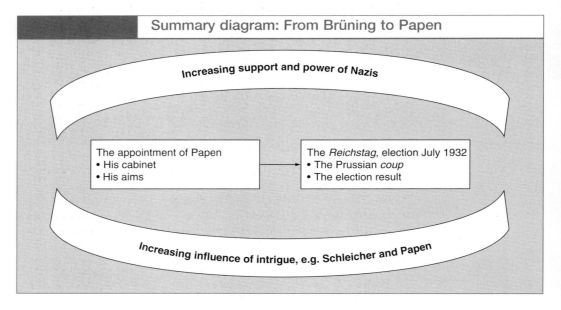

Summary diagram: From Brüning to Papen

Increasing support and power of Nazis

The appointment of Papen
- His cabinet
- His aims

The *Reichstag*, election July 1932
- The Prussian *coup*
- The election result

Increasing influence of intrigue, e.g. Schleicher and Papen

5 | The Death of the Weimar Republic

It is now clear that Weimar democracy was really dead before the establishment of the Nazi dictatorship in early 1933 (see pages 139–43). The problem for the historian is trying to determine when the Weimar Republic expired and why.

Three major themes stand out as fundamental weaknesses of the Weimar Republic.

Key question
Why did Weimar democracy fail?

(i) The hostility of Germany's vested interests

From the very start, the Weimar Republic faced the hostility of Germany's established élites. Following military defeat and the threat of revolution, this opposition was at first limited. However, the fact that so many key figures in German society and business rejected the idea of a democratic republic was a major problem for Weimar. They worked against the interests of Weimar and hoped for a return to the pre-war situation. This was a powerful handicap to the successful development of the Republic in the 1920s and, in the 1930s, it was to become a decisive factor in its final collapse.

(ii) Ongoing economic problems

The Republic was also troubled by an almost continuous economic crisis that affected all levels of society. It inherited the enormous costs of the First World War followed by the burden of post-war reconstruction, Allied reparations and the heavy expense of the new welfare benefits. So, even though the inflation crisis of 1923 was overcome, problems in the economy were disguised and remained unresolved. These were to have dramatic consequences with the onset of the world economic crisis in 1929.

(iii) Limited base of popular support

Weimar democracy never enjoyed widespread political support. There was never total acceptance of, and confidence in, its system and its values. From the Republic's birth its narrow base of popular support was caught between the extremes of left and right. But, as time went by, Weimar's claims to be the legitimate government became increasingly open to question. Sadly, Weimar democracy was associated with defeat and the humiliation of the Treaty of Versailles and reparations. Its reputation was further damaged by the crisis of 1922–3. Significantly, even the mainstays of the Weimar Republic had weaknesses:

- The main parties of German liberalism, DDP and DVP, were losing support from 1924.
- The ZP and DNVP were both moving to the political right.
- Even the loyalty and the commitment of the SPD to democracy has to be balanced against its failure to join the coalitions in the mid-1920s and its conflict with its left-wing partner, the KPD.

In short, a sizeable proportion of the German population never had faith in the existing constitutional arrangements and, as the years passed, more were looking for change.

These unrelenting pressures meant that Weimar democracy went through a number of phases:

- The difficult circumstances of its birth in 1918–19 left it handicapped. It was in many respects, therefore, a major achievement that it survived the problems of the period 1919–23.
- The years of relative stability from 1924 to 1929, however, amounted to only a short breathing space and did not result in any strengthening of the Weimar system. On the eve of the world economic crisis it seemed that Weimar's long-term chances of survival were already far from good.
- In the end, the impact of the world depression, 1929–33, intensified the pressures that brought about Weimar's final crisis.

In the view of some historians, Weimar had been a gamble with no chance of success. For others, the Republic continued to offer the hope of democratic survival right until mid-1932, when the Nazis became the largest party in the July *Reichstag* election. However, the manner of Brüning's appointment and his decision to rule by emergency decree created a particular system of presidential government. This fundamentally undermined the Weimar system and was soon followed by the electoral breakthrough of the Nazis. From this time, democracy's chance of surviving was very slim indeed. Democracy lived on with ever increasing weakness before it reached its demise in July 1932. However, in truth, democratic rule in Weimar Germany was terminal from the summer of 1930.

Summary diagram: The death of the Weimar Republic

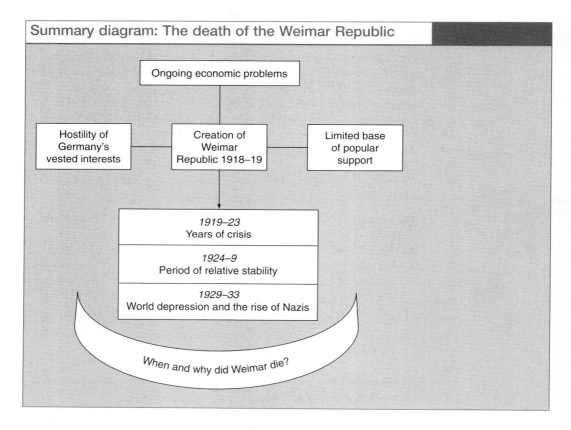

Study Guide: AS Question

In the style of Edexcel

How far do you agree that the Weimar Republic collapsed because the economic crisis of 1929–32 revealed its 'fundamental weaknesses'? (30 marks)

Exam tips

The cross-references are intended to take you straight to the material that will help you to answer the question.

This question asks you to explain why the Weimar Republic collapsed, but it has a precise focus on whether the Republic was weak and fragile from the beginning ('a gamble with no chance of success', page 119). How serious were its fundamental weaknesses? Did the economic crises simply reveal these weaknesses, or did the post-1929 period represent a set of exceptional circumstances and introduce new issues which forced the collapse?

In exploring the fundamental weaknesses of the Republic you could consider:

- The hostility of powerful vested interests from the beginning (pages 25 and 117–18).
- Ongoing economic problems and how far the period of stability (1924–9) disguised rather than resolved them (pages 47–53 and 59–62).
- The limited base of popular support for Weimar democracy (page 119).

For the impact of events and circumstances after 1929 you could consider:

- The impact of world depression in intensifying problems and creating political crisis and undermining support for the Weimar Republic (pages 101–4 and 105–8).
- The link between the economic crisis and the electoral breakthrough and growing strength of the Nazis (pages 123–33).
- The undermining of democracy during the 'presidential governments' of Brüning, von Papen and von Schliecher in 1930–2 (pages 109–16).

You will need to come to an overall conclusion. You may decide to emphasise the importance of the events and circumstances post-1929, or to show that the collapse of the Weimar Republic came about primarily because of its fundamental weaknesses.

7 The Nazi Road to Dictatorship 1932–4

POINTS TO CONSIDER

Although Weimar democracy was, in effect, dead by the summer of 1932, it should not be assumed that Hitler's appointment was inevitable. The purpose of this chapter is to consider two questions that are inextricably linked: 'Why did Hitler and the Nazis become so politically powerful?' and 'Why was Weimar Germany replaced by a Nazi dictatorship?' The main points are:

- The creation of a Nazi mass movement: who voted for the Nazis and why?
- Nazi political methods: propaganda and violence
- Political intrigue: the appointment of Hitler as chancellor
- The establishment of the Nazi dictatorship, January–March 1933
- Co-ordination
- The Night of the Long Knives

Key dates

1932	May	Brüning dismissed as chancellor and replaced by Papen
	July	*Reichstag* election: Nazis won 230 seats (37.3 per cent)
	September	*Reichstag* passed a massive vote of 'no confidence' in Papen's government (512 votes to 42)
	November	*Reichstag* election: Nazi vote dropped to 33.1 per cent, winning 196 seats
	December	Papen dismissed as chancellor and replaced by Schleicher
1933	January 30	Schleicher dismissed and Hitler appointed as chancellor
	February 27	*Reichstag* fire: Communists blamed
	March 5	Final *Reichstag* elections according to Weimar Constitution
	March 21	The 'Day of Potsdam'
	March 23	Enabling Act passed
	July 14	All political opposition to NSDAP declared illegal

| 1934 | June 30 | Night of the Long Knives: destruction of the SA by the SS |
| | August 2 | Death of Hindenburg: Hitler combined the offices of chancellor and president. Oath of loyalty taken by the army |

1 | The Creation of a Nazi Mass Movement

Key question
Who voted for the Nazis?

The point is often made that Hitler and the Nazis never gained an overall majority in *Reichstag* elections. However, such an occurrence was unlikely because of the number of political parties in Weimar Germany and the operation of the proportional representation system. Considering this, Nazi electoral achievements by July 1932 were very impressive. The 13,745,000 voters who had supported them represented 37.3 per cent of the electorate, thus making Hitler's party the largest in the *Reichstag*. Only one other party on one other occasion had polled more: the SPD in the revolutionary atmosphere of January 1919. Nazism had become a mass movement with which millions identified and, as such, it laid the foundations for Hitler's coming to power in January 1933. Who were these Nazi voters and why were they attracted to the Nazi cause?

Key date
Nazis won 230 seats out of 608 (37.3 per cent) in *Reichstag* election: July 1932

The results of the elections 1928–32 show the changing balance of the political parties (see pages 107 and 114–18), although really these figures on their own are limited in what they show us about the nature of Nazi support. However, the graph and table in Figure 7.1 reveal a number of significant points about the kind of people who actually voted for the Nazis.

From this it seems fairly clear that the Nazis made extensive gains from those parties with a middle-class and/or a Protestant identity. However, it is also apparent that the Catholic parties, the Communist Party and, to a large extent, the Social Democrats were able to withstand the Nazi advances.

Geography and denomination

These political trends are reflected in the geographical base of Nazi support, which was generally higher in the north and east of the country and lower in the south and west. Right across the North German Plain, from East Prussia to Schleswig-Holstein, the Nazis gained their best results and this seems to reflect the significance of two important factors – religion and the degree of urbanisation.

In those areas where Catholicism predominated (see Figure 7.2) the Nazi breakthrough was less marked, whereas the more Protestant regions were more likely to vote Nazi. Likewise, the Nazis fared less well in the large industrial cities, but gained greater support in the more rural communities and in residential suburbs.

The Nazi vote was at its lowest in the Catholic cities of the west, such as Cologne and Düsseldorf. It was at its highest in the

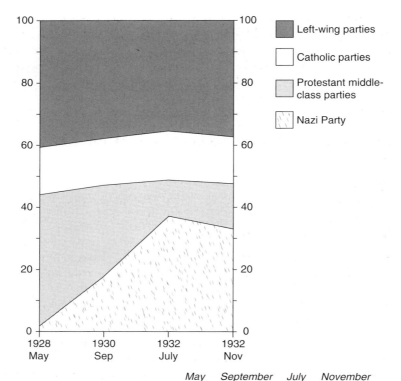

	May 1928	September 1930	July 1932	November 1932
Nazi Party	2.6	18.3	37.3	33.1
Protestant middle-class parties (DNVP, DDP, DVP and others)	41.8	29.3	11.1	14.6
Catholic parties (ZP and BVP)	15.2	14.8	15.7	15.0
Left-wing parties (SPD and KPD)	40.4	37.6	35.9	37.3

Figure 7.1:
Percentage of vote gained by each major political grouping in the four *Reichstag* elections 1928–32

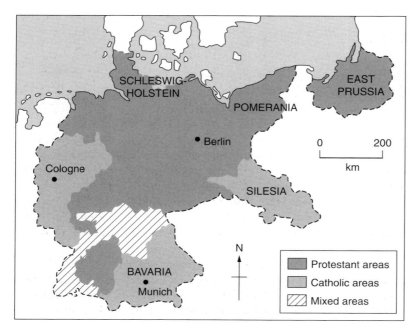

Figure 7.2:
Electoral split by religion

Protestant countryside of the north and north-east, such as Schleswig-Holstein and Pomerania. Ironically, therefore, Bavaria, a strongly Catholic region, and the birthplace of Nazism, had one of the lowest Nazi votes in Germany. Such a picture does not of course take into account the exceptions created by local circumstances. For instance, parts of the province of Silesia, although mainly Catholic and urbanised, still recorded a very high Nazi vote. This was probably the result of nationalist passions generated in a border province, which had lost half its land to Poland.

Class
Nazi voters also reflected the rural/urban division in terms of their social groupings. It seems that the Nazis tended to win a higher proportion of support from:

- the peasants and farmers
- the '*Mittelstand*' (the lower middle classes, e.g. artisans, craftsmen and shopkeepers)
- the established middle classes, e.g. teachers, **white-collar workers**, public employees.

This tendency is shown in the figures of the Nazi Party's membership lists, which can be seen in Figure 7.3.

From this it is clear that a significantly higher proportion of the middle-class subsections tended to join the Nazi Party than the other classes, i.e. government officials/employees, self-employed, white-collar workers. However, it is worth bearing in mind two other points. First, although the working class did join the Nazi party in smaller proportions, it was still the largest section in the NSDAP. Secondly, although the peasants tended to vote for the Nazis, the figures show they did not join the NSDAP in the same proportion.

The appeal of Nazism
It is clear that more of the Protestants and the middle classes voted for Nazism in proportion to their percentage in German society. The real question is why were those with a loyalty to Catholicism or socialism not so readily drawn to voting for the Nazis?

- First, both of them represented well-established ideologies in their own right and both opposed Nazism on an intellectual level.
- Secondly, the organisational strength of each movement provided an effective counter to Nazi propaganda. For socialism, there was the trade union structure. For Catholicism, there was the Church hierarchy, extending right down to the local parish priest.
- Thirdly, both movements had suffered under the Imperial German regime. As so often happens, persecution strengthened commitment. It was, therefore, much harder for the Nazis to break down the established loyalties of working-class and

Key term

White-collar workers
Workers not involved in manual labour.

Key question
Why were the Protestants, the middle classes and the young more attracted to Nazism?

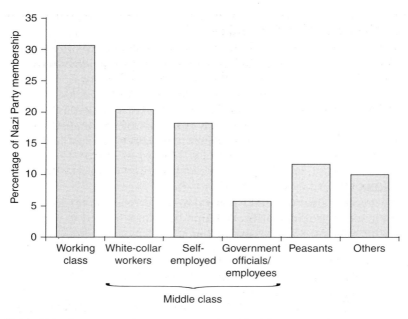

Figure 7.3: Nazi Party members in 1932

Table 7.1: German society as a whole in 1933 (%)

Working class	Middle class			Peasants	Others
	White-collar workers	Self-employed	Government officials/ employees		
46.3	12.4	9.6	4.8	20.7	6.2

Catholic communities and their traditional '**associationism**', or identity, remained strong. In contrast, the Protestants, the farmers and the middle classes had no such loyalties. They were therefore more likely to accept the Nazi message.

Associationism
Having a strong identity or affiliation with a particular group.

Key term

The 'politics of anxiety'

What was common among many Nazi voters was their lack of faith in, and identity with, the Weimar system. They believed that their traditional role and status in society was under threat. For many of the middle classes (see Figure 7.3 above) the crisis of 1929–33 was merely the climax of a series of disasters since 1918. Hitler was therefore able to exploit what is termed 'the politics of anxiety', as expressed by the historian T. Childers in his book *The Nazi Voter*:

> [By 1930] the NSDAP had become a unique phenomenon in German electoral politics, a catch-all party of protest, whose constituents, while drawn primarily from the middle class electorate were united above all by a profound contempt for the existing political and economic system.

In this way Hitler seemed able to offer to many Germans an escape from overwhelming crisis and a return to former days.

Profile: Adolf Hitler 1889–1945

1889	April	–	Born at Braunau-am-Inn, Austria
1905		–	Left school with no real qualifications
1907–13		–	Lived as a dropout in Vienna
1914		–	Joined the German army
1918	August	–	Awarded the Iron Cross, first class
	October	–	Gassed and stayed in hospital at the time of Germany's surrender
1919	September	–	Joined the DAP led by Drexler
1920	February	–	Drew up the Party's 25 points programme with Drexler. The Party was renamed the NSDAP
1921	July	–	Appointed leader of the Party
1923	November 8–9	–	Beer Hall *putsch* at Munich
1924		–	Found guilty of treason and sentenced to five years, reduced to nine months. Wrote *Mein Kampf*
1925	February 27	–	NSDAP refounded at Munich
1925–33		–	Committed the Party to a legality policy
		–	Restructured the Party
1930	September	–	Nazi breakthrough in the *Reichstag* election: 107 seats won
1932	July	–	Nazis elected the largest party in the *Reichstag* election
	August	–	Requested the post of chancellor, but rejected by Hindenburg
1933	January 30	–	Appointed chancellor of coalition government by Hindenburg
	March 23	–	Given dictatorial powers by the Enabling Act
1934	June 30	–	Ordered the purge of the SA, known as the Night of the Long Knives
	August 2	–	Combined the posts of chancellor and president on the death of Hindenburg. Thereafter, referred to as *Der Führer*
1935		–	Declaration of military conscription
1936	March	–	Remilitarisation of the Rhineland
1937	November	–	Hossbach Conference
1938	February	–	Blomberg–Fritsch crisis. Purge of army generals and other leading conservatives
1938	March	–	*Anschluss* with Austria
	September	–	Czech crisis resulting in the take-over of Sudetenland
1939	September 1	–	Ordered the invasion of Poland (resulting in the declaration of war by Britain and France on 3 September)
1941	June 22	–	Ordered the invasion of the USSR
	December 11	–	Declared war on the USA after Japan attacked Pearl Harbor
1944	July 20	–	Stauffenberg Bomb Plot
1945	April 30	–	Committed suicide in the ruins of Berlin

Background

Hitler's upbringing has provoked much psychological analysis, and the character that has emerged has been seen as repressed, lonely and moody. It also seems that much of Hitler's outlook on life was shaped by his unhappy years in Vienna (1907–13) when he failed to become an art student. It was here, too, that the real core of his political ideas was firmly established: anti-Semitism, German nationalism, anti-democracy and anti-Marxism. Hitler himself found a real purpose in the First World War. His belief in

German nationalism and the camaraderie of the troops combined to give him direction. However, the shock of hearing of Germany's surrender in November 1918 confirmed all his prejudices.

The early years of the Nazi Party

Hitler in 1919 was drawn to the DAP, which was just one of many ultra-right-wing racist parties in post-war Germany. His dynamic speeches and his commitment quickly resulted in his becoming the NSDAP's leader by 1921 and it was he who prompted many of the Party's early features, which gave it such a dynamic identity. Nevertheless, despite all the noise and trouble he caused, Hitler was still only the leader of a fringe political party in Bavaria. So when Germany hit the problems of 1923, Hitler grossly overestimated the potential of the *putsch* in November 1923 and it ended in disaster.

Hitler used the next few months to good effect. He exploited his trial by turning himself into a hero of the right-wing nationalists and in prison he wrote *Mein Kampf*. He also reassessed his long-term strategy to one based on legality. The following years were relatively stable and economically prosperous years for Weimar, and the election results for Hitler and the Nazi Party in 1928 were very disappointing. Nevertheless, he managed to restore his leadership and restructure the Party and its organisation.

The road to power 1929–33

The Great Depression created the environment in which Hitler could exploit his political skills. His charisma, his speeches and his advanced use of propaganda, directed by his disciple Goebbels, were the key features of his political success. Nevertheless, although he emerged by 1932 as the leader of the largest party and the most serious opponent to Weimar democracy, he was only invited to be chancellor in January 1933 when he joined a coalition with other nationalists and conservatives.

Dictator 1933–45

Hitler established his dictatorship with immense speed. He was given unlimited powers by the Enabling Act, which provided the legal basis for the suppression of political opposition, and he destroyed the dissident faction in his own Party on the Night of the Long Knives. After the death of Hindenburg, he styled himself *Führer* of Germany.

Hitler was portrayed as the all-powerful dictator, but there has been considerable debate about the image and reality of his direction of daily affairs (see page 228) Nevertheless, it is fair to conclude that Hitler leadership directed German events:

- by upholding the creation of a one-party state maintained by the brutal SS-Police system, which was totally loyal to him (see pages 229–34)
- by supporting the gradualist racial policy that culminated in the genocide (see pages 215–24)
- by pursuing an expansionist foreign policy to establish a 'greater Germany' by means of *Lebensraum* (see pages 245–50).

Below the surface Hitler's regime was chaotic; but the cult of the *Führer* was upheld by Goebbels's propaganda machine as well as by the diplomatic and military successes from 1935–41. However, the winter of 1942–3 marked the 'turn of the tide' and Hitler increasingly deluded himself and refused to consider surrender. It was only when the Red Army closed in on the ruins of Berlin that the spell of the *Führer*'s power was finally broken – by his own suicide in the bunker on 30 April 1945.

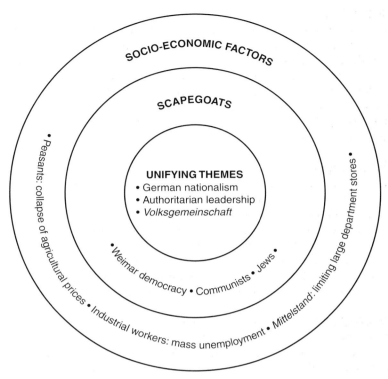

Figure 7.4: Nazi propaganda

Key question
Did SA violence
advance the rise of
Nazism?

Violence

There was one other strand to the political style of this Nazi
revolution: the systematic encouragement and use of violence.
Weimar politics had been a bloody affair from the start, but the
growth of the SA and SS unleashed an unprecedented wave of
violence, persecution and intimidation.

The growth of unemployment resulted in a phenomenal
expansion of the SA, led by Röhm, in 1921–3 and 1930–4.
Understandably, many people joined as members of the SA out of
desperation, for food and accommodation, although much of it
was just thuggery. The SA mainly was responsible for the violence
against the opposition, especially the Communists. All this helped
to destabilise the already difficult situation in Germany and, in
the wake of the presidential election (see pages 109–13), the SA
was actually banned for three months. However, it was restored by
the new chancellor, Papen, in June 1932. So, during the
campaign of July 1932, there were 461 political riots in Prussia
alone: battles between Communists and Nazis on 10 July left 10
people dead; a week later, 19 died after the Nazis marched
through a working-class suburb of Hamburg.

Such violent activities were encouraged by the Nazi leadership,
as control of the streets was seen as essential to the expansion of
Nazi power. The ballot box of democracy remained merely a
means to an end, and, therefore, other non-democratic tactics
were considered legitimate in the quest for power. The Nazis

poured scorn on rational discussion and fair play. For them the end did justify the means. For their democratic opponents, there was the dilemma of how to resist those who exploited the freedoms of a democratic society merely to undermine it.

The Stennes' revolt

Despite the Nazi violence, Hitler became increasingly keen to maintain the policy of legality. He felt it was important to keep discipline, so he could maintain the image of a Party that could offer firm and ordered government. The SA had generally supported the radical socialist aspects of Nazism, and yet Hitler was concerned increasingly with appealing to the middle-class conservative Nazi voters. The most serious disagreement between the SA and the Party leadership has become known as the Stennes' revolt in February 1931.

Walther Stennes, the leader of the Berlin SA, rebelled against the orders of Hitler and Goebbels to act legally and to limit the violence. Hitler defeated the revolt with a small purge, but it underlined the fact that the relationship between the Party leadership and the SA was at times very difficult. These differences were not really resolved until the infamous **Night of the Long Knives** in 1934 (see pages 147–52).

Night of the Long Knives
A crucial turning point when Hitler arranged for the SS to purge the SA leadership and murder about 200 victims, including Ernst Röhm, Gregor Strasser and Kurt von Schleicher.

Key term

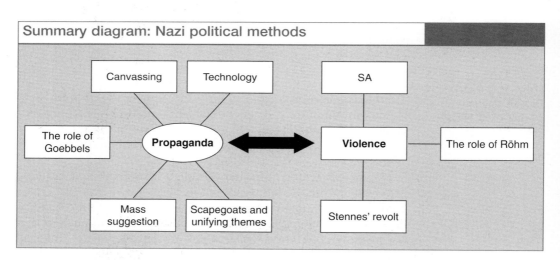

Summary diagram: Nazi political methods

- Canvassing
- Technology
- SA
- The role of Goebbels
- Propaganda
- Violence
- The role of Röhm
- Mass suggestion
- Scapegoats and unifying themes
- Stennes' revolt

3 | Political Intrigue, July 1932 to January 1933

The political strength of the Nazi Party following the July 1932 *Reichstag* elections was beyond doubt (see pages 114–18). However, there still remained the problem for Hitler of how to translate this popular following into real power. He was determined to take nothing less than the post of chancellor for himself. This was unacceptable to both Schleicher and Papen, who were keen to have Nazis in the cabinet, but only in positions of limited power. Therefore, the meeting between Hitler, Papen and Hindenburg on 13 August ended in deadlock.

Key question
Why did Papen fail to prevent Hitler's coming to power?

Key dates

Reichstag passed a massive vote of 'no confidence' in Papen's government (512 votes to 42): September 1932

Nazi vote dropped to 33.1 per cent and won 196 seats in the *Reichstag* election: November 1932

Papen's failure

As long as Papen retained the sympathy of Hindenburg, Hitler's ambitions would remain frustrated. Indeed, a leading modern historian, Jeremy Noakes, describes the period from August to December 1932 as 'the months of crisis' for the Nazis, since 'it appeared the policy of legality had led to a cul-de-sac'. Party morale declined and some of the wilder SA members again became increasingly restless.

On the other hand, Papen was humiliated when on 12 September the *Reichstag* passed a massive vote of 'no confidence' in Papen's government (512 votes to 42). Consequently, he dissolved the new *Reichstag* and called for yet another election. In some respects

'A Breakdown: A Pleasing Phenomenon!' Cartoon by Oskar Garvens mocking the German people in 1932 for showing no interest in the competing political parties.

Papen's reading of the situation was sound. The Nazis were short of money, their morale was low and the electorate was growing tired of repeated elections. These factors undoubtedly contributed to the fall in the Nazi vote on 6 November to 11.7 million (33.1 per cent), which gave them 196 seats. However, Papen's tactics had not achieved their desired end, since the fundamental problem of overcoming the lack of majority *Reichstag* support for his cabinet remained. Hitler stood firm: he would not join the government except as chancellor.

In his frustration, Papen began to consider a drastic alternative; the dissolution of the *Reichstag*, the declaration of martial law and the establishment of a presidential dictatorship. However, such a plan was completely opposed by Schleicher, who found Papen's growing political desperation and his friendship with President Hindenburg additional causes for concern. Schleicher still believed that the popular support for the Nazis could not be ignored, and that Papen's plan would give rise to civil commotion and perhaps civil war. When he informed Hindenburg of the army's lack of confidence in Papen, the President was forced, unwillingly, to demand the resignation of his friendly chancellor.

> **Key date**
>
> Papen dismissed as chancellor and replaced by Schleicher: December 1932

Schleicher's failure

> **Key question**
> Why did Schleicher fail to prevent Hitler's coming to power?

Schleicher at last came out into the open. Over the previous two years he had been happy to play his role behind the scenes, but he now decided to become the dominant player, when he gained the favour of Hindenburg and was appointed chancellor on 2 December. Schleicher's aims, rather ambitiously, were to achieve political stability and restore national confidence by creating a more broadly based government. He had a two-pronged strategy:

- First, to gain some support from elements of the political left, especially the trade unions, by suggesting a programme of public works.
- Second, to split the Nazis and attract the more socialist wing of the Nazi Party, under Gregor Strasser, by offering him the position of vice-chancellor.

With these objectives Schleicher, therefore, intended to project himself as the chancellor of national reconciliation. However, his political manoeuvres came to nothing.

First, the trade unions remained deeply suspicious of his motives and, encouraged by their political masters from the SPD, they broke off negotiations. Moreover, the idea of public works alienated some of the landowners and businessmen. Second, although Schleicher's strategy to offer Strasser the post of vice-chancellor was a very clever one, in the end it did not work. Strasser himself responded positively to Schleicher's overtures and he was keen to accept the post, but the fundamental differences between Hitler and Strasser led to a massive row. Hitler retained the loyalty of the Party's leadership and Strasser was left isolated and promptly forced to resign from the Party.

Profile: Kurt von Schleicher 1882–1934

1882		– Born in Brandenburg, Prussia
1900–18		– Professional soldier and became an officer in Hindenburg's regiment
1919–32		– Worked in the German civil service in the Defence Ministry
1932	June	– Appointed defence minister in Papen's presidential government
	December	– Chancellor of Germany, until his forced resignation on 28 January 1933
1933	January	– Dismissed by Hindenburg
1934	June	– Murdered in the Night of the Long Knives

Schleicher was a shadowy figure and yet, he still had an important influence in the years 1930–3. He really preferred to exert political power behind the scenes and he did not take any high-ranking post until he became defence minister in June 1932. Nevertheless, he was undoubtedly the 'fixer', who set up the appointments of Brüning and Papen before, through Hindenburg, he finally contrived his own chancellorship. As a general, his primary aim was to preserve the interests and values of the German army, but in the end he was unable to control the intrigue – and a year later he lost his own life.

Nevertheless, the incident had been a major blow to Party morale and tensions remained high in the last few weeks of 1932, as the prospect of achieving power seemed to drift away.

Hitler's success

Key question
Why did President Hindenburg eventually appoint Hitler as chancellor?

Hitler's fortunes did not begin to take a more favourable turn until the first week of 1933. Papen had never forgiven Schleicher for dropping him. Papen was determined to regain political office and he recognised he could only achieve this by convincing Hindenburg that he could muster majority support in the *Reichstag*. Consequently, secret contacts were made with Nazi leaders, which culminated in a meeting on 4 January 1933 between Papen and Hitler. Here it was agreed in essence that Hitler should head a Nazi–Nationalist coalition government with Papen as vice-chancellor.

Back-stage intrigue to unseat Schleicher now took over. Papen looked for support for his plan from major landowners, leaders of industry and the army. It was only now that the conservative establishment thought that they had identified an escape from the threat of communism and the dangerous intrigues of Schleicher. But, above all, Papen had to convince the president himself. Hindenburg, undoubtedly encouraged by his son, Oskar, and his state secretary, Meissner, eventually gave in. Schleicher had failed in his attempt to bring stability. In fact, he had only succeeded in frightening the powerful vested interests with his ambitious plans. Hindenburg, therefore, heeded the advice of Papen to make Hitler chancellor of a coalition government, secure in the knowledge that those traditional conservatives and Nationalists would control the Nazis. On 28 January 1933, Hindenburg withdrew his support for Schleicher as chancellor.

It was only in this situation that Hindenburg finally agreed, on the suggestion of Papen, to appoint Hitler as chancellor in the mistaken belief Hitler could be controlled and used in the interests of the conservative establishment. Papen believed that Hitler would be a chancellor in chains and so two days later, on 30 January 1933, Hindenburg agreed to sanction the creation of a Nazi–Nationalist coalition.

> **Key date**
>
> Schleicher dismissed and Hitler appointed as chancellor:
> 30 January 1933

Nazi parade celebrating Hitler's appointment as chancellor near the Brandenburg Gate during the evening of 30 January 1933.

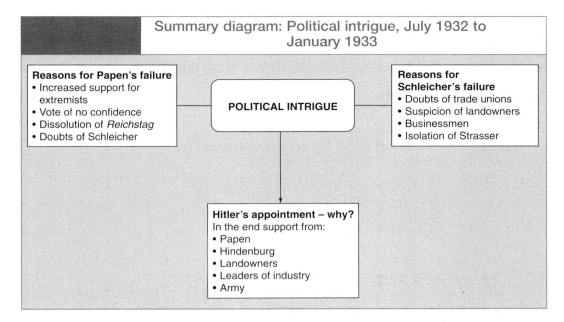

Summary diagram: Political intrigue, July 1932 to January 1933

Reasons for Papen's failure
- Increased support for extremists
- Vote of no confidence
- Dissolution of *Reichstag*
- Doubts of Schleicher

POLITICAL INTRIGUE

Reasons for Schleicher's failure
- Doubts of trade unions
- Suspicion of landowners
- Businessmen
- Isolation of Strasser

Hitler's appointment – why?
In the end support from:
- Papen
- Hindenburg
- Landowners
- Leaders of industry
- Army

4 | The Nazi 'Legal Revolution', January–March 1933

Although Hitler had been appointed chancellor, his power was by no means absolute. Hindenburg had not been prepared to support Hitler's appointment until he had been satisfied that the chancellor's power would remain limited. Such was Papen's confidence about Hitler's restricted room for manoeuvre that he boasted to a friend, 'In two months we'll have pushed Hitler into a corner so hard that he'll be squeaking.'

The limitations of Hitler as chancellor

Key question
What were the political constraints on Hitler?

At first sight, the confidence of the conservatives seemed to be justified, since Hitler's position was weak in purely constitutional terms:

- There were only two other Nazis in the cabinet of 12: Wilhelm Frick as minister of the interior, and Hermann Göring as a minister without portfolio (a minister with no specific responsibility) (see profile, page 168). There were, therefore, nine other non-Nazi members of the cabinet, all from conservative-nationalist backgrounds, such as the army, industry and landowners.
- Hitler's coalition government did not have a majority in the *Reichstag*, suggesting that it would be difficult for the Nazis to introduce any dramatic legislation.
- The chancellor's post, as the previous 12 months had clearly shown, was dependent on the whim of President Hindenburg, and he openly resented Hitler. Hindenburg had made Hitler chancellor but he could as easily sack him.

Hitler was very much aware of the potential power of the army and the trade unions. He could not alienate these forces, which could break his government. The army could arrange a military *coup* or the trade unions could organise a general strike, as they had done in 1920 (see pages 39–40).

Hitler's strengths

Within two months, the above weaknesses were shown not to be real limitations when Hitler became a dictator. Moreover, power was to be achieved by carrying on with the policy of legality which the Party had pursued since 1925. Hitler already possessed several key strengths when he became chancellor:

Key question
What were Hitler's main political strengths?

- He was the leader of the largest political party in Germany, which was why the policy of ignoring him had not worked. During 1932 it had only led to the ineffectual governments of Papen and Schleicher. Therefore, political realism forced the conservatives to work with him. They probably needed him more than he needed them. The alternative to Hitler was civil war or a Communist *coup* – or so it seemed to many people at the time.
- More importantly, the Nazi Party had now gained access to the resources of the state. For example, Göring (see page 168) not only had a place in the cabinet but was also minister of the interior in Prussia, with responsibility for the police. It was a responsibility that he used blatantly to harass opponents, while ignoring Nazi crimes. Goebbels (see pages 237–8), likewise, exploited the propaganda opportunities on behalf of the Nazis. 'The struggle is a light one now,' he confided in his diary, '… since we are able to employ all the means of the state. Radio and press are at our disposal.'
- Above all, however, Hitler was a masterly political tactician. He was determined to achieve absolute power for himself whereas Papen was really politically naïve. It soon became clear that 'Papen's political puppet' was too clever to be strung along by a motley collection of ageing conservatives.

The *Reichstag* election, 5 March 1933

Hitler lost no time in removing his strings. Within 24 hours of his appointment as chancellor, new *Reichstag* elections had been called. He felt new elections would not only increase the Nazi vote, but also enhance his own status.

Key question
How did Hitler create a dictatorship in two months?

The campaign for the final *Reichstag* elections held according to the Weimar Constitution had few of the characteristics expected of a democracy: violence and terror dominated with meetings of the Socialists and Communists being regularly broken up by the Nazis. In Prussia, Göring used his authority to enrol an extra 50,000 into the police; nearly all were members of the SA and SS. Altogether 69 people died during the five-week campaign.

The Nazis also used the atmosphere of hate and fear to great effect in their election propaganda. Hitler set the tone in his 'Appeal to the German People' of 31 January 1933. He blamed the prevailing poor economic conditions on democratic government and the terrorist activities of the Communists. He

'Not the most comfortable seat.' A US cartoon drawn soon after Hitler's appointment as chancellor. What does it suggest about Hitler's political position at that time?

cultivated the idea of the government as a 'national uprising' determined to restore Germany's pride and unity. In this way he played on the deepest desires of many Germans, but never committed himself to the details of a political and economic programme.

Another key difference in this election campaign was the improved Nazi financial situation. At a meeting on 20 February with 20 leading industrialists, Hitler was promised three million *Reichsmarks*. With such financial backing and Goebbels' exploitation of the media, the Nazis were confident of securing a parliamentary majority.

The *Reichstag* fire

As the campaign moved towards its climax, one further bizarre episode strengthened the Nazi hand. On 27 February the *Reichstag* building was set on fire, and a young Dutch Communist, van der Lubbe, was arrested in incriminating circumstances. At the time, it was believed by many that the incident was a Nazi plot to support the claims of a Communist *coup*, and thereby to justify Nazi repression. However, to this day the episode has defied satisfactory explanation. A major investigation in 1962 concluded that van der Lubbe had acted alone; a further 18 years later the West Berlin authorities posthumously acquitted him; whereas the recent biography of Hitler by Ian Kershaw remains convinced that van der Lubbe acted on his own in a series of three attempted arsons within a few weeks. So, it is probable that the true explanation will never be known. The real significance of the *Reichstag* fire is the cynical way it was exploited by the Nazis to their advantage.

On the next day, 28 February, Frick drew up, and Hindenburg signed, the 'Decree for the Protection of People and State'. In a few short clauses most civil and political liberties were suspended and the power of central government was strengthened. The justification for the decree was the threat posed by the Communists. Following this, in the final week of the election campaign, hundreds of anti-Nazis were arrested, and the violence reached new heights.

Key dates

The Nazis blame the Communists for the *Reichstag* fire: 27 February 1933

Final elections according to the Weimar Constitution: 5 March 1933

Election result

In this atmosphere of fear, Germany went to the polls on 5 March. The election had a very high turnout of 88 per cent – a figure this high suggests the influence and intimidation of the SA, corruption by officials and an increased government control of the radio.

Somewhat surprisingly, the Nazis increased their vote from 33.1 per cent to only 43.9 per cent, thereby securing 288 seats. Hitler could claim a majority in the new *Reichstag* only with the help of the 52 seats won by the Nationalists. It was not only disappointing; it was also a political blow, since any change in the existing Weimar Constitution required a two-thirds majority in the *Reichstag*.

The Enabling Act, March 1933

Despite this constitutional hurdle, Hitler decided to propose to the new *Reichstag* an Enabling Act that would effectively do away with parliamentary procedure and legislation and which would instead transfer full powers to the chancellor and his government for four years. In this way the dictatorship would be grounded in legality. However, the successful passage of the Act depended on gaining the support or abstention of some of the other major political parties in order to get a two-thirds majority.

A further problem was that the momentum built up within the lower ranks of the Nazi Party was proving increasingly difficult for Hitler to contain in the regional areas. Members were impatiently taking the law into their own hands and this gave the impression

Key term

Revolution from below

The radical elements in the Party, e.g. the SA, that wanted to direct the Nazi revolution from a more local level rather than from the leadership in Berlin.

Key dates

Day of Potsdam ceremony: 21 March 1933

Enabling Act passed: 23 March 1933

of a '**revolution from below**'. It threatened to destroy Hitler's image of legality, and antagonise the conservative vested interests and his DNVP coalition partners. Such was his concern that a grandiose act of reassurance was arranged. On 21 March, at Potsdam Garrison Church, Goebbels orchestrated the ceremony to celebrate the opening of the *Reichstag*. In the presence of Hindenburg, the Crown Prince (the son of Kaiser Wilhelm II), and many of the army's leading generals, Hitler symbolically aligned National Socialism with the forces of the old Germany.

Two days later the new *Reichstag* met in the Kroll Opera House to consider the Enabling Act, and on this occasion the Nazis revealed a very different image. The Communists (those not already in prison) were refused admittance, while the deputies in attendance faced a barrage of intimidation from the ranks of the SA who surrounded the building.

However, the Nazis still required a two-thirds majority to pass the Act and, on the assumption that the Social Democrats would vote against, they needed the backing of the Centre Party. Hitler thus promised in his speech of 23 March to respect the rights of the Catholic Church and to uphold religious and moral values. These were false promises, which the ZP deputies deceived themselves into believing. In the end only the Social Democrats voted against, and the Enabling Act was passed by 444 to 94 votes.

Germany had succumbed to what Karl Bracher, a leading German scholar, has called 'legal revolution'. Within the space of a few weeks Hitler had legally dismantled the Weimar Constitution. The way was now open for him to create a one-party totalitarian dictatorship.

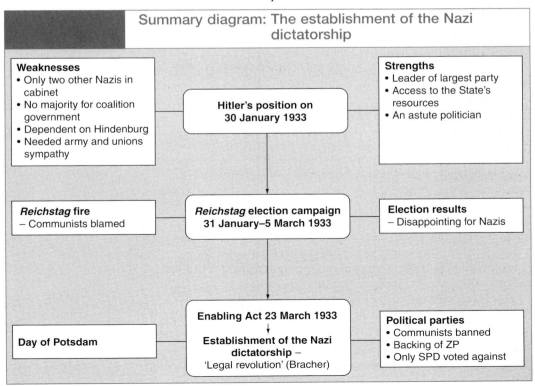

Summary diagram: The establishment of the Nazi dictatorship

Weaknesses
- Only two other Nazis in cabinet
- No majority for coalition government
- Dependent on Hindenburg
- Needed army and unions sympathy

Strengths
- Leader of largest party
- Access to the State's resources
- An astute politician

Hitler's position on 30 January 1933

Reichstag fire
– Communists blamed

Reichstag election campaign 31 January–5 March 1933

Election results
– Disappointing for Nazis

Day of Potsdam

Enabling Act 23 March 1933
↓
Establishment of the Nazi dictatorship –
'Legal revolution' (Bracher)

Political parties
- Communists banned
- Backing of ZP
- Only SPD voted against

5 | Co-ordination: *Gleichschaltung*

Key question
What was
Gleichschaltung?

The Enabling Act was the constitutional foundation stone of the Third Reich. In purely legal terms the Weimar Constitution was not dissolved until 1945, but in practice the Enabling Act provided the basis for the dictatorship which evolved from 1933. In that legal way, the intolerance and violence used by the Nazis to gain power could now be used as tools of government by the dictatorship of Hitler and the Party.

The degeneration of Weimar's democracy into the Nazi state system is usually referred to as **Gleichschaltung** or co-ordination. In practice, it applied to the Nazifying of German society and structures and refers specifically to the establishment of the dictatorship, 1933–4. To some extent it was generated by the power and freedom exploited by the SA at the local level – in effect a 'revolution from below'. But it was also directed by the Nazi leadership from the political centre in Berlin – a 'revolution from above'. Together, these two political forces attempted to 'co-ordinate' as many aspects of German life as possible along Nazi lines, although differences over the exact long-term goals of National Socialism laid the basis for future conflict within the Party (see pages 147–52).

Gleichschaltung
'Bringing into line'
or 'co-ordination'.

Key term

In practice, co-ordination has been viewed rather neatly as the 'merging' of German society with Party associations and institutions in an attempt to Nazify the life of Germany. At first many of these Nazi creations had to live alongside existing bodies, but over the years they gradually replaced them. In this way, much of Germany's cultural, educational and social life became increasingly controlled (see Chapter 9). However, in the spring and summer of 1933 the priority of the Nazi leadership was to secure its political supremacy. So its real focus of attention was the 'co-ordination' of the federal states, the political parties and the independent trade unions – which were at odds with Nazi political aspirations.

Main features of co-ordination
The federal states

Key question
In what ways did
Nazism achieve
co-ordination?

The regions had a very strong tradition in Germany history. Even after the creation of the German Empire in 1871 the previously independent states had carried on as largely self-governing federal states. And in 1919 the Weimar Constitution had agreed on a federal structure with 17 *Länder* (regional states), e.g. Prussia, Bavaria and Saxony (see page 22). Yet, this stood in marked contrast to Nazi desires to create a fully unified country.

Nazi activists had already exploited the climate of February–March 1933 to intimidate opponents and to infiltrate federal governments. Indeed, their 'political success' rapidly degenerated into terror and violence that seemed even beyond the control of Hitler, who called for restraint because he was afraid of losing the support of the conservatives. Consequently, the situation was resolved in three legal stages:

- First, by a law of 31 March 1933, the regional parliaments (*Landtage*) were dissolved and then reformed with acceptable majorities, which allowed the Nazis to dominate regional state governments.
- Secondly, a law of 7 April 1933 created Reich Governors (*Reichstatthalter*) who more often than not were the local party *Gauleiters* with full powers.
- The process of centralisation was finally completed in January 1934 when the regional parliaments were abolished. Federal governments and governors were subordinated to the authorities of the ministry of the interior in the central government.

By early 1934 the federal principle of government was as good as dead. Even the Nazi Reich governors existed simply 'to execute the will of the supreme leadership of the Reich'.

The trade unions

Germany's trade union movement was powerful because of its mass membership and its strong connections with socialism and Catholicism. Back in 1920 it had clearly shown its industrial muscle when it had successfully ended a right-wing *putsch* against the Weimar government by calling a general strike. On the whole, German organised labour was hostile to Nazism and, so, posed a major threat to the stability of the Nazi state.

Yet, by May 1933 it was shown to be a spent force. Admittedly, the depression had already severely weakened it by reducing membership and lessening the will to resist. However, the trade union leaders deceived themselves into believing that they could work with the Nazis and thereby preserve a degree of independence and at least the structure of trade unionism. Their hope was that:

- in the short term, trade unionism would continue to serve its social role to help members
- in the long term, it could provide the framework for development in the post-Nazi era.

However, the labour movement was deceived by the Nazis.

The Nazis surprisingly declared 1 May (the traditional day of celebration for international socialist labour) a national holiday, which gave the impression to the trade unions that perhaps there was some scope for co-operation. This proved to be the briefest of illusions. The following day, trade union premises were occupied by the SA and SS, union funds were confiscated and many of the leaders were arrested and sent to the early concentration camps, such as Dachau.

Independent trade unions were then banned and in their place all German workers' organisations were absorbed into the German Labour Front (*Deutscher Arbeitsfront*, DAF), led by Robert Ley. DAF became the largest organisation in Nazi Germany with 22 million members, but it acted more as an instrument of control than as a genuine representative body of workers' interests and concerns (see page 178). Also, it lost the most fundamental right to negotiate wages and conditions of work. So, by the end of 1933, the power of the German labour movement had been decisively broken.

Political parties

It was inconceivable that *Gleichschaltung* could allow the existence of other political parties. Nazism openly rejected democracy and any concessions to alternative opinions. Instead, it aspired to establish authoritarian rule within a one-party state. This was not difficult to achieve:

- The Communists had been outlawed since the *Reichstag* fire (see page 142).
- Soon after the destruction of the trade unions the assets of the Social Democrats were seized and they were then officially banned on 22 June.
- Most of the major remaining parties willingly agreed to dissolve themselves in the course of late June 1933 – even the Nationalists (previously coalition partners to the Nazis) obligingly accepted.
- Finally, the Catholic Centre Party decided to give up the struggle and followed suit on 5 July 1933.

Thus, there was no opposition to the decree of 14 July that formally proclaimed the Nazi Party as the only legal political party in Germany.

> **Key date**
> All political opposition to NSDAP declared illegal: 14 July 1933

Success of *Gleichschaltung* in 1933

By the end of 1933 the process of *Gleichschaltung* was well advanced in many areas of public life in Germany. However, it was certainly far from complete. In particular, it had failed to make any impression on the role and influence of the churches, the army and big business. Also, the civil service and education had only been partially co-ordinated. This was mainly due to Hitler's determination to shape events through the 'revolution from above' and to avoid antagonising such powerful vested interests. Yet, there were many in the lower ranks of the Party who had contributed to the 'revolution from below' and who now wanted to extend the process of *Gleichschaltung*. It was this internal party conflict which laid the basis for the bloody events of June 1934.

> **Key question**
> How advanced was the process of Nazi co-ordination by the end of 1933?

A photograph of Prussian policemen in Berlin in 1933. Although they wore the traditional helmet with the insignia, they are 'brought into line' by carrying Nazi flags and give the Nazi salute.

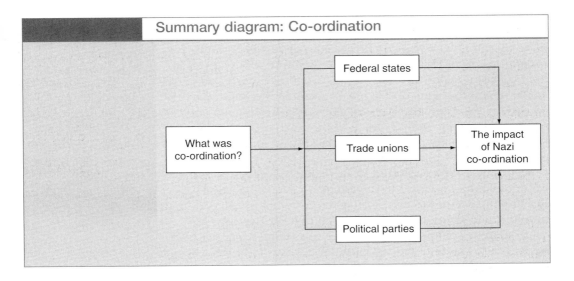

Summary diagram: Co-ordination

What was co-ordination? → Federal states → The impact of Nazi co-ordination

Trade unions

Political parties

Key question
What exactly was the political dilemma faced by Hitler in 1933?

6 | From Chancellor to *Führer*

Within just six months of coming to power Hitler had indeed managed to turn Germany into a one-party dictatorship. However, in a speech on 6 July 1933 to the Reich Governors, Hitler warned of the dangers posed by a permanent state of revolution. He therefore formally declared an end to the revolution and demanded that 'the stream of revolution must be guided into the safe channel of evolution'.

Hitler was caught in a political dilemma. He was increasingly concerned that the behaviour of Party activists was running beyond his control. This was likely to create embarrassment in his relations with the more conservative forces whose support he still depended on, e.g. big business, civil service and, above all, the army. Hitler's speech amounted to a clear-cut demand for the Party to accept the realities of political compromise and also the necessity of change from above.

The position of the SA

However, Hitler's appeal failed to have the desired effect. If anything, it reinforced the fears of many Party members that the Nazi leadership was prepared to dilute the ideology of National Socialism. Such concerns came in particular from within the ranks of the SA giving rise to calls for **'a second revolution'**.

Table 7.2: SA membership 1931–4

	1931	1932	1933	1934
Membership figures	100,000	291,000	425,000	3,000,000

SA membership grew at first because of the large number of unemployed young men, but from 1933 many joined as a way to advance themselves.

The SA represented the radical, left wing of the Nazi Party and to a large extent it reflected a more working-class membership, which in the depression was often young and unemployed. It placed far more emphasis on the socialist elements of the Party programme than Hitler ever did and, therefore, saw no need to hold back simply for the sake of satisfying the élites. It had played a vital role in the years of struggle by winning the political battle on the streets, and many of its members were embittered and frustrated over the limited nature of the Nazi revolution. They were also disappointed by their own lack of personal gain from this acquisition of power.

Such views were epitomised by the leader of the SA, Ernst Röhm, who openly called for a genuine 'National Socialist Revolution'. Röhm was increasingly disillusioned by the politics of his old friend Hitler and he recognised that the developing confrontation would decide the future role of the SA in the Nazi state. In a private interview in early 1934 with a local Party boss, Rauschning, Röhm gave vent to his feelings and his ideas:

> Adolf is a swine. He will give us all away. He only associates with the reactionaries now. ... Getting matey with the East Prussian generals. They're his cronies now ... Adolf knows exactly what I want. I've told him often enough. Not a second edition of the old imperial army.

Key term

'A second revolution'
Refers to the aims of the SA, led by Ernst Röhm, which wanted social and economic reforms and the creation of a 'people's army' merging the German army and the SA. The aims of 'a second revolution' were more attractive to the 'left-wing socialist Nazis' or 'radical Nazis', who did not sympathise with the conservative forces in Germany.

Profile: Ernst Röhm 1887–1934

1887		– Born in Munich
1914–18		– Served in the First World War and reached the rank of captain
1919		– Joined the *Freikorps*
		– Met Hitler and joined the Nazi Party
1921		– Helped to form the SA and became its leader in the years 1921–3
1923	November	– Participated in the Munich Beer Hall *putsch*
1924		– Initially jailed, but soon released on probation
1925–30		– Left for Bolivia in South America
1930		– Returned to Germany at Hitler's request
1930–4		– SA leader
1933	December	– Invited to join the cabinet
1934	June	– Arrested and then murdered in the Night of the Long Knives

Röhm was always a controversial character. He was an open homosexual, a heavy drinker and enjoyed the blood and violence of war and political street battles. Yet, he was one of Hitler's closest friends in the years 1919–34, which partially explains why Hitler found it so painful to destroy the SA and its leader.

He played a key role in the earliest years, when he introduced Hitler to the Nazi Party in 1919. He formed the SA in 1921, but he left Germany after the Beer Hall *putsch*. Most significantly, in the years 1930–3 Röhm was given the responsibility by Hitler of reorganising the SA and restoring its discipline. By intimidation and street violence Röhm's SA had turned itself into a powerful force by 1931, although conflict between the Party leadership and the SA grew increasingly serious.

After the Nazi consolidation of power, Röhm was committed to pursue 'a second revolution' that reflected the reforms of the 'left-wing socialist Nazis' or 'radical Nazis'. He did not sympathise with the conservative forces in Germany and, above all, aimed to create a 'people's army' by merging the German army and the SA. This fundamental difference culminated in the Night of the Long Knives and his own death.

Röhm, therefore had no desire to see the SA marches and rallies degenerating into a mere propaganda show now that the street-fighting was over. He wanted to amalgamate the army and the SA into a people's militia – of which he would be the commander.

The power struggle between the SA and the army

However, Röhm's plan was anathema to the German army which saw its traditional role and status being directly threatened. Hitler was therefore caught between two powerful, but rival, forces – both of which could create considerable political difficulties for him.

On the one hand, the SA consisted of three million committed Nazis with his oldest political friend leading it. It had fought for Hitler in the 1923 Munich *putsch* and also in the battle of the streets, 1930–3. The SA was also far larger than the army.

On the other hand, the army was the one organisation that could unseat Hitler from his position of power. The officer class was suspicious of Hitler and it had close social ties with many of the powerful interests, e.g. civil service and *Junkers*. Moreover, the army alone possessed the military skills which were vital to the success of his foreign policy aims. Also, however large the SA was, it could never hope to challenge the discipline and professional expertise possessed by the army.

So, political realities dictated that Hitler had to retain the backing of the army but, in the winter of 1933–4, he was still loath to engineer a showdown with his old friend, Röhm. He tried to make concessions to Röhm by bringing him into the cabinet. He also called a meeting in February between the leaders of the army, the SA and the SS in an attempt to reach an agreement about the role of each organisation within the Nazi state. However, the tension did not ease. Röhm and the SA resented Hitler's apparent acceptance of the privileged position of the army. Moreover, the unrestrained actions and ill-discipline of the SA only increased the feelings of dissatisfaction among the generals.

Junkers
The landowning aristocracy, especially those from eastern Germany.

Key term

The Night of the Long Knives

The developing crisis came to a head in April 1934 when it became apparent that President Hindenburg did not have much longer to live. The implications of his imminent death were profound; for Hitler wanted to assume the presidency without opposition. He certainly did not want a contested election, nor did he have any sympathy for those who wanted the restoration of the monarchy. It seems that Hitler's hand was forced by the need to secure the army's backing for his succession to Hindenburg.

The support of the army had become the key to the survival of Hitler's regime in the short term, while in the long term it offered the means to fulfil his ambitions in the field of foreign affairs. Whatever personal loyalty Hitler felt for Röhm and the SA was finally put to one side. The army desired their elimination and an end to the talk of a 'second revolution' and a 'people's militia'. By agreeing to this, Hitler could gain the favour of the army generals, secure his personal position and remove an increasingly embarrassing millstone from around his neck.

Without primary written evidence it is difficult to establish the exact details of the events in June 1934. However, it seems highly probable that, at a meeting on the battleship *Deutschland* in April 1934, Hitler and the two leading generals, Blomberg and Fritsch, came to an agreed position against Röhm and the SA. Furthermore, influential figures within the Nazi Party, in particular Göring and Himmler, were also manoeuvring behind the scenes. They were aiming for a similar outcome in order to further their own ambitions by removing a powerful rival. Given

Key question
When and why did the political conflict come to a head?

all that, Hitler probably did not decide to make his crucial move to solve the problem of the SA until mid-June when Vice-Chancellor Papen gave a speech calling for an end to SA excesses and criticised the policy of co-ordination. Not surprisingly, these words caused a real stir and were seen as a clear challenge. Hitler now recognised that he had to satisfy the conservative forces – and that meant he had to destroy the power of the SA immediately.

The purge

On 30 June 1934, the Night of the Long Knives, Hitler eliminated the SA as a political and military force once and for all. Röhm and the main leaders of the SA were shot by members of the SS – although the weapons and transport were actually provided by the army. There was no resistance of any substance. In addition, various old scores were settled: Schleicher, the former chancellor, and Strasser, the leader of the radical socialist wing of the Nazi Party, were both killed. Altogether it is estimated that 200 people were murdered.

From a very different perspective, on 5 July 1934 the *Völkischer Beobachter* (*The People's Observer*), the Nazi newspaper, reported on the Reich cabinet meeting held two days earlier:

> Defence Minister General Blomberg thanked the *Führer* in the name of the cabinet and the army for his determined and courageous action, by which he had saved the German people from civil war … .
>
> The Reich cabinet then approved a law on measures for the self-defence of the state. Its single paragraph reads: 'The measures taken on 30 June and 1 and 2 July to suppress the acts of high treason are legal, being necessary for the self-defence of the state.'

The significance of the Night of Long Knives

It would be difficult to overestimate the significance of the Night of the Long Knives. In one bloody action Hitler overcame the radical left in his own Party, and the conservative right of traditional Germany. By the summer of 1934, the effects of the purge could be seen clearly:

- The German army had clearly aligned itself behind the Nazi regime, as was shown by Blomberg's public vote of thanks to Hitler on 1 July. Perhaps, even more surprisingly, German soldiers agreed to take a personal oath of loyalty to Hitler.
- The SA was rendered almost unarmed and it played no significant role in the political development of the Nazi state. Thereafter its major role was to attend propaganda rallies as a showpiece force.
- More ominously for the future, the incident marked the emergence of the SS. German generals had feared the SA, but they failed to recognise the SS as the Party's élite institution of terror.
- Above all, Hitler had secured his own personal political supremacy. His decisions and actions were accepted, so in effect

Key question
How significant was the Night of the Long Knives?

he had managed to legalise murder. From that moment, it was clear that the Nazi regime was not a traditional authoritarian one, like Imperial Germany 1871–1918; it was a personal dictatorship with frightening power.

Consequently, when Hindenburg died on 2 August, there was no political crisis. Hitler was simply able to merge the offices of chancellor and president, and also to take on the new official title of *Führer*. The Nazi regime had been stabilised and the threat of a 'second revolution' had been completely removed.

Führer
Meaning leader. Hitler was declared leader of the Nazi Party in 1921. In 1934 he became leader of the country after the death of Hindenburg.

Key term

Night of the Long Knives – destruction of SA by SS: 30 June 1934

Death of Hindenburg: Hitler combined the offices of chancellor and president. Oath of loyalty taken by army: 2 August 1934

Key dates

A cartoon/photomontage published by the German communist John Heartfield in July 1934. The image is of a Stormtrooper who has been murdered on Hitler's order in the Night of the Long Knives. What is ironic about his Heil Hitler salute?

Summary diagram: From Chancellor to *Führer*

7 | Conclusions: Why was Weimar Germany Replaced by a Nazi Dictatorship?

In 1932 only 43 per cent of the electorate voted in the July *Reichstag* elections for pro-Republican parties. The majority of the German people had voted in a free (and reasonably fair) election to reject democracy, despite the fact that there was no clear alternative. So, Germany did not necessarily have to end up with a Nazi dictatorship. Yet, within just six months Hitler had assumed the mantle of power and by 1934 he was the leader of a brutal dictatorship.

Key question
Why was Hitler appointed as chancellor?

The appointment of Hitler

The depression transformed the Nazis into a mass movement. Admittedly, 63 per cent of Germans never voted for them, but 37 per cent of the electorate did, so the Nazis became by far the strongest party in a multi-party democracy. The depression had led to such profound social and economic hardship that it created an environment of discontent, which was easily exploited by the Nazis' style of political activity. Indeed, it is questionable whether Hitler would have become a national political figure without the severity of that economic downturn. However, his mixture of racist, nationalist and anti-democratic ideas was readily received by a broad spectrum of German people, and especially by the disgruntled middle classes.

Other extreme right-wing groups with similar ideas and conditions did not enjoy similar success. This is partially explained by the impressive manner in which the Nazi message was communicated: the use of modern propaganda techniques, the violent exploitation of scapegoats – especially the Jews and

Communists – and the well-organised structure of the Party apparatus. All these factors undoubtedly helped but, in terms of electoral appeal, it is impossible to ignore the powerful impact of Hitler himself as a charismatic leader with a cult following. Furthermore, he exhibited a quite extraordinary political acumen and ruthlessness when he was involved in the detail of political in-fighting.

Nevertheless, the huge popular following of the Nazis, which helped to undermine the continued operation of democracy, was insufficient on its own to give Hitler power. In the final analysis, it was the mutual recognition by Hitler and the representatives of the traditional leaders of the army, the landowners and heavy industry that they needed each other, which led to Hitler's appointment as chancellor of a coalition government on 30 January 1933. Since September 1930 every government had been forced to resort almost continuously to the use of presidential emergency decrees because they had lacked a popular mandate.

In the chaos of 1932 the only other realistic alternative to including the Nazis in the government was some kind of military regime – a presidential dictatorship backed by the army, perhaps. However, that, too, would have faced similar difficulties. Indeed, by failing to satisfy the extreme left and the extreme right, there would have been a very real possibility of civil war. A coalition with Hitler's Nazis, therefore, provided the conservative élites with both mass support and some alluring promises: a vigorous attack on Germany's political left wing and rearmament as a precursor to economic and political expansion abroad. For Hitler, the inclusion of Papen and Hugenberg gave his cabinet an air of conservative respectability.

The establishment of the Nazi dictatorship

In the end, Hitler became chancellor because the political forces of the left and centre were too divided and too weak, and because the conservative right wing was prepared to accept him as a partner in government in the mistaken belief that he could be tamed. With hindsight, it can be seen that 30 January 1933 was decisive and Hitler was entrenched in power.

These are the key factors which help to explain the establishment of the dictatorship:

- *Terror*. The Nazis used violence – and increasingly so without legal restriction, e.g. the Night of the Long Knives and the arrest of the Communists. Nazi organisations also employed violence at a local level to intimidate opposition.
- *Legality*. The use of law by the Nazis gave a legal justification for the development of the regime, e.g. the Enabling Act, the Emergency Decree of 28 February 1933, the dissolution of the parties.
- *Deception*. Hitler misled powerful groups in order to destroy them, e.g. the trade unions and the SA.
- *Propaganda*. The Nazis successfully cultivated powerful images – especially when Goebbels took on responsibility for the

Key question
In what ways was Hitler able to consolidate Nazi power between 1933 and 1934?

Propaganda Ministry. Myths were developed about Hitler as a respectable statesman, e.g. the Day of Potsdam (see page 143).

- *Weaknesses of the opposition.* In the early Weimar years, the left had considerable potential power, but it became divided between the Social Democrats and the Communists – and was marred by the economic problems of the depression.
- *Sympathy of the conservative right.* Many of the traditional vested interests, e.g. the army, civil service, were not wholly committed to Weimar and they really sympathised with a more right-wing authoritarian regime. They accepted the Night of the Long Knives.

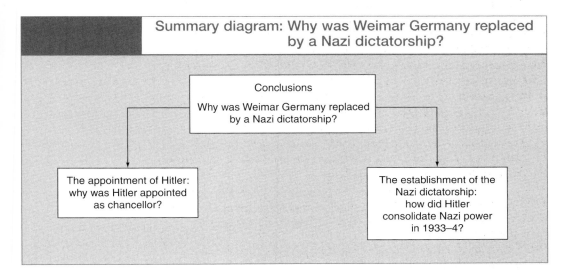

Summary diagram: Why was Weimar Germany replaced by a Nazi dictatorship?

Conclusions

Why was Weimar Germany replaced by a Nazi dictatorship?

The appointment of Hitler: why was Hitler appointed as chancellor?

The establishment of the Nazi dictatorship: how did Hitler consolidate Nazi power in 1933–4?

Study Guide: AS Question

In the style of Edexcel

How far did the Nazi regime rely on terror and violence to consolidate its hold on power in the years 1933–4?   (30 marks)

Exam tips

The cross-references are intended to take you straight to the material that will help you to answer the question.

The critical requirement is that you address the 'to what extent' part of the question. You are not being asked simply to describe the Nazi consolidation of power 1933–4, but to evaluate the significance of the role of terror against other factors. In order to do this, you should examine:

- The Nazi methods of terror such as:
  - intimidation, e.g. the March 1933 election (pages 140–2); the swelling numbers of SA recruits and their effect (page 148)
  - persecution and arrest of opponents, such as the treatment of Communists following the *Reichstag* fire (page 142)
  - the significance of the Night of the Long Knives in removing the threat of a second revolution (pages 151–2).
- Other methods of consolidation, such as:
  - legal means of consolidation – Hitler's rise to chancellor; the Enabling Act; the gradual elimination of political opposition leaving the Nazi Party as the only legal party by 14 July 1933 (pages 141–6)
  - deception and persuasion in the form of propaganda, and exploitation of the fears felt by many in society at the time (pages 103–4 and 154–5)
  - the appeal of Nazi ideology in the changing social and economic climate of the time (pages 153–4).

A thoughtful conclusion is essential and you must weigh up the balance between the various factors. There are differences of view between historians here. There is a debate about how far it can be said that Hitler's consolidation of power in this period was chiefly by legal means. The question gives you the chance to explore this issue and decide for yourself on which side the balance of evidence appears to be.

8 The Nazi Economy

POINTS TO CONSIDER

The purpose of this chapter is to consider Nazi economic policies and their effects on the performance of the Nazi economy over the years of the Third Reich. The economy went through various stages and to appreciate the significance of these, it is important to consider the following main themes:

- The economic background to the establishment of the Nazi regime
- The economic recovery of Germany 1933–6
- The introduction of the Four-Year Plan 1936–9
- The economy at war 1939–45

Key dates

1933	March	Appointment of Schacht as President of the *Reichsbank*
1934	July	Appointment of Schacht as Minister of Economics
	September	New Plan introduced
1936	October	Four-Year Plan established under Göring
1937	November	Resignation of Schacht as Minister of Economics
1939	December	War Economy decrees
1941	December	Rationalisation Decree issued by Hitler
1942	February	Appointment of Albert Speer as Minister of Armaments
1944	August	Peak of German munitions production

1 | The Economic Background

Key question
Did the Nazis have an economic policy?

In the years before 1933, Hitler had been careful not to become tied down to the details of an economic policy. Hitler even told his cabinet in February 1933 to 'avoid all detailed statements concerning an economic programme of the government'.

However, Hitler was also politically astute enough to realise that his position depended on bringing Germany out of depression and so during 1932 the Nazi leadership had begun to consider a number of *possible* approaches to the management of the economy.

- First were the socio-economic aspects of the Nazi Party's original aims, as outlined in the anti-capitalist sentiments of the **25-points programme** of the Nazi Party of 1920 such as:
  - profit sharing in large industrial enterprises
  - the extensive development of insurance for old age
  - the **nationalisation** of all businesses.

  Hitler accepted these points in the early years because he recognised their popular appeal but he himself never showed any real commitment to such ideas. As a result, they created important differences within the Party, as a faction within it still demanded these.
- Secondly, attention was given to the emerging idea of deficit financing. This found its most obvious expression in the theories of the British economist J.M. Keynes and the new President of the USA, F.D. Roosevelt, from 1933. By spending money on public works, deficit financing was intended to create jobs, which would then act as an artificial stimulus to demand within the economy. Indeed, work schemes were actually started in Germany in 1932 by Chancellors Papen and Schleicher.
- Finally, there was the idea of the *Wehrwirtschaft* (defence economy), whereby Germany's peacetime economy was geared to the demands of total war. This was to avoid a repetition of the problems faced during the First World War when a long, drawn-out conflict on two fronts eventually caused economic collapse. Related to this was the policy of **autarky**. This envisaged a scheme for the creation of a large trading area in Europe under the dominating influence of Germany, which could be developed to rival the other great economic powers. It played upon the idea of German power and harked back to the expansionist views of some First World War nationalists (see page 36).

Of these three economic approaches, Hitler identified his long-term political and military aims most clearly with the defence economy. However, there were important differences within the Party over economic planning so, despite the consideration given to such policies by the Nazi leaders, no coherent plan had emerged by January 1933. Hitler had no real understanding of economics and to a large extent the implementation of economic policy was initially left to bankers and civil servants.

From the start, then, there was a lack of real direction and elements of all three approaches can be detected in the economic history of the Third Reich. This suggests that economic policy tended to be pragmatic. It evolved out of the demands of the situation rather than being the result of careful planning. As the leading historian A. Schweitzer stated, 'no single unified economic system prevailed throughout the entire period of the Nazi regime'.

Key terms

25-Points programme
Hitler drew up the Party's 25-points programme in February 1920 with the Party's founder, Anton Drexler.

Nationalisation
The socialist principle that the ownership of key industries should be transferred to the state.

Autarky
The aim for self-sufficiency in the production of food and raw materials, especially when at war.

Key question
How serious were Germany's economic problems in the Great Depression 1929–33?

Germany's economic condition in 1933

Germany had faced continuing economic problems since the end of the First World War. However, as can be seen on pages 101–4, the sheer scale of the world economic depression that began in 1929 meant that Germany undoubtedly suffered in a particularly savage way:

- *Trade*. Germany depended heavily on its capacity to sell manufactured goods. In the slump of global trade, the demand for German exports declined rapidly and its sale of manufactured goods, e.g. steel, machinery and chemicals, collapsed.
- *Industry*. Despite its post-war problems, Germany was an industrial power. However, when it began to lose economic confidence from 1929, demand fell and businesses cut production, or worse, collapsed.
- *Employment*. The most obvious feature of the industrial contraction was mass long-term unemployment. The length and severity of the economic recession greatly increased the number of unemployed, with all the associated social problems. In 1932 the figure rose to 5.6 million. If the number of unregistered unemployed is added, the total without work was about eight million in 1932.
- *Agriculture*. The situation in the countryside was no better than in the towns. The agricultural depression deepened, leading to widespread rural poverty. As global demand fell, agricultural prices, farmers' wages and incomes fell sharply, which forced some to sell off their farms.
- *Finance*. Because of war debts, reparations and inflation, German banking had faced serious financial problems in the years even *before* 1929. The onset of the depression undermined the confidence of the financial sector: foreign investment disappeared, German share prices collapsed and five major banks collapsed in 1931.

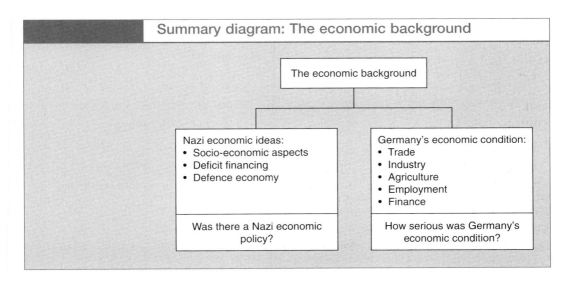

Summary diagram: The economic background

The economic background

Nazi economic ideas:
- Socio-economic aspects
- Deficit financing
- Defence economy

Germany's economic condition:
- Trade
- Industry
- Agriculture
- Employment
- Finance

Was there a Nazi economic policy?

How serious was Germany's economic condition?

2 | Economic Recovery 1933–6

Schacht's economic strategy

In the early years Nazi economic policy was under the control of Hjalmar Schacht, President of the *Reichsbank* (1933–9) and Minister of Economics (1934–7). This reflected the need of the Nazi leadership to work with the powerful forces of big business. Schacht was already a respected international financier because of his leading role in the creation of the new currency in the wake of the 1923 hyperinflation.

It is certainly true that the economic depression reached its low-point in the winter of 1932–3 and that afterwards the trade cycle began to improve. This undoubtedly worked to the political and economic advantage of the Nazis. Nevertheless, there was no single, easy 'quick fix' solution.

The heart of economic recovery lay in the major revival of public investment led, for the most part, by the state itself, which embarked on a large-scale increase in its own spending in an effort to stimulate demand and raise national income. So, under Schacht's guidance and influence, deficit financing was adopted through a range of economic measures.

Banking and the control of capital

Initially, because the German banking system had been so fundamentally weakened, the state increasingly assumed greater responsibility for the control of capital within the economy. It then proceeded to set interest rates at a lower level and to reschedule the large-scale debts of local authorities.

Assistance for farming and small businesses

Particular financial benefits were given to groups such as farmers and small businesses. This not only stimulated economic growth, but also rewarded some of the most sympathetic supporters of the Nazis in the 1930–3 elections. Some of the measures included (see also pages 180–4):

- maintaining tariffs on imported produce in order to protect German farmers
- the Reich Food Estate giving subsidies as part of a nationally planned agricultural system (see pages 182–3)
- the Reich Entailed Farm Law reducing debts by tax concessions and lower interest rates in an attempt to offer more security of land ownership to small farmers (see also pages 182–3)
- giving allowances to encourage the re-hiring of domestic servants
- allocating grants for house repairs.

State investment – public works

However, of the greatest significance was the direct spending by the state on a range of investment projects. In June 1933 the Law to Reduce Unemployment was renewed and expanded (from a scheme which had originally been started by Papen in 1932) and

Key question
How did Schacht's policies stimulate economic recovery?

Appointment of Schacht as President of the *Reichsbank*: March 1933

Key date

the RAD (*Reichsarbeitsdienst*, Reich Labour Service) was expanded to employ 19–25 year olds. For a long time most historians assumed that rearmament was the main focus of investment, but the figures for public expenditure show that this was initially spread among rearmament, construction and transportation. So the investment in the first three years was directed towards work creation schemes such as:

* reforestation
* land reclamation
* motorisation – the policy of developing the vehicle industry and the building of improved roads, e.g. the autobahns (motorways)
* building – especially the expansion of the housing sector and public buildings.

The cumulative effect of these policies was to triple public investment between 1933 and 1936 and to increase government expenditure by nearly 70 per cent over the same period. By early 1936 the economic recovery was well advanced and then emphasis began to turn even more towards rearmament.

Table 8.1: Public investment and expenditure by billion *Reichsmarks* (RM)

	1928	1932	1933	1934	1935	1936
Total public investment	6.6	2.2	2.5	4.6	6.4	8.1
Total government expenditure	11.7	8.6	9.4	12.8	13.9	15.8

Table 8.2: Public expenditure by category by billion *Reichsmarks* (RM)

	1928	1932	1933	1934	1935	1936
Construction	2.7	0.9	1.7	3.5	4.9	5.4
Rearmament	0.7	0.7	1.8	3.0	5.4	10.2
Transportation	2.6	0.8	1.3	1.8	2.1	2.4

Table 8.3: Unemployment and production in Germany 1928–36

	1928	1929	1930	1931	1932	1933	1934	1935	1936
Unemployment (millions)	1.4	1.8	3.1	4.5	5.6	4.8	2.7	2.2	1.6
Industrial production (1928 = 100)	100	100	87	70	58	66	83	96	107

As a result of these strategies, there was a dramatic growth in jobs. From the registered peak of 5.6 million unemployed in 1932, the official figure of 1936 showed that it had declined to 1.6 million. For those many Germans who had been desperately out of work, it seemed as if the Nazi economic policy was to be welcomed. Even in other democratic countries scarred by mass unemployment, observers abroad admired Germany's achievement of job creation.

Yet, even in 1936, the government public deficit certainly did not run out of control, since Schacht maintained taxes at a relatively high level and encouraged private savings in state savings banks. Of course, it must be remembered that all this took place as the world economy began to recover and Schacht was aided by the natural upturn in the business cycle after its low-point in winter 1932. Nevertheless, it is difficult to believe that such a marked turnaround in investment and employment could have been achieved without Nazi economic policy.

The balance of payments problem

Germany made an impressive economic recovery between 1933 and 1936, but two underlying worries remained:

- the fear that a rapid increase in demand would rekindle inflation
- the fear that a rapid increase in demand would lead to the emergence of a **balance of trade** deficit.

In fact, the problem of inflation never actually materialised – partly because there was a lack of demand in the economy, but also because the regime established strict controls over prices and wages. This had been helped by the abolition of the trade unions in May 1933 (see pages 145–6). On the other hand, what was to be a recurring balance of payments problem emerged for the first time in the summer of 1934. This was a consequence of Germany's importing more raw materials while failing to increase its exports. Its gold and foreign currency reserves were also low.

Key question
Why was Germany's balance of trade problem so significant?

Balance of trade
Difference in value between exports and imports. If the value of the imports is above that of the exports, the balance of the payments has a deficit that is often said to be 'in the red'.

Key term

Unemployed men (with shovels) enrol for work on one of the autobahns in September 1933.

The balance of payments problem was not merely an economic issue, for it carried with it large-scale political implications. If Germany was so short of foreign currency, which sector of the economy was to have priority in spending the money? The early Economics Minister, Schmitt, wanted to try to reduce unemployment further by manufacturing more consumer goods for public consumption, e.g. textiles. However, powerful voices in the armed forces and big business were already demanding more resources for major programmes, e.g. rearmament.

Hitler could not ignore such pressure – especially as this economic problem coincided with the political dilemma over the SA. Consequently, Schmitt's policy was rejected and he was removed, thereby allowing Schacht to combine the offices of Minister of Economics and President of the *Reichsbank*.

Key dates

Appointment of Schacht as Minister of Economics: July 1934

New Plan introduced: September 1934

Key question
How did Schacht try to resolve the balance of payments problem?

Schacht's 'New Plan'

By the law of 3 July, Schacht was given dictatorial powers over the economy, which he then used to introduce the 'New Plan' of September 1934. This provided for a comprehensive control by the government of all aspects of trade, tariffs, capital and currency exchange in an attempt to prevent excessive imports. From that time the government decided which imports were to be allowed or disapproved. For example, imports of raw cotton and wool were substantially cut, whereas metals were permitted in order to satisfy the demands of heavy industry.

The economic priorities were set by a series of measures:

- *Bilateral trade treaties*
  Schacht tried to promote trade and save foreign exchange by signing bilateral trade treaties, especially with the countries of south-east Europe, e.g. Romania and Yugoslavia. These often took the form of straightforward barter agreements (thus avoiding the necessity of formal currency exchange). In this way Germany began to exert a powerful economic influence over the Balkans long before it obtained military and political control.

- *The* Reichsmark *currency*
  Germany agreed to purchase raw materials from all countries it traded with on the condition that *Reichsmarks* could only be used to buy back German goods (at one time it is estimated that the German *Reichsmark* had 237 different values depending on the country and the circumstances).

- *Mefo bills*
  Mefo were special government money bills (like a credit note) designed by Schacht. They were issued by the *Reichsbank* and guaranteed by the government as payment for goods, and were then held for up to five years earning 4 per cent interest per annum. The main purpose of Mefo bills was that they successfully disguised government spending.

Schacht was never a member of the Nazi Party, but he was drawn into the Nazi movement and the regime. His proven economic

Profile: Hjalmar Schacht 1877–1970

1877		– Born in North Schleswig, Germany
1899		– Graduated in political economy
1916		– Appointed as Director of the National Bank
1923	November	– Appointed as Reich currency commissioner to set up the new currency, *Rentenmark*
	December	– Appointed President of the *Reichsbank*
1930	March	– Resigned in protest at the Young Plan
1931		– Became increasingly sympathetic to Nazism. Agreed to raise money for the Nazi Party through his contacts in banking and industry, e.g. Gustav and Alfred Krupp
1932	November	– Played a leading role in organising the letter from the petition of German industrialists who pressed Hindenburg to support Hitler's appointment
1933	March	– Re-appointed as President of the *Reichsbank*
1934	July	– Appointed as Minister of Economics
	September	– Drew up and oversaw the New Plan
1937	November	– Resigned as Minister of Economics
1939	January	– Resigned as President of the *Reichsbank* in protest at Nazi economic policy
1939–43		– Remained in the government as Minister without Portfolio, but became increasingly at odds with the Nazi regime
1944–5		– In contact with the anti-Nazi resistance and arrested after the 20 July Bomb Plot. Held in Ravensbrück concentration camp until the end of war
1945–6		– Charged at the Nuremberg War Crimes Trials, but acquitted
1950–63		– Private financial consultant to the government of many countries
1970	June	– Died in Munich

Schacht was undoubtedly an economic genius. He built his reputation on the way he stabilised the German economy by the creation of the new currency, the *Rentenmark*, in 1923. He served as President of the *Reichsbank* to all the Weimar governments 1923–30, but he was a strong nationalist and eventually resigned over the Young Plan.

Schacht was increasingly taken in by Hitler's political programme. From 1930, his influence went through three clear stages.

- In 1930–3 he played an essential role in encouraging big business to finance the rise of the Nazis and he backed Hitler's appointment as chancellor.
- In the years 1933–6 Schacht was in effect economic dictator of Germany and it was he who shaped Germany's economic recovery by deficit financing and the New Plan of 1934.
- However, he fundamentally disagreed with the emphasis on rearmament in the Four-Year Plan and after 1936 his influence was gradually eclipsed.

Adolf Hitler opens the first stretch of the autobahn between Frankfurt am Main and Darmstadt on 19 May 1935. The first autobahn was not initiated by the Nazis, but was prompted by the mayor of Cologne, Adenauer; the stretch from Cologne to Bonn was opened in 1932. Nevertheless, 3000 km of motorway roads were developed before the onset of the war. They served as an economic stimulus, but were also used politically as a propagandist tool. Their military value has been doubted.

skills earned him respect both in and outside the Party and it was he who laid the foundations for economic recovery. By mid-1936:

- unemployment had fallen to 1.5 million
- industrial production had increased by 60 per cent since 1933
- GNP had grown over the same period by 40 per cent.

However, such successes disguised fundamental structural weaknesses that came to a head in the second half of 1936 over the future direction of the German economy.

Summary diagram: Economic recovery 1933–6

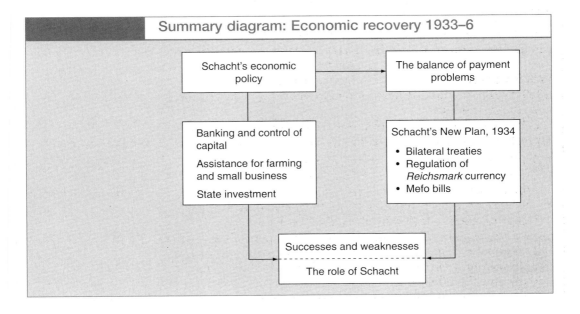

3 | Implementation of the Four-Year Plan 1936

In many respects, as Schacht himself was only too aware, he had merely hidden the balance of payments problem by a series of clever financial tricks. And, despite his apparent sympathy for deficit financing, Schacht believed that a combination of a budget deficit and a balance of payments deficit could not be maintained indefinitely. In early 1936 it became clear to him that, as the demands for rearmament and consumption of goods increased, the German balance of payments would go deeply into the red. He therefore suggested a reduction in arms expenditure in order to increase the production of industrial goods that at least could be exported so as to earn foreign exchange. Such a solution had its supporters, especially among industries geared to exporting, e.g. electrics, tools. However, it was unacceptable to the armed forces and to the Nazi leadership. By the mid-1930s, then, this debate was popularly summed up by the question: should the economy concentrate on producing '**Guns or Butter?**'

Key question
What was the main purpose of the Four-Year Plan?

Guns or Butter?
A phrase used to highlight the controversial economic choice between rearmament and consumer goods.

Key term

Guns or Butter? A cartoon published by the German magazine *Simplicissimus* in 1933. Critics of the new Nazi regime felt that it was more interested in rearmament than encouraging trade and peace.

The aims and objectives of the Plan

Most significantly, Hitler himself expressed his position in a secret memorandum in August 1936. This has been seen as one of the most important documents of Nazi history, as it provides a clear insight into Hitler's war aims and the development of the Nazi economy. He concluded by writing:

> There has been time enough in four years to find out what we cannot do. Now we have to carry out what we can do. I thus set the following tasks.
>
> (i) The German armed forces must be operational within four years
> (ii) The German economy must be fit for war within four years.

Key date

Four-Year Plan established under Göring: October 1936

The politico-economic crisis of 1936 was resolved by the introduction of the Four-Year Plan under the control of Hermann Göring who, in October of that year, was appointed 'Plenipotentiary of the Four-Year Plan'. Its aims were clearly to expand rearmament and autarky to make Germany as self-sufficient as possible in food and industrial production. In order to achieve this, the Plan highlighted a number of objectives:

- To regulate imports and exports, so as to prioritise strategic sectors, e.g. chemicals and metals at the expense of agricultural imports.
- To control the key sectors of the labour force, so as to prevent price inflation, e.g. the creation of a Reich Price Commissioner and increased work direction by DAF (see page 178).
- To increase the production of raw materials, so as to reduce the financial cost of importing vital goods, e.g. steel, iron and aluminium.
- To develop *ersatz* (substitute) products, e.g. oil (from coal), artificial rubber (buna).
- To increase agricultural production, so as to avoid imported foodstuffs, e.g. grants for fertilisers and machinery.

Key question

Why was the creation of the Four-Year Plan so significant?

The effects of the Four-Year Plan

The decision to implement the Four-Year Plan marked an important turning point in the Nazi regime. Nazi control over the German economy became much tighter, as Schacht described in his own book written in 1949:

> … On December 17th 1936, Göring informed a meeting of big industrialists that it was no longer a question of producing economically, but simply of producing. And as far as getting hold of foreign exchange was concerned it was quite immaterial whether the provisions of the law were complied with or not … Göring's policy of recklessly exploiting Germany's economic substance necessarily brought me into more and more acute conflict with him, and for his part he exploited his powers, with Hitler and the Party behind him, to counter my activity as Minister of Economics to an ever-increasing extent.

Profile: Hermann Göring 1893–1946

1893		– Born in Bavaria, the son of the governor of German Southwest Africa
1914–18		– Served in the First World War and became a pilot officer of the Richthofen Squadron
1922		– Dropped out of university and joined the Party as an SA commander
1923	November	– Took part in the Munich *putsch* and was seriously injured
1928	May	– Elected to the *Reichstag*
1933	January	– Appointed to the cabinet of Hitler's government as Minister without Portfolio
	February	– Exploited the *Reichstag* fire to discredit the Communists
	March	– Organised the terror to impose the dictatorship and to uphold co-ordination
1934	June	– Helped to organise the Night of the Long Knives
1935		– Commander-in-Chief of the new *Luftwaffe* (airforce)
1936	October	– Appointed Plenipotentiary of the Four-Year Plan by Hitler
1939		– Named as Hitler's successor, and at the height of his power and influence
1940–1		– After the failures of the *Luftwaffe* to win the Battle of Britain, his influence declined
1941–5		– He retained most of his offices, but he was increasingly isolated within the Nazi leadership
1946		– Committed suicide two hours before he was due to be executed at the Nuremberg trials

Göring played a crucial role in the rise of Nazism and during the consolidation of its power 1933–40. He came from a well-to-do family and with this status and the contacts provided by his aristocratic first wife, he was able to give Nazism a more respectable image in high society.

Göring's approach was uncompromising and brutal. During 1933–4 he organised the infiltration of the German police with the SA and SS – and willingly used violence and murder in the terror to secure Nazi power. He was deeply involved in the *Reichstag* fire (see page 142) and the Night of the Long Knives (see pages 150–2).

At first, he was popular because of his witty and charming conversation, but he became increasingly resented for his ambition and greed – he was given a whole host of titles and posts. From 1936 he became in effect economic dictator, though after the failures of the *Luftwaffe* to win the Battle of Britain, his influence sharply declined.

Resignation of
Schacht as Minister
of Economics:
November 1937

Schacht had no real respect for Göring, who had no economic expertise and deliberately and increasingly ignored Schacht's advice. Schacht recognised that his influence was on the wane and eventually in November 1937 he resigned. He was replaced by the weak Walther Funk, although from this time Göring himself became the real economic dictator.

The success of the Plan was mixed over the years (see Table 8.4). On the one hand, production of a number of key materials, such as aluminium and explosives, had expanded greatly, or at least at a reasonable rate. On the other hand, it fell a long way short of the targets in the essential commodities of rubber and oil, while arms production never reached the levels desired by the armed forces and Hitler. All in all, the Four-Year Plan had succeeded in the sense that Germany's reliance on imports had not increased. However, this still meant that when war did break out Germany was dependent on foreign supplies for one-third of its raw materials.

Germany found itself at war in September 1939 really because of diplomatic miscalculation. Its economy was still a long way from being fully mobilised, but it was certainly on more of a war footing than Britain or France. The question now was whether Germany could complete the economic mobilisation and thereby bring about military victory.

Table 8.4: The Four-Year Plan, launched in 1936

Commodity (in thousands of tons)	Four-Year Plan target	Actual output 1936	Actual output 1938	Actual output 1942
Oil	13,830	1,790	2,340	6,260
Aluminium	273	98	166	260
Rubber (buna)	120	0.7	5	96
Explosives	223	18	45	300
Steel	24,000	19,216	22,656	20,480
Hard coal	213,000	158,400	186,186	166,059

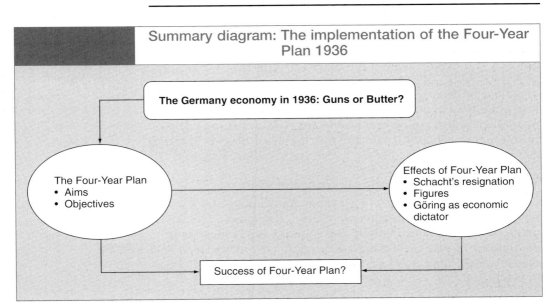

Summary diagram: The implementation of the Four-Year Plan 1936

The Germany economy in 1936: Guns or Butter?

The Four-Year Plan
• Aims
• Objectives

Effects of Four-Year Plan
• Schacht's resignation
• Figures
• Göring as economic dictator

Success of Four-Year Plan?

4 | The Nazi Economy at War 1939–45

The string of military successes achieved by the German armed forces with their use of *Blitzkrieg* strategy up to December 1941 won Hitler and the regime valuable popular support. Moreover, it gave the impression of an economy that had not been over-strained by the demands of war. Such a view, however attractive, does not actually square with either Nazi intentions or the economic statistics.

The expansion of the Nazi economy

First, Hitler himself was determined to avoid the problems faced by Germany in the First World War and to fight the coming war with an economy thoroughly prepared for a major and perhaps extended conflict. To this end, a series of war economy decrees was issued by Hitler in December 1939 outlining vast programmes for every possible aspect of war production, e.g. submarines and aircraft. These plans suggest that the Nazis went well beyond the demands of *Blitzkrieg* and a limited war.

Secondly, in real and percentage terms, German military expenditure doubled between 1939 and 1941, as shown by Table 8.5. (However, the figures have important implications, as Britain trebled expenditure in the same categories.)

Table 8.5: Military expenditure of Germany and Britain

	Germany (RM billions)			Britain (£ billions)		
Year	GNP	Military expenditure	Military expenditure as a % of GNP	GNP	Military expenditure	Military expenditure as a % of GNP
1937	93	11.7	13	4.6	0.3	7
1938	105	17.2	17	4.8	0.4	8
1939	130	30.0	23	5.0	1.1	22
1940	141	53.0	38	6.0	3.2	53
1941	152	71.0	47	6.8	4.1	60

Thirdly, food rationing in certain items was introduced from the very start of the war and the German labour force was rapidly mobilised for war so that, by the summer of 1941, 55 per cent of the workforce was involved in war-related projects – a figure which then only crept up to a high-point of 61 per cent by 1944. In this light it is hardly surprising that the first two years of war also witnessed a 20 per cent decline in civilian consumption.

The limitations of economic mobilisation

However, despite the intent of wholesale mobilisation the actual results, in terms of armaments production, remained disappointingly low. Admittedly, there was a marked increase in the number of submarines, but amazingly, Germany's airforce had only increased from 8290 aircraft in 1939 to 10,780 in 1941 while in Britain over the same period the number of aircraft had trebled to 20,100. Likewise, Hitler was astonished to learn when

---

Key question
How did the German economy expand?

Blitzkrieg
Literally 'lightning war'. It was the name of the military strategy developed to avoid static war. It was based on the use of dive-bombers, paratroopers and motorised infantry.

Key term

Hitler's War Economy decrees: December 1939

Key date

Key question
To what extent did the Nazis fail to mobilise the economy during the war?

drawing up plans for the invasion of the USSR that the Germans' armoured strength totalled only 3500 tanks, which was just 800 more than for the invasion of the West.

It seems that despite the Nazi image of German order and purposefulness, the actual mobilisation of the German economy was marred by inefficiency and poor co-ordination. The pressures resulting from the premature outbreak of war created problems, since many of the major projects were not due to be ready until 1942–3. So, at first, there was undoubtedly confusion between the short-term needs and long-term plans of the Nazi leadership.

Nevertheless, this should not have been an impossible barrier if only a clear and authoritative central control had been established over the economy. Instead, a host of different agencies all continued to function in their own way and often in a fashion which put them at odds with each other. So, although there was a Ministry of Armaments, it existed alongside three other interested governmental ministries, those of Economics, Finance and Labour. In addition, there was political infighting between the leading Nazi figures – for example, the *Gauleiters* tried to control their local areas at the expense of the plans of the state and the Party (see page 233) – and also considerable financial corruption.

(see page 233)

There were a number of groups responsible for armaments: the Office of the Four-Year Plan, the SS bodies and the different branches of the armed forces, **Wehrmacht**, *Luftwaffe* and navy. The armed forces, in particular, were determined to have their way over the development of munitions with the very best specifications possible and as a result the drive for quality was pursued at the expense of quantity. The consequence of all this was that after two years of war, and with the armed forces advancing into the USSR, Germany's economic mobilisation for total war had not achieved the expected levels of armaments production.

Total war 1941–5

By the end of 1941, Germany was at war with Britain, the USSR and the USA and yet its armaments production remained inferior to that of Britain. Preparations for a new approach had begun in the autumn of 1941 and Hitler himself had issued a **'Rationalisation Decree'** in December of that year.

However, it was the appointment of Albert Speer as Minister of Armaments in February 1942 that marked the real turning point. Speer had previously been the *Führer*'s personal architect and he enjoyed excellent relations with Hitler. He now used the *Führer*'s authority to cut through the mass of interests and to implement his programme of 'industrial self-responsibility' to provide mass production. The controls and constraints previously placed upon business, in order to fit in with Nazi wishes, were relaxed. In their place a Central Planning Board was established in April 1942, which was in turn supported by a number of committees, each representing one vital sector of the economy. This gave the industrialists a considerable degree of freedom, while ensuring

Key terms

Wehrmacht
The German army.

Rationalisation Decree
An intended reform of the economy to eliminate the waste of labour and materials.

Key question
How effectively did the German economy respond to the demands of 'total war'?

that Speer as the director of Central Planning was able to maintain overall control of the war economy. Speer also encouraged industrialists and engineers to join his ministerial team. At the same time, wherever possible, he excluded military personnel from the production process.

Speer was what would now be called a 'technocrat'. He simply co-ordinated and rationalised the process of war production and more effectively exploited the potential of Germany's resources and labour force. Speer was able to exert influence because of his friendship with Hitler and he used his personal skills to charm or blackmail other authorities. In his way, he took a whole range of other personal initiatives to improve production, such as:

- employing more women in the arms factories
- making effective use of concentration camp prisoners as workers
- preventing skilled workers being lost to military conscription.

Rationalisation Decree issued by Hitler: December 1941

Appointment of Albert Speer as Minister of Armaments: February 1942

Key dates

Profile: Albert Speer 1905–81

1905		– Born in Mannheim
1924–8		– Trained as an architect at Karlsruhe, Munich and Berlin
1931	January	– Joined the Nazi Party
1934		– Became Hitler's personal architect
1942		– Minister of Armaments
1946	October	– Sentenced to 20 years as a result of the Nuremberg trials
1966		– Released from Spandau prison
1969		– Publication of his books, *Inside the Third Reich* and *Spandau: The Secret Diaries*
1981		– Died in London on a visit

Speer remains as an interesting, and significant, figure on several counts:

- He was a talented and able architect who was commissioned for the design of the German pavilion at the Paris Exhibition in 1937, the Reich Chancellery in Berlin and the Party Palace in Nuremberg. His close friendship with Hitler and their common interest in architecture allowed him to exert increasing political influence.
- He quickly proved himself a skilful manager of the war economy, resulting in a fundamental increase in armaments production, 1942–4.
- Despite his friendship with Hitler, he clashed with leading Nazis, particularly Himmler.
- He always claimed after the war that he opposed forced labour in the occupied countries, yet his opponents maintained that this policy had more to do with efficiency than morality, and even claimed that he was aware of the treatment of the Jews.

The successes and limitations of Speer's economic rationalisation

In a famous speech in February 1943, after the German army surrender at Stalingrad, Joseph Goebbels invited the crowd to support 'total war'. However, the transformation of the Nazi economy really pre-dated Goebbels's propagandist appeal to 'total war' and was down to the work of Speer. As a result of Speer's first six months in power:

- ammunition production increased by 97 per cent
- tank production rose by 25 per cent
- total arms production increased by 59 per cent.

By the second half of 1944, when German war production peaked, it can be noted that there had been more than a three-fold increase since early 1942.

Despite Speer's economic successes, Germany probably had the capacity to produce even more and could have achieved a level of output close to that of the USSR or the USA. He was not always able to counter the power of the Party *Gauleiters* at a local level and the SS remained a law unto themselves, especially in the conquered lands. Indeed, although the occupied territories of the Third Reich were well and truly plundered, they were not exploited with real economic efficiency. Above all, though, from 1943 Speer could not reverse the detrimental effects of Anglo-American bombing.

After the war, 'blanket bombing' by the Allies was condemned by some on moral grounds and its effectiveness denied; indeed, critics pointed to Speer's production figures as proof that the strategy had failed to break the German war economy. However, it is probably more accurate to say that the effects of bombing

Table 8.6: Number of German, British, US and Soviet tanks produced 1940–5

	Germany	Britain	USA	USSR
1940	1,600	1,400	300	2,800
1941	3,800	4,800	4,100	6,400
1942	6,300	8,600	25,000	24,700
1943	12,100	7,500	29,500	24,000
1944	19,000	4,600	17,600	29,000
1945	3,900	N/A	12,000	15,400

Table 8.7: Number of German, British, US and Soviet aircraft produced 1940–5

	Germany	Britain	USA	USSR
1940	10,200	15,000	6,100	7,000
1941	11,000	20,100	19,400	12,500
1942	14,200	23,600	47,800	26,000
1943	25,200	26,200	85,900	37,000
1944	39,600	26,500	96,300	40,000
1945	N/A	12,100	46,000	35,000

prevented Germany from increasing its levels of arms production even further. The results of Allied bombing caused industrial destruction and breakdown in communications. Also, Germany was forced to divert available resources towards the construction of anti-aircraft installations and underground industrial sites. Because of this Germany was unable to achieve a total war economy. As it was, German arms production peaked in August 1944 at a level well below its full potential.

In the end, the Nazi economy had proved incapable of rising to the demands of total war and the cost of that failure was all too clearly to be seen in the ruins and economic collapse of 1945. (See also Chapter 12.)

Peak of German munitions production: August 1944

Key date

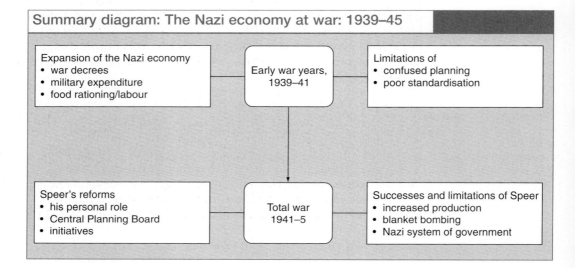

Summary diagram: The Nazi economy at war: 1939–45

Expansion of the Nazi economy
• war decrees
• military expenditure
• food rationing/labour

Early war years, 1939–41

Limitations of
• confused planning
• poor standardisation

Speer's reforms
• his personal role
• Central Planning Board
• initiatives

Total war 1941–5

Successes and limitations of Speer
• increased production
• blanket bombing
• Nazi system of government

Study guide: AS Question

In the style of Edexcel

How successful were Nazi economic policies in the years
1933–45?   (30 marks)

Exam tips

*The cross-references are intended to take you straight to the material
that will help you to answer the question.*

This is a very broad question that covers all aspects of this chapter.
Note that the dates in the question cover the peace years as well as
the war years. You should start by outlining a clear criterion to
assess 'successful', e.g. against the aims of the economic policy or
its results. You should then choose the relevant material carefully to
test your criterion, but be careful not to get lost in too much detail.
Avoid mere narrative but, instead, aim to analyse the extent of
success at each stage:

- the strengths and weaknesses of Germany's economic recovery
  1933–6 (see pages 160–5)
- the strengths, problems and implications of the Four-Year Plan
  1936–9 (pages 166–9)
- the successes and failures of the war economy (see pages 170–4).

In your conclusion, you have to remember that the condition of the
German economy was not static – it changed over time.

9 Nazi Society

POINTS TO CONSIDER
The purpose of this chapter is to consider Nazi social aims
and policies and their effects on the Third Reich. However,
this chapter will introduce the concept of *Volksgemeinschaft*,
which is essential to an understanding of German society in
the period. It will examine the following themes of German
social history and should help you to answer the historical
question of whether *Volksgemeinschaft* fundamentally
changed German society during the Third Reich:

• Nazi views on society: *Volksgemeinschaft*
• Social groups
• Education and youth
• Religion
• Women and the family
• Culture
• Outsiders
• The Nazi social revolution

The major issue of anti-Semitism will be covered in
Chapter 10, The Racial State.

Key dates

1933	May	The burning of the books
		Creation of German Labour Front
	July	Concordat signed with the Papacy
1934		Reich Ministry of Education created: control of education was taken away from *Länder*
		Creation of the Confessional Church
1937	March	Papal encyclical, *Mit Brennender Sorge*, issued
1941	August	Bishop Galen's sermon against euthanasia
1944	November	Execution of 12 Edelweiss Pirates in Cologne

1 | The Nazi *Volksgemeinschaft*

Key question
What was the
purpose of the Nazis
in creating the
Volksgemeinschaft?

When Nazi ideology developed in the 1920s it was based on three
key elements: racism, nationalism and authoritarianism (for
details see pages 91–4 in Chapter 5). However, Hitler always
claimed that National Socialism was more than just a political
ideology. It was a movement that aimed to transform German
society. It rejected the values of communism, liberalism and
Christianity and in their place upheld the concept of
Volksgemeinschaft.

Volksgemeinschaft was probably the vaguest element of Nazi
ideology and it is therefore difficult to define precisely. Indeed,
historians are divided between those who see it as a 'pseudo-
ideology' built on image alone, and those who see it as a more
concrete movement with genuine support.

The essential purpose of the *Volksgemeinschaft* was to overcome
the old German divisions of class, religion and politics and to
bring about a new collective national identity by encouraging
people to work together. This new social mentality aimed to bring
together the disparate elements and to create a German society
built on the Nazi ideas of race and struggle.

Very closely associated with Nazi racism was the aim of
Volksgemeinschaft to get people working together for the benefit of
the nation by promoting traditional German values. The ideal
German image was that of the classic peasant working on the soil
in the rural community; this was exemplified in the concept of
'Blood and Soil' (*Blut und Boden*) (see pages 180–3) and the
upholding of traditional roles by the two sexes.

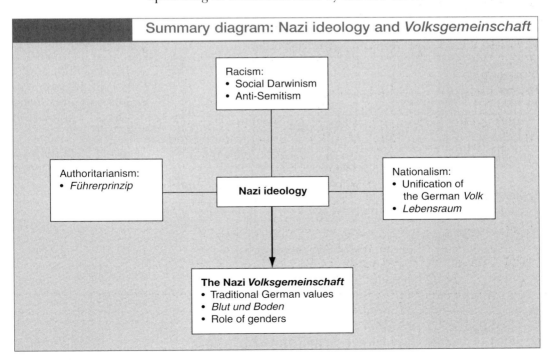
Summary diagram: Nazi ideology and *Volksgemeinschaft*

2 | Social Groups

The revival of the economy (see pages 160–5) in conjunction with Hitler's diplomatic successes (see page 246) contributed greatly to the German people's acceptance, or at least tolerance, of the regime. In the pre-war years it really did seem to many Germans as if the Nazis had pulled their country out of the economic quagmire. However, in material terms the effects varied considerably from one class to another.

Industrial workers

The working class was by far the largest social group in German society (see Table 9.1). The Nazi regime definitely could not assume that the workers could be won over to the promised ideas of the *Volksgemeinschaft*. Under Weimar, many workers had belonged to independent trade unions and politically they had generally voted for the left-wing parties – the Social Democrats and Communists.

At first, the Nazi regime simply wanted to establish its authority and so it closed down all the established trade unions (see pages 145–6). As a result, workers completely lost the right of industrial bargaining. Consequently management and the government controlled pay increases and were able to limit workers' freedom of movement.

Key question
Did the workers benefit under the Third Reich?

Table 9.1: German society

	Working class	Middle classes			Peasants	Others
		White-collar workers	Self-employed	Government officials/ employees		
German society as a whole in 1933 (%)	46.3	12.4	9.6	4.8	20.7	6.2

In the place of the unions, from May 1933, the only available option to workers was to join the German Labour Front (DAF, *Deutsche Arbeitsfront*). Led by Robert Ley, DAF became the largest Nazi organisation in the Third Reich with a membership that increased from five million in 1933 to 22 million in 1939. It became responsible for virtually all areas of work such as:

- setting working hours and wages
- dealing harshly with any sign of disobedience, strikes or absenteeism
- running training schemes for apprenticeships
- setting stable rents for housing
- supervising working conditions through the DAF subsection called the Beauty of Labour (SdA, *Schönheit der Arbeit*). The SdA aimed to provide cleaning, meals, exercise, etc.
- organising recreational facilities through the Strength through Joy (KdF, *Kraft durch Freude*). It provided very real opportunities

Creation of German Labour Front: May 1933

Key date

to millions of workers: cultural visits, sports facilities and holiday travel – although such benefits were only available to the loyal workers.

However, assessing the material effects of the Nazi regime on the workers is a highly complicated issue mainly because there are so many variables, such as age, occupation and geographical location. The obvious and most significant benefit for industrial workers was the creation of employment. For the many millions who had suffered from the distress of mass unemployment, the creation of jobs was accepted gratefully (see pages 160–2).

A Nazi propaganda poster advertising the benefits of saving for 'Your own KdF car'. Workers enthusiastically paid millions of marks to the scheme but the Volkswagen was never actually produced until after the war.

Profile: Robert Ley 1890–1945

1890	– Born in the Rhineland, the son of a farmer
1914	– Graduated with a degree in chemistry
1914–17	– First World War pilot
1920–8	– Worked with the major chemicals company IG Farben, but sacked for drunkenness
1924	– Joined the NSDAP
1930	– Elected to the *Reichstag*
1933–45	– Leader of the German Labour Front. Used the money to fund KdF (the Volkswagen scheme, see pages 178–9) and the élite training schools, *Ordensburgen* (see page 187)
1939–45	– Lost influence to Todt and Speer
1945	– Captured by US forces, but committed suicide before trial

Ley enjoyed a very significant power-base as the leader of DAF, which was the largest Nazi organisation in the Third Reich. However, he personally failed to develop the institution to its political potential and simply exploited the position for his own self-advancement. He became an alcoholic and although he retained his position, he lost the support of other leading Nazis.

Indeed, by the late 1930s Germany had achieved full employment and there was a growing shortage of workers.

Yet, to put that major benefit into context, it is important to bear in mind a number of key factors:

- Average workers' **real wages** only rose above 1929 levels in 1938. Also, workers were forced to pay extensive contributions for DAF and insurance/tax.
- The generalised picture disguises the fact that the biggest gains were clearly made by the workers associated with the boom in the rearmament industries, whereas those in consumer goods struggled to maintain their real incomes.
- Working hours increased over time. The average working week was officially increased from 43 hours in 1933 to 47 hours in 1939 – and as military demands grew, there was pressure on many workers to do more overtime.

So, there is considerable evidence to suggest there was workers' discontent even before 1939. Once the war set in, pressures increased further – especially from 1942 when bombing began to hit German industrial urban sectors. By 1944 the working week had grown to 60 hours.

Peasants and small farmers

The farming community had been attracted to the Nazi cause by the promise of financial aid, as they had suffered from a series of economic problems from the mid-1920s. Moreover, peasants felt

Real wages
The actual purchasing power of income taking into account inflation/deflation and also the effect of deductions, e.g. taxes.

Key term

Key question
Did the peasantry and small farmers benefit under the Third Reich?

Profile: Richard Darré 1895–1953

1895		– Born in Buenos Aires, Argentina, of German and Swedish parents
1914–18		– Served in the First World War and reached the rank of lieutenant
1920–5		– Studied at Halle and gained a doctorate in agriculture specialising in animal breeding
1928–30		– Publication of three books on Nazi views of race; the most significant was *The Peasantry as the Life-source of the Nordic Race*
1930	June	– Created a Nazi agrarian political organisation
	July	– Joined the Nazi Party
1933	May 28	– Appointed Reich Peasant Leader
	June 29	– Appointed Minister of Agriculture and Food
	September	– Responsible for introducing the Reich Entitled Law and the Reich Food Estate (see pages 160, 182–3)
1938	September	– Made leader of the Central Office for Race and Settlement (RuSHA)
1940		– Delivered his infamous speech outlining the fate of the British people in his plans for race and settlement
1942		– Forced to resign from all his positions
1945		– Arrested and held by Allied forces
1949		– Sentenced to seven years in prison for confiscating Jewish and Polish property
1953		– Died in Munich

Darré was more intellectual than many Nazi leaders. He was well travelled, fluent in four languages and eventually was awarded a doctoral degree for his studies. In 1930 he was drawn into the NSDAP and played an important role in the rise of the Nazis by creating an agrarian political organisation. He effectively exploited the rural unrest winning electoral support in the countryside.

There were two elements to Darré's thinking:

- to restore the role and values of the countryside and to reverse the drive towards urbanisation by promoting the concept of 'Blood and Soil'
- to support the expansionist policy of *Lebensraum* and to create a German racial aristocracy based on selective breeding.

Initially, his agricultural reforms were well received by the Nazi regime and certainly helped to enable many farmers to recover in the mid-1930s. In particular, his ideas were supported by Himmler and they worked closely together in the RuSHA. The extent of Darré's racism is shown in his speech of 1940:

As soon as we beat England we shall make an end of you Englishmen once and for all. Able-bodied men and women between the ages of 16 and 45 will be exported as slaves to the Continent. The old and weak will be exterminated.

All men remaining in Britain as slaves will be sterilised; a million or two of the young women of the Nordic type will be segregated in a number of stud farms where, with the assistance of picked German sires, during a period of 10 or 12 years, they will produce annually a series of Nordic infants to be brought up in every way as Germans.

However, Darré increasingly fell out with the leadership. His idealistic vision of a rural utopia was at odds with the economic demands of war production and in 1942 he was forced to resign by Hitler.

increasingly that they were losing out to the growing urban society of industrial Germany. Yet, it seemed from Nazi ideology of 'Blood and Soil' promoted by Richard Darré (see profile on page 181) that there was a real sympathy for the role of the peasants in society. It portrayed the peasantry as racially the purest element of the *Volk*, the providers of Germany's food and as the symbol of traditional German values.

The Nazi regime certainly took initiatives on agriculture:

- A substantial number of farm debts and mortgages were written off and small farmers were given low interest rates and a range of tax allowances.
- The government maintained extensive tariffs to reduce imports.
- The introduction of the Reich Entailed Farm Law of 1933 gave security of tenure to the occupiers of medium-sized farms between 7.5 and 125 hectares and forbade the division of farms.
- The Reich Food Estate, established in 1933, supervised every aspect of agricultural production and distribution – especially food prices and working wages (although its bureaucratic meddling became the focus of much resentment, when, for example, it stipulated that each hen had to lay 65 eggs per year).

The economic realities meant that in practice the impact of Nazi agricultural policy was rather mixed. At first, all farmers benefited from an increase in prices between 1933 and 1936 and so farmers' incomes did improve markedly – though they only recovered to 1928 levels in 1938. However, it seems that by 1936–7 any benefits were giving way to a growing peasant disillusionment. This was for several reasons:

- Although the regime succeeded in increasing agricultural production by 20 per cent from 1928 to 1938, there continued to be a significant drift of workers to the towns where wages were higher. German agriculture just did not have the economic power to compete with other sectors of the economy. As a result, 3 per cent of the German population drifted from the countryside to the town.

- Of course, the positive aspects of the Reich Food Estate were accepted, but the regulation became increasingly resented.
- The Reich Entailed Farm Law also caused resentment and family discontent. In trying to solve one problem by passing on farms to just one child, farmers faced the very real dilemma of not being able to provide a future for their remaining children.

With the onset of the war in 1939 the peasantry's pressures developed in all sorts of ways. Men were increasingly conscripted to the military fronts – so the problem of the shortage of agricultural labour was exacerbated. This resulted in the transportation to Germany of cheap forced labour of peasants from eastern Europe, e.g. Poles and Czechs. This also conflicted with Nazi thinking since the labourers were not even viewed as racially acceptable.

Landowners

Key question
Did the landowners lose out?

The landed classes had been initially suspicious of the idea of radical social change. They resented the political interference of the Party, but above all they feared the Nazis would redistribute the large landed estates. However, they soon learned to live quite comfortably with the Nazi regime and in the years before 1939 their economic interests were not really threatened. Indeed, German victories in the early years of the war offered the chance of acquiring more cheap land.

The real blow for the landowners actually came in 1945 when the occupation of eastern Germany by the USSR resulted in the nationalisation of land. The traditional social and economic supremacy of the German landowners was broken.

Mittelstand

Key question
Did the *Mittelstand* benefit under the Third Reich?

Another social class that expected to benefit from the Nazi regime was the *Mittelstand*. The problems confronting the *Mittelstand* were in many ways comparable to the problems faced by the peasantry. It had suffered from the decline in commerce in Germany since the First World War and it found it difficult to compete with the increasing power of big business and trade unions.

Research has shown that in the elections 1930–3 the *Mittelstand* had voted for Nazism in greater proportion than the rest of German society and the Nazi regime was keen to take sympathetic measures to maintain that support:

- The government used the money available from the confiscation of Jewish businesses to offer low interest rate loans.
- It introduced the Law to Protect Retail Trade (1933) against large department stores, of which many were Jewish. This

banned the opening of new department stores and taxed the existing ones.
- It imposed a host of new trading regulations to protect small craftsmen.

However, despite the Nazis' attempt to implement their electoral promises before 1933 and the economic recovery, the position of the *Mittelstand* continued the decline that had started with Germany's industrialisation. The costs of small businesses meant that they could not compete with the lower costs of the large department stores. Moreover the problem was made worse because of the Nazi preference for big business, whose support was required for rearmament.

In 1933, 20 per cent of the owners of small businesses were under 30 years old and 14 per cent over 60. By 1939 the corresponding figures were 10 per cent under 30 and 19 per cent over 60, which highlighted the ageing trend of the *Mittelstand*. And in the years 1936–9 it is reckoned that the number of traditional skilled craftsmen declined by 10 per cent. The truth is that the *Mittelstand* found itself being significantly squeezed out.

Big business

The influence of big business remained very significant and generally it benefited from the Nazis' economic programme. So despite the increasing range of government controls, the financial gains were impressive. The value of German industry steadily increased, as shown by the following:

Key question
Why did big business benefit?

- The share price index increased from 41 points in 1932 to 106 in 1940, while annual dividends to investors grew from an average 2.83 per cent to 6.6 per cent over the same period.
- The improvement in salaries of management from an average 3700RM in 1934 to 5420RM in 1938 also reflected the economic growth.

Moreover, from 1939 the onset of the war provided enormous opportunities for taking over foreign property, land and companies. For example, Oskar Schindler (1908–74), a German businessman, set up business in Krakow in 1939 and drew much of his workforce from the Jewish labour camp. After initially exploiting these workers he eventually saved thousands from extermination.

Summary diagram: Social groups

Mittelstand
• Problems
• Nazi initiatives
• Decline
- - - - - - - - - - - - - - -
Did it benefit?

Peasants and small farmers
• Nazi initiatives
• Benefits and disillusion
• Darré's ideas
- - - - - - - - - - - - - - -
Did the peasantry benefit?

Nazi social groups

Industrial workers
• Loss of rights
• Robert Ley and DAF
• Material effects
- - - - - - - - - - - - - - -
Did they benefit in the Third Reich?

Landowners
• Comfortable survival
• Post-1945 losses
- - - - - - - - - - - - - - -
Did the landowners lose out?

Big business
• Financial gains
• Initial advantages of war
- - - - - - - - - - - - - - -
Why did big business benefit?

3 | Education and Youth

Key question
What were the aims of Nazi education?

In Nazi Germany, education became merely a tool for the consolidation of the Nazi system. Hitler expressed his views chillingly in 1933:

> When an opponent declares, 'I will not come over to your side', I calmly say, 'Your child belongs to us already … What are you? You will pass on. Your descendants, however, now stand in the new camp. In a short time they will know nothing else but this new community.'

Education in the Third Reich was therefore intended to **indoctrinate** its youth so completely in the principles and ethos of National Socialism that the long-term survival of the 'New Order' would never be brought into question. A National Socialist Teachers' League official wrote pompously in 1937:

Indoctrination
Inculcating and imposing a set of ideas.

> German youth must no longer – as in the Liberal era in the cause of so-called objectivity – be confronted with the choice of whether it wishes to grow up in a spirit of materialism or idealism, of racism or internationalism, of religion or godlessness, but it must be consciously shaped according to the principles which are

recognised as correct and which have shown themselves to be correct: according to the principles of the ideology of National Socialism.

This was to be achieved not only through the traditional structure of the educational system, but also by the development of various Nazi youth movements.

Schools

The actual organisation of the state educational system was not fundamentally altered, although by a law of 1934 control was taken from the regional states and centralised under the Reich Ministry of Education, Culture and Science led by Reich Minister Bernhard Rust. The Ministry was then able to adapt the existing system to suit Nazi purposes.

First, the teaching profession itself was 'reconditioned'. Politically unreliable individuals were removed and Jewish teachers were banned, and many women were encouraged to conform to Nazi values by returning to the home (see pages 198–203). Special training courses were arranged for those teachers who remained unconvinced by the new requirements. In addition, the National Socialist Teachers' League (NSLB, *Nationalsozialistische Lehrerbund*) was established and its influence and interference continued to grow. By 1937, it included 97 per cent of all teachers and two-thirds of the profession had been on special month-long courses on Nazi ideology and the changes to the curriculum.

Secondly, the curricula and syllabuses were adapted. To fit in with the Nazi Aryan ideal, a much greater emphasis was placed on physical education, so that 15 per cent of school time was given over to it, and games teachers assumed an increased status and importance in the school hierarchy. On the academic front, Religious Studies were dropped to downgrade the importance of Christianity, whereas German, Biology and History became the focus of special attention:

- German language and literature were studied to create 'a consciousness of being German', and to inculcate a martial and nationalistic spirit. Among the list of suggested reading for 14-year-old pupils was a book entitled *The Battle of Tannenberg*, which included the following extract: 'A Russian soldier tried to bar the infiltrator's way, but Otto's bayonet slid gratingly between the Russian's ribs, so that he collapsed groaning. There it lay before him, simple and distinguished, his dream's desire, the Iron Cross.'
- Biology became the means by which to deliver Nazi racial theory: ethnic classification, **population policy** and racial genetics were all integrated into the syllabus.
- History, not surprisingly, was also given a special place in the Nazi curriculum, so that the glories of German nationalism could be emphasised.

Key question
How did German schools change under the Nazis?

Reich Ministry of Education created – control of education was taken away from *Länder*: 1934 — *Key date*

Population policy
In 1933–45 the Nazi government aimed to increase the birth rate. — *Key term*

One final innovation was the creation of various types of élite schools. They were intended to prepare the best of Germany's youth for future political leadership, were modelled on the principles of the Hitler Youth, and focused on physical training, paramilitary activities and political education. The 21 *Napolas* (National Political Educational Institutions) and the 10 Adolf Hitler Schools were both for boys of secondary school age, and the three *Ordensburgen* for boys of college age.

Hitler Youth

Key question
How did the Hitler
Youth try to
indoctrinate
Germany's young
people?

The responsibility for developing a new outlook lay with the youth movements. There was already a long and well-established tradition of youth organisation in Germany before 1933, but at that time the Hitler Youth (HJ, *Hitler Jugend*) represented only 1 per cent of the total.

The term 'Hitler Youth' in fact embraced a range of youth groups under the control of its leader Baldur von Schirach and in the next six years the structure and membership of the HJ grew remarkably – although this was partly because parents were pressurised to enrol the children and by 1939 membership became compulsory.

Profile: Baldur von Schirach 1907–74

1907	– Born in Berlin, the son of an aristocratic German father and an American mother
1924	– Joined the NSDAP as a student of art history at Munich
1928	– Leader of National Socialist German Students' League
1933–9	– Youth Leader of the German Reich
1939–40	– Joined the German army and won the Iron Cross
1940–5	– *Gauleiter* of Vienna
1945	– Arrested by the Allies
1946–66	– Sentenced to 20 years' imprisonment at the Nuremberg War Crimes Trials
1967	– Publication of his book, *I believed in Hitler*
1974	– Lived privately in West Germany until his death

Schirach's only real significant role was as 'Youth Leader of the German Reich', which gave him the responsibility to supervise all the youth organisations, 1933–9. He became obsessed with Hitler from the mid-1920s – he even wrote poetry to the *Führer*! He was not greatly respected by other leading Nazis, partly because of his effeminate nature. However, his loyalty and charm allowed him to remain influential with Hitler and he was appointed *Gauleiter* of Vienna.

Schirach denied responsibility for war crimes, but the Nuremberg Trials found him guilty of having deported the Jews from Austria.

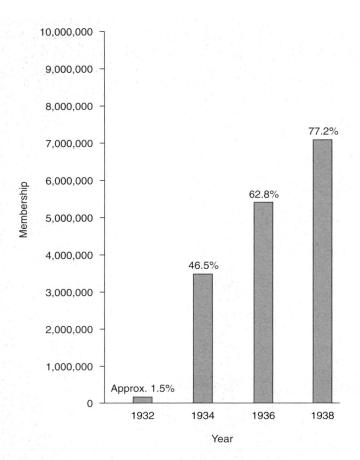

Figure 9.1: Hitler Youth movements. The percentages indicate the percentage of total youth population aged 10–18 years who were members

Table 9.2: Youth groups

Boys 10–14 years old	German Young People (DJ, *Deutsche Jungvolk*)
Boys 14–18 years old	Hitler Youth (HJ, *Hitler Jugend*)
Girls 10–14 years old	League of Young Girls (JM, *Jungmädel*)
Girls 14–18 years old	League of German Girls (BDM, *Bund Deutscher Mädel*)

In all four groups shown in Table 9.2 there was a great stress on political indoctrination, emphasising the life and achievements of the *Führer*, German patriotism, athletics and camping. In addition, the sexes were moulded for their future roles in Nazi society. Boys engaged in endless physical and military-type activities, e.g. target shooting, and girls were prepared for their domestic and maternal tasks, e.g. cooking.

'Youth serves the *Führer*. Every ten year old into the Hitler Youth.' The Nazi propaganda poster cleverly plays on the combined images of the young boy and Hitler sharing a common vision.
It was produced in 1940, by which time war had started and membership was compulsory.

Successes and failures

Key question
Did Nazi education succeed?

It is difficult to assess the success of any educational system. It depends on the criteria chosen and the 'evidence' is open to conflicting interpretations. Therefore, conclusions must be tentative.

The teaching profession certainly felt its status to be under threat, despite its initial sympathy for the regime. Thirty-two per cent were members of the Party in 1936 – a figure markedly higher than the figure of 17 per cent of the Reich Civil Service as a whole. The anti-academic ethos and the crude indoctrination alienated many, while the Party's backing of the HJ and its activities caused much resentment. Not surprisingly, standards in traditional academic subjects had fallen by the early years of the war. This was particularly the case in the various élite schools, where physical development predominated. By 1938 recruitment of teachers had declined and there were 8000 vacancies – and only 2500 were coming out of the teacher training colleges. In higher education, the number of students had halved even before the onset of the war. The overall effect of these changes was described in 1937 in a report from the teachers' organisation in Bavaria:

> Many pupils believe that they can simply drift through for eight years and secure their school leaving certificate with minimal intellectual performance. The schools receive no support whatsoever from the Hitler Youth units; on the contrary, it is those pupils who are in positions of leadership there who often display unmannerly behaviour and laziness at school. School discipline has declined to an alarming extent.

The impact of the HJ seems to have been very mixed. In some respects the emphasis on teamwork and extracurricular activities was to be commended – especially when compared to the limited provision available in many European countries. So, the provision for sports, camping and music genuinely excited many youngsters – and for those from poorer backgrounds, the HJ really offered opportunities. However, the organisation suffered from its over-rapid expansion and the leadership was inadequate. When the war started it became even more difficult to run the movement effectively and, as a result, the increasing Nazi emphasis on military drill and discipline was certainly resented by many adolescents. This point was made by a BDM leader in her memoirs:

> Apart from its beginnings during the 'years of struggle', the Hitler Youth was not a youth movement at all: it became more and more the 'state youth organisation', that is to say, it became more and more institutionalised, and finally became the instrument used by the National Socialist regime to run its ideological training of young people and the war work for certain age groups.

Moreover, much recent research suggests that sizeable pockets of the adolescent population had not been won over by 1939 and that, during the war, alienation and dissent increased quite markedly. The regime even established a special youth section of the secret police and a youth concentration camp was set up at Neuwied.

A number of youth groups developed deliberately exhibiting codes of behaviour at odds with the expected social values of Nazism. 'Swing Youth' was one such craze among mainly middle-class youngsters who took up the music and imagery associated with the dance-bands of Britain and the USA. The **Edelweiss Piraten** was a general name given to a host of working-class youths who formed gangs, such as the 'Roving Dudes' and 'Navajos'. Their members had been alienated by the military emphasis and discipline of the Hitler Youth. They met up and organised their own hikes and camps which then came into conflict with the official ones. In several instances, 'Pirates' became involved in more active resistance, most famously at Cologne in 1944 when 12 of them were publicly hanged because of their attacks on military targets and the assassination of a *Gestapo* officer.

key date

Execution of 12 Edelweiss Pirates in Cologne: November 1944

key term

Edelweiss
A white alpine flower which served as a symbol of opposition.

Kittelbach Pirates from 1937. 'Pirates' was the label chosen by dissenting German youth. In what ways could these boys be seen as challenging Nazi ideals?

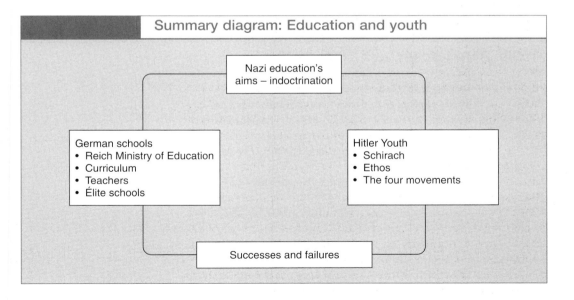

Summary diagram: Education and youth

Nazi education's aims – indoctrination

German schools
• Reich Ministry of Education
• Curriculum
• Teachers
• Élite schools

Hitler Youth
• Schirach
• Ethos
• The four movements

Successes and failures

4 | Religion

In the 1930s the majority of German people were Christian, two-thirds of whom were **Protestant** and the remaining one-third Catholic. The rise of Nazism posed fundamental political and ethical problems for the Christian Churches, while Nazism could not ignore those Churches, which were well-established and powerful institutions.

In his rise to power Hitler avoided direct attacks on the Churches and number 24 of the Party's 25-points programme spoke in favour of 'positive Christianity' which was closely linked to racial and national views (see page 87). However, there can be little doubt that Nazism was based on a fundamentally anti-Christian philosophy. Where Nazism glorified strength, violence and war, Christianity taught love, forgiveness and neighbourly respect. Moreover, Christianity was regarded as the product of an inferior race – Jesus was a Hebrew – and therefore, it could not be reconciled with Nazi *völkisch* thought. Some leading Nazis, such as Himmler and his deputy, Heydrich, openly revealed their contempt for Christianity. Hitler himself was more cautious, although what were probably his true feelings were revealed in a private conversation in 1933:

> Neither of the denominations – Catholic or Protestant, they are both the same – has any future left … That won't stop me stamping out Christianity in Germany root and branch. One is either a Christian or a German. You can't be both.

Key question
How did the Nazis regard religion?

Key terms

Protestant
General name for the reformed Churches created in sixteenth-century Europe that split from the Roman Catholic Church. There were 28 different Protestant Churches in Germany, of which the largest was the Lutheran (the German state Church, like the Church of England).

Völkisch
Nationalist views associated with racism (especially anti-Semitism).

Profile: Alfred Rosenberg 1893–1946

1893	– Born in Russian Estonia, but of German parents
1919	– Joined the Party as one of its earlier members
1923	– Took part in the Munich Beer Hall *putsch*
1924–5	– Leader of the Party while Hitler was in prison
1930	– Elected as a member of the *Reichstag*
	– Published his book on racial theory, *The Myth of the Twentieth Century*
1941	– Minister for the Occupied Territories
1945	– Arrested by Allied forces
1946	– Executed after the Nuremberg War Trials

Rosenberg was not really an effective political leader. He was an educated and scholarly figure, but he only exerted influence with a limited number within the Party. He was portrayed as the Party's main 'ideologue' and in his lengthy book he expressed his commitment to racism, anti-Semitism and anti-Christianity. His major significance lay in his promotion of the German Faith Movement.

Teutonic paganism
The non-Christian beliefs of the Germans in ancient history (heathens).

Cult of personality
Using the power and charisma of a political leader to dominate the nation.

The German Faith Movement

In place of Christianity, the Nazis aimed to cultivate a **teutonic paganism**, which became known as the German Faith Movement. Although a clear Nazi religious ideology was never fully outlined, the development of the German Faith Movement, promoted by the Nazi thinker Alfred Rosenberg, revolved around four main themes:

- the propagation of the 'Blood and Soil' ideology (see pages 180–3)
- the replacement of Christian ceremonies – marriage and baptism – by pagan equivalents
- the wholesale rejection of Christian ethics – closely linked to racial and nationalist views
- the **cult of** Hitler's **personality**.

However, the Nazi government knew that religion was a very delicate issue and it initially adopted a cautious conciliatory stance towards both the Churches.

Kulturkampf
'Cultural struggle'. Refers to the tension in the 1870s between the Catholic Church and the German state, when Bismarck was chancellor.

Concordat
An agreement between Church and state.

Conciliation and conflict 1933–5

In his very first speech as Chancellor, Hitler paid tribute to the Churches as being integral to the well-being of the nation. Members of the SA were even encouraged to attend Protestant Church services. This was done to give weight to the idea that the Nazi state could accommodate Protestantism. The 'Day of Potsdam' (see page 143) further gave the impression of a unity between the Protestant Church and the state.

Likewise, the Catholic Church responded sympathetically to the overtures of the Nazis. Catholic bishops, in particular, were frightened of the possibility of a repeat of the so-called *Kulturkampf* in the late nineteenth century. So, Catholic bishops were concerned to safeguard the position of the Church under the Nazis and in July 1933 a **Concordat** was signed between the Papacy and the regime (represented by Vice-Chancellor Papen who was a Catholic). In the agreement it was decided that:

- the Nazis would guarantee the Catholic Church religious freedom
- the Nazis would not interfere with the Catholic Church's property and legal rights
- the Nazis would accept the Catholic Church's control over its own education
- in return, the Catholic Church would not interfere in politics and would give diplomatic recognition to the Nazi government.

In the short term the Concordat seemed to be a significant success. However, the courting of both of the Churches by the Nazis was totally insincere. They were merely being lulled into a false sense of security while the dictatorship was being established. By the end of 1933 Nazi interference in religious affairs was already causing resentment and disillusionment in both Catholic and Protestant Churches.

Profile: Pastor Martin Niemöller 1892–1984

1892 – Born in Lippstadt
1914–18 – U-boat commander and won the Iron Cross
1920–4 – Studied theology and ordained as a Protestant pastor in Berlin
1934 – Co-founder of the Confessional Church
1937 – A critical sermon resulted in his arrest
1937–45 – Held in the concentration camps of Sachsenhausen and Dachau
1946 – President of the Protestant Church in Hessen
1946–84 – A strong supporter of the World Peace Movement
1984 – Died in Wiesbaden, Germany

In the 1920s Niemöller was a nationalist, anti-communist and against the Weimar Republic – he even sympathised with Hitler in the rise of Nazism. However, during 1933 his doubts emerged because of Nazism's anti-Semitism and its attempt to control the Churches. Therefore, he played a crucial role in the formation of the Confessional Church in 1934 and after a highly critical sermon he was imprisoned from 1937 to 1945. Although his actions in the Third Reich were limited, his words have resonated through the years:

> When the Nazis came for the Communists
> I stayed quiet:
> I was not a Communist.
>
> When they came for the Social Democrats
> I stayed quiet:
> I was not a Social Democrat.
>
> When they came for the Trade Unionists
> I stayed quiet:
> I was not a Trade Unionist.
>
> When they came for the Jews
> I stayed quiet:
> I was not a Jew.
>
> Then they came for me
> And there was no-one left to protest.

The Nazi regime hoped that the Protestant Churches would gradually be 'co-ordinated' through the influence of the group known as the German Christians (*Deutsche Christen*). This group hoped to reconcile their Protestant ideas with Nazi nationalist and racial thinking by finding common ground. So, a new Church constitution was formulated in July 1933 with the Nazi sympathiser Ludwig Müller as the first Reich Bishop – an interesting application of the *Führerprinzip*.

Key dates

Creation of the
Confessional Church:
1934

Papal encyclical, *Mit
Brennender Sorge*,
issued: 1937

Key question
How did the
relationship between
the Churches and
state change over
time?

However, such Nazi policies alienated many Protestant pastors, and there soon developed an opposition group, the Confessional Church (*Bekennende Kirche*), which upheld orthodox Protestantism and rejected Nazi distortions. Led by Pastor Niemöller, by 1934 the Confessional Church gained the support of about 7000 pastors out of 17,000. They claimed to represent the true Protestant Churches of Germany.

Churches and state 1935–45

By 1935 it was clear that the Nazi leadership had achieved only limited success in its control over the Churches. It was torn between a policy of total suppression, which would alienate large numbers of Germans, and a policy of limited persecution, which would allow the Churches an unacceptable degree of independence outside state control. In fact, although the ultimate objective was never in doubt, Nazi tactics degenerated into a kind of war of attrition against the Churches.

In order to destabilise the Churches, the Ministry of Church Affairs, led by Hanns Kerrl, was established. He adopted a policy of undermining both the Protestant and Catholic Churches by a series of anti-religious measures, including:

- closure of Church schools
- undermining of Catholic youth groups
- personal campaigns to discredit and harass the clergy, e.g. monasteries were accused of sexual and financial malpractices
- confiscation of Church funds
- campaign to remove crucifixes from schools
- arrest of more and more pastors and priests.

The standing of the Churches was undoubtedly weakened by this approach, but it also stimulated individual declarations of opposition from both Protestants and Catholics:

- Niemöller delivered a sermon in which he said that 'we must obey God rather than man'; he was interned in 1937 and for the next eight years he was held in various concentration camps.
- The Pope, Pius XI, eventually vehemently attacked the Nazi system in his encyclical, or public letter, of 1937 entitled *With Burning Concern* (*Mit Brennender Sorge*).

Clearly, the conflict between the Churches and the state was set to continue.

The outbreak of war initially brought about a more cautious policy, as the regime wished to avoid unnecessary tensions. However, following the easy military victories against Poland and France (1939–40), and then the invasion of atheistic Soviet Union (1941), the persecution intensified. This was the result of pressure applied by anti-Christian enthusiasts, such as Bormann and Heydrich (see page 222) and the SS hierarchy.

So, once again, monasteries were closed, Church property was attacked and Church activities were severely restricted. Even so, religion was such a politically sensitive issue that Hitler did not allow subordination of the Churches to give way to wholesale suppression within Germany. It was only in the occupied territory of Poland – the area designated as an experimental example of the 'New Order' – that events were allowed to run their full course. Here, many of the Catholic clergy were executed and churches were closed down. In the end the Nazi persecution of the Churches failed, but only because the war itself was lost.

Conclusion

The Nazis achieved only limited success in their religious policy. The German Faith Movement was a clearly a failure. Neo-paganism never achieved support on any large scale. The 1939 official census recorded only 5 per cent of the population as members, although it shows the direction that might have been taken, if the likes of Himmler had won the war.

Key question
Did Nazi religious policy succeed in its aims?

There were numerous individual Christians who made brave stands against the Nazis. This made the dictatorship wary of launching a fundamental assault on religion. As a result, German loyalty to the Christian faith in the Protestant and Catholic Churches survived in the long term despite Nazism. The historian J.R.C. Wright says: 'The Churches were severely handicapped but not destroyed. Hitler's programme needed time: he was himself destroyed before it had taken root.'

However, both the Catholic and Protestant Churches failed because of their inability to provide effective opposition to Nazism. Neither of the Christian Churches was 'co-ordinated' and therefore, both enjoyed a measure of independence. So they both could have provided the focus for active resistance. Instead, they preferred, as institutions, to adopt a pragmatic policy towards Nazism. They stood up for their own religious practices and traditions with shows of dissent, but generally they refrained from wholesale denunciations of the regime.

Key question
Did the Churches effectively oppose the Nazis?

The reasons for the Churches' reluctance to show opposition to the regime lay in their conservatism:

- They distrusted the politics of the left which seemed to threaten the existing order of society. The most extreme form of communism rejected the existence of religion itself.
- There was a nationalist sympathy for Nazism, especially after the problems of 1918–33. For many Church leaders it was too easy to believe that Hitler's 'national renewal' was simply a return to the glorious days before 1914. This was particularly true of the Lutheran Protestant Church, which had been the state Church in Prussia under Imperial Germany.
- Both Churches rightly feared the power of the Nazi state. They believed that any gestures of heroic resistance were more than likely to have bloody consequences. In such a situation, their emphasis on pastoral and spiritual comfort was perhaps the most practical and realistic policy for them.

Effective Christian resistance, therefore, remained essentially the preserve of individual churchmen who put their own freedom and

Profile: Dietrich Bonhoeffer 1906–45

1906		– Born at Breslau, Germany
1923–31		– Studied at Tübingen, Berlin, Rome, Barcelona and New York
1931–3		– Lecturer and student pastor at Berlin University
1933–5		– Worked as a pastor on the outskirts of London
1935		– Returned to Germany and joined the Confessing Church
1935–40		– Ran a college to train pastors
1936		– His college was closed
1940–43		– Banned from preaching and made contact with the active resistance movement
1943	April	– Arrested by the *Gestapo*
1943–45		– Held in various prisons and camps.
1945	April	– Murdered in Flossenbürg concentration camp

From the very start Bonhoeffer was a consistent opponent of Hitler and Nazism. However, by 1940, he had moved from religious dissent to political resistance. Over the next three years he:

- helped Jews to emigrate
- was drawn into the Kreisau Circle and actively worked with the underground movement
- travelled secretly to Sweden to see an English bishop, Bell, in the hope that Britain would help the resistance (the British authorities remained very cautious).

When he was sentenced to death the SS doctor later wrote: 'in nearly 50 years as a doctor I never saw another man go to his death so possessed of the spirit of God'.

lives at risk in order to uphold their beliefs or to give pastoral assistance.

It has been estimated that 40 per cent of the Catholic clergy and over 50 per cent of the Protestant pastors were harassed by the Nazis. Most famous were:

Key date

Bishop Galen's sermon against euthanasia: August 1940

- Bishop Galen of Münster, whose outspoken sermon attacking Nazi euthanasia policy (see page 208) in 1941 proved so powerful that the authorities recoiled from arresting him and actually stopped the programme.
- Martin Niemöller, the founder of the Confessional Church, who languished in a concentration camp from 1937 (see page 194).
- Dietrich Bonhoeffer, whose opposition started as religious dissent but, from 1940, developed into political resistance which brought him into direct contact with elements of the conservative resistance (see above).

Such heroic examples were by no means exceptional and hundreds of priests and pastors were to die in the camps for their refusal to co-operate with the regime. Their sacrifice is therefore eloquent testimony to the limits to which people would go to defy conformity. But it also bears witness to the fact that such courageous resistance was rarely able to restrain the regime.

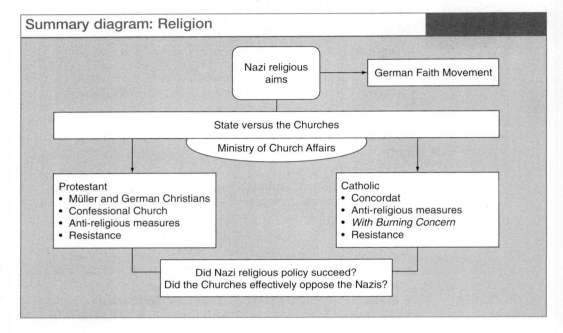

Summary diagram: Religion

5 | Women and the Family

Key question
How and why was German society changed in the twentieth century?

The first quarter of the twentieth century witnessed two important social changes in German family life:

- Germany's population growth had decelerated markedly – which is *not* to say that the actual population had declined. In 1900 there had been over two million live births per annum, whereas by 1933 the figure was below one million.
- Over the same period female employment expanded by at least a third, far outstripping the percentage increase in population.

Both of these trends had been partially brought about by long-term changes in social behaviour common to many industrialised countries. It was recognised that the use of contraception to limit family size would improve the standard of living and give the better-educated female population the opportunity to have a vocation as well as children. However, Germany's recent past history exaggerated these developments. Economic mobilisation during the First World War had driven women into the factories, while the post-war difficulties caused by the inflation had encouraged them to stay on working out of economic necessity. In addition, the war had left a surplus of 1.8 million marriageable women, as well as many wives with invalided husbands. Finally, the changing balance of the economy in the 1920s had led to an increased demand for non-manual labour and the growth of mass-production techniques requiring more unskilled workers. These factors tended to favour the employment of women, who could be paid less than men.

The Nazi view towards women

Key question
What was the ideal role of women in Nazi society?

The ideology of National Socialism was in stark contrast to the above social trends. Nazism fundamentally opposed social and economic female emancipation and had the following aims for women:

- To have more children and to take responsibility for bringing them up.
- To care for the house and their husbands.
- To stop paid employment except for very specialist vocations such as midwifery.

In the view of the Nazis, nature had ordained that the two sexes should fulfil entirely different roles, and it was simply the task of the state to maintain this distinction. What this amounted to was that 'a woman's place was to be in the home'. Or, as the Nazi slogan presented it, they were to be devoted to the three German Ks – 'Kinder, Küche, Kirche' ('children, kitchen and Church' – see the 'Ten commandments' for choosing a spouse, below). Such dogma was upheld by the Party, even before 1933 – there was not a single female Nazi deputy in the *Reichstag*, and a Party regulation of 1921 excluded women from all senior positions within its structure.

> ## Nazi Ten Commandments for the choice of a spouse
> 1. Remember that you are German!
> 2. If you are genetically healthy, do not stay single.
> 3. Keep your body pure.
> 4. Keep your mind and spirit pure.
> 5. Marry only for love.
> 6. As a German, choose only a spouse of similar or related blood.
> 7. In choosing a spouse, ask about his forebears.
> 8. Health is essential to physical beauty.
> 9. Don't look for a playmate but for a companion in marriage.
> 10. You should want to have as many children as possible.

Nazis' views on women tied in with their concern about the demographic trends. A growing population was viewed as a sign of national strength and status – a reflection of Germany's aspiration to the status of an international power. How could they demand nationalist expansionism in eastern Europe, if the number of Germans was in fact levelling out? It was therefore considered essential to increase the population substantially and, to this end, women were portrayed as primarily the mothers of the next generation – an image that suited Nazi anti-feminism.

Female employment

Key question
Did the Nazis reduce the number of women in employment?

Initially, attempts to reduce the number of women in work seem to have been quite successful. Between 1933 and 1936 married women were in turn debarred from jobs in medicine, law and the higher ranks of the civil service. Moreover, the number of female teachers and university students was reduced considerably – only 10 per cent of university students could be female. Such laws had a profound effect on professional middle-class women, although their actual number was small.

Nazi incentives

In other sectors of the economy a mixture of Party pressure and financial inducements was employed to cajole women out of the workplace and back into the home. From June 1933 interest-free loans of 600RM were made available to young women who withdrew from the labour market in order to get married. The effects of the Depression also worked in favour of Nazi objectives. They not only drastically reduced the number of female workers (although proportionately far less than male workers), but also enabled the government to justify its campaign for women to give up work for the benefit of unemployed men. On these grounds, **labour exchanges** and employers were advised to discriminate positively in favour of men. As a result of all this, the percentage of women in employment fell from 37 per cent to 31 per cent of the total from 1932 to 1937.

Nazi women's organisations

Women were quite specifically excluded from the Nazi machinery of government. The only employment opportunities available to them were within the various Nazi women's organisations, such as the National Socialist Womanhood (NSF, *National Sozialistische Frauenschaft*) and the German Women's Enterprise (DFW, *Deutsches Frauenwerk*), led by Gertrud Scholtz-Klink. Yet, the NSF and DFW were regarded by the Party as mere tools for the propagation of the **anti-feminist** ideology by means of cultural, educational and social programmes. And so, when a campaign started in the NSF for enhanced opportunities for women within the Party, its organisers were officially discredited.

Effects

However, by 1937 Nazi ideological convictions were already threatened by the pressures of economic necessity. The introduction of conscription and the rearmament boom from the mid-1930s soon led to an increasing shortage of labour, as the Nazi economy continued to grow. The anti-feminist ideology could only be upheld if economic growth was slowed down and that, in turn, would restrict the rearmament programme. Of course, Hitler was not prepared to sanction this. Consequently, market forces inevitably began to exploit this readily available

Labour exchanges
Local offices created by the state for finding employment. Many industrialised countries had labour exchanges to counter mass unemployment.

Anti-feminist
Opposing female advancement.

Key terms

pool of labour, and the relative decline in female employment was reversed. Between 1937 and 1939 it rose from 5.7 million to 7.1 million, and the percentage of women increased from 31 per cent to 33 per cent of the total workforce (see Table 9.3) At this point the government decided to end the marriage loan scheme (see page 202) for women who withdrew from the labour market.

Table 9.3: Women in regular manual and non-manual employment

	1932	1937	1939
Millions of women	4.8	5.7	7.1
Women as a percentage of the total	37	31	33

Note: the comparative figure for 1928 was 7.4 million.

The contradictions between theory and practice of female employment were exacerbated further with the onset of war. So, although the trend of female employment continued to increase, the Nazi regime did not fully exploit the valuable resource of women as munitions workers – and the figures show that women remained underemployed right to the end of the war. This was due to:

- Germany's poor economic mobilisation. At first it was badly organised and (see pages 171–2) there was no general conscription of female labour. When in 1943 Speer did try to mobilise the economy on a total war footing by suggesting the conscription of women workers, he encountered opposition from Bormann, Sauckel (the Plenipotentiary for Labour) and indeed from Hitler himself, who was always concerned about civilian morale.
- The appeal for women to do war work was not convincing. Long hours in an arms factory made life very arduous, especially if there were the added responsibilities of maintaining a household and raising children. In addition, the Nazi government had also given all sorts of financial incentives to have more children with welfare benefits (see page 202).
- Farming responsibilities. One reason that distorts the picture of female employment was that women had traditionally played an important part in German farming. The shortage of agricultural labour had created major problems from the 1930s (see pages 182–3), but once the young men were sent away for the war it got worse. As a result many German women experienced considerable hardship meeting the continuous demands of running a farm. By 1944 it is estimated that 65 per cent of the agricultural workforce were women.

The Nazis were caught in the contradictions of their own ideology. They were motivated by military expansionism which needed to employ women effectively, so, in the final two years of the Nazi state, more and more women ended up at work. Yet, the government could not bring itself to renounce fully its anti-feminist stance. As an official in the NSF wrote, 'It has always been our chief article of faith that a woman's place is in the home – but since the whole of Germany is our home we must serve wherever we can best do so.'

Marriage and family

Key question
What were the effects of Nazi population policy?

The Nazi state was obsessed with a desire to increase Germany's population and a series of measures was promptly introduced:

- Marriage loans. The loan was worth just over half a year's earnings and a quarter of it was converted into a straight gift for each child that was born. (The scheme was introduced in June 1933, but progressively reduced from 1937.)
- Family allowances were improved dramatically, particularly for low-income families.
- Income tax was reduced in proportion to the number of children and those families with six or more did not pay any.
- Maternity benefits were improved.
- The anti-abortion law introduced under the Weimar Republic was enforced much more strictly.
- Contraceptive advice and facilities were restricted.

Inevitably, these incentives and laws were backed up by an extensive propaganda campaign, which glorified motherhood and the large family. There were also rewards: the Honour Cross of the German Mother in bronze, silver and gold, awarded for four, six and eight children, respectively. Such glorification reached its climax in the coining of the Nazi slogan 'I have donated a child to the *Führer*' (as contemporary humorists soon pointed out, this was presumably because of Hitler's personal unwillingness or inability to father children of his own).

Table 9.4: Social trends in Nazi Germany 1933–9

	Marriages per 1000 inhabitants	Divorces per 10,000 existing marriages	Births per 1000 inhabitants
1933	9.7	29.7	14.7
1936	9.1	32.6	19.0
1939	11.1	38.3	20.3

The statistics in Table 9.4 show several trends:

- From 1933 the birth rate increased significantly, reaching a peak in 1939 (although thereafter it again slowly declined).
- The divorce rate continued to increase.
- The figure of marriages was fairly consistent (apart from the blips in 1934 and 1939 – probably connected to the improving economy and the onset of the war).

The real problem for the historian is deciding whether Nazi population policy was actually *responsible* for the demographic trends. Interpreting population statistics is difficult because it involves so many different factors – social, economic and even psychological factors. Also, it is extremely hard to assess the *relative* significance of Nazi population policy when it is set against the importance of events such as the Depression and later on the Second World War.

Lebensborn

Nazi population policy not only aimed to increase the number of children being born, but also tried to improve 'racial standards'. It led to the establishment of one of the most extraordinary features of Nazi social engineering, **Lebensborn**, set up by Himmler and the SS. Initially, the programme provided homes for unmarried mothers of the increasing number of illegitimate children who were seen as racially correct. Later, the institution also made the necessary arrangements for girls to be 'impregnated' by members of the SS in organised brothels. It is reckoned that by the end of the regime about 11,000 children were born under these circumstances.

Key term

Lebensborn
Literally, the 'spring' or 'fountain of life'. Founded by Himmler and overseen by the SS to promote doctrines of racial purity.

Key question
How successful was Nazi policy on women and family?

Conclusion

Feminist historians have been highly critical of Nazi population and family policy that had reduced the status of women. One historian, Gisela Bock, in the 1980s viewed Nazi thinking on women as a kind of secondary racism in which women were the victims of a sexist–racist male regime that reduced women to the status of mere objects. Such an interpretation would, of course, have been denied by the Nazis who claimed to regard women as different rather than inferior. But some modern-day non-feminist historians have tried to explain the positive features of Nazi policy on women. Improved welfare services made life easier for women, especially in more isolated rural areas. Also, with so many husbands away during the war, women were protected from having to combine paid work with bringing up a family and running the household.

Yet, despite these different perspectives, Nazi policy objectives for women and the family could not really be squared with the social realities of twentieth-century Germany. With the changing population trend and the increasing employment of women, Nazi views on women and the family were idealistic but impractical. Consequently, Nazi policy towards women and the family was contradictory and incoherent.

Summary diagram: Women and the family

Social background
- Slowing down of Germany's population growth
- Expansion of female employment
- Effects of war

Nazi views towards women
- Three German Ks
- More children
- Care for home
- Reduce paid employment

Female work
- Nazi incentives
- Nazi women's organisations
- Effects – short term and long term

Marriage and family
- Nazi measures
- Effects

Conclusion

How successful was Nazi policy on women and family?

6 | Culture

Key question
What was the purpose of Nazi culture?

During the evening of 10 May 1933, in the middle of a square just off the centre of Berlin, there took place an event that soon became known as 'the burning of the books'. Thousands of volumes seized from private and public libraries were hurled into the flames by Nazi activists and university students because they were considered undesirable on account of their Jewish, socialist or pacifist tendencies. For a nation whose literary heritage was one of the greatest in Europe, it was seen by many as an act of mindless barbarism. It also rather aptly set the tone for the cultural life of Nazi Germany.

Key date

The burning of the books: 10 May 1933

Nazi culture was no longer to be promoted merely as 'art for art's sake'. Rather, it was to serve the purpose of moulding public opinion, and, with this in mind, the Reich Chamber of Culture was supervised by the Propaganda Ministry. Germany's cultural life during the Third Reich was simply to be another means of achieving censorship and indoctrination, although Goebbels expressed it in more pompous language:

> What we are aiming for is more than a revolt. Our historic mission is to transform the very spirit itself to the extent that people and things are brought into a new relationship with one another.

Culture was therefore 'co-ordinated' by means of the Reich Chamber of Culture, established in 1933, which made provision for seven subchambers: fine arts, music, the theatre, the press, radio, literature and films. In this way, just as anyone in the media had no option but to toe the Party line (see pages 216–17),

Anti-modernism
Strand of opinion that rejects, objects to or is highly critical of changes to society and culture brought about by technological advancement.

Key question
In what ways did the Nazis shape German culture?

so all those involved in cultural activities had to be accountable for their creativity. Nazi culture was dominated by a number of key themes reflecting the usual ideological prejudices:

• anti-Semitism
• militarism and the glorification of war
• nationalism and the supremacy of the Aryan race
• the cult of the *Führer* and the power of absolutism
• **anti-modernism** and the theme of 'Blood and Soil'
• neo-paganism and a rejection of traditional Christian values.

Major cultural themes
Music
The world of music managed to survive reasonably well in the Nazi environment, partly because of its less obvious political overtones. Also, Germany's rich classical tradition from the works of Bach to Beethoven was proudly exploited by the regime. However, Mahler and Mendelssohn, both great Jewish composers, were banned, as were most modern musical trends. Also the new 'genres' of jazz and dance-band were respectively labelled 'Negroid' and 'decadent'.

Literature
Over 2500 of Germany's writers left their homeland during the years 1933–45 in reaction to the new cultural atmosphere. Among those who departed were Thomas Mann, Bertolt Brecht and Erich Maria Remarque (see page 78). Their place was taken by a lesser literary group, who either sympathised with the regime or accepted the limitations.

Actors, like the musicians, tended to content themselves with productions of the classics – Schiller, Goethe (and Shakespeare) – in the knowledge that such plays were politically acceptable and in the best traditions of German theatre.

Visual arts
The visual arts were also effectively limited by the Nazi constraints. Modern schools of art were held in total contempt and Weimar's rich cultural awakening was rejected as degenerate and symbolic of the moral and political decline of Germany under a system of parliamentary democracy. Thus, the following were severely censored:

• 'New functionalism' artists, like Georg Grosz and Otto Dix, wanted to depict ordinary people in everyday life – and by their art they aimed to comment on the state of society.
• The Bauhaus style started by Walter Gropius influenced all aspects of design. It emphasised the close relationship between art and technology, which is underlined by its motto 'Art and Technology – a new unity' (see page 78).

The modern style of art was resented by Nazism so much that in July 1937 two contrasting art exhibitions were launched entitled 'Degenerate Art' and 'Great German Art'. The first one was deliberately held up to be mocked and many of the pieces were destroyed; the second one glorified all the major Nazi themes of *Volksgemeinschaft* and celebrated classic styles and traditional nineteenth-century romanticism. Most admired were:

• the sculptor Arno Breker (see below)
• the architect Albert Speer, who drew up many of the great plans for rebuilding the German cities and oversaw the 1936 Berlin Olympics stadium.

Cinema

Only in the field of film can it be said that the Nazi regime made a genuine cultural contribution. Many of the major film studios were in the hands of nationalist sympathisers. However, Jewish film actors and directors such as Fritz Lang were removed – and then decided to leave Germany. Perhaps the most famous

Arno Breker, *Comrades*. Breker was sculptor-in-chief to the Third Reich. By collaborating closely with Albert Speer he undertook numerous government commissions. His statue celebrated Aryan physical perfection and the importance of comradeship.

German émigrée was Marlene Dietrich, who swiftly established a new career in Hollywood.

Goebbels recognised the importance of expanding the film industry, not only as a means of propaganda, but also as an entertainment form – this explains why, out of 1097 feature films produced between 1933 and 1945, only 96 were specifically at the request of the Propaganda Ministry. The films can be divided into three types:

- Overt propaganda, e.g. *The Eternal Jew* (*Ewige Jude*), a tasteless, racist film that portrayed the Jews like rats, and *Hitlerjunge Queux*, based on the story of a Nazi murdered by the communists.
- Pure escapism, e.g. *The Adventures of Baron von Münchhausen*, a comedy based on an old German legend which gives the baron the powers of immortality.
- Emotive nationalism, e.g. *Olympia*, Leni Riefenstahl's docu-drama of the Berlin Olympics, *Triumph of the Will*, Riefenstahl's film about the 1934 Nuremberg Rally, and *Kolberg*, an epic produced in the final year of the war, which played on the national opposition to Napoleon. These last two films are still held in high regard by film critics for their use of subtle cinematic techniques despite the clear underlying political messages.

Key question
Did the Third Reich manage to create a cultural identity of its own?

In the play *Schlageter* (1934) by Hanns Johst there is the line, 'Whenever I hear the word culture, I reach for my gun'. It is a phrase that is often, and incorrectly, attributed to Göring, but it still neatly underlines the anti-culture approach of the Nazis. Cultural life during the Third Reich was effectively silenced – it could only operate within the Nazi strait-jacket and to that extent Goebbels succeeded in censoring it. However, the regime most certainly failed in its attempts to create a new Nazi cultural identity firmly rooted in the minds of the *Volk*.

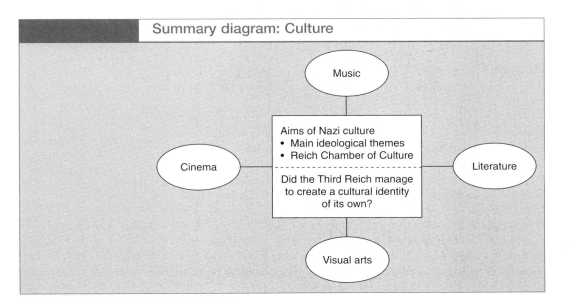

Summary diagram: Culture

Music

Aims of Nazi culture
- Main ideological themes
- Reich Chamber of Culture
- -
Did the Third Reich manage to create a cultural identity of its own?

Cinema

Literature

Visual arts

7 | Outsiders

Key question
Who were the
outsiders in the
Volksgemeinschaft?

Despite all its claims to create a *Volksgemeinschaft*, Nazism believed
that certain people were not allowed to join the Third Reich –
and they were to be discriminated against and persecuted.
Nazism was an all-embracing society, but only of those who
conformed to their criteria – and there were certain groups who
were definitely 'outsiders'.

Ideological opponents

This term could most obviously be applied to the Communists,
so many of whom were sent to the early concentration camps in
1933 (see page 145). However, it increasingly became a term
to cover anyone who did not politically accept the regime and, as
the years went on, a broader range of political and ideological
opponents was imprisoned or worse, e.g. Pastor Niemöller (see
pages 194 and 195) and General Stauffenberg (see page 244).

The 'biologically inferior'

This covered all the races that, according to the Nazis, were
'inferior' or subhuman, such as the Gypsies, Slavs and Jews (see
Chapter 10).

It also included those who were mentally and physically
disabled. As early as July 1933 the Nazis proclaimed 'The Law for
the Prevention of Hereditarily Diseased Offspring', which allowed
for the compulsory sterilisation of those with hereditary
conditions – examples included schizophrenia, Huntington's
chorea, hereditary blindness or deafness. Over the 12 years of the
Nazi period, 350,000 people were sterilised under this law.

However, the policy went much further from 1939, when Hitler
himself initiated the idea of using euthanasia for children with
severe disabilities (such as Down's syndrome and cerebral palsy)
by using the phrase 'mercy death'. No specific law permitted this,
but patients were killed in asylums under the name of 'Operation
T4'. About 70,000 were gassed in 1940–1 but, following public
rumours and Catholic opposition, the operation was stopped (see
page 197).

Asocials

The term was used very broadly to cover anyone whose behaviour
was not viewed as acceptable.

These social outcasts included alcoholics, prostitutes, criminals,
tramps and the workshy. Those asocials who were 'orderly' but
avoided work were rounded up and organised into a compulsory
labour force; and those who were judged as 'disorderly' were
imprisoned and sometimes sterilised or experimented on.

Homosexuals were also classed as asocials. They were seen as
breaking the laws of nature and undermining traditional Nazi
family values. In 1936 the Reich Central Office for the
Combating of Homosexuality and Abortion was established.
Between 10,000 and 15,000 homosexuals were imprisoned and
those sent to camps were forced to wear pink triangles (it is worth
noting that lesbians were not persecuted).

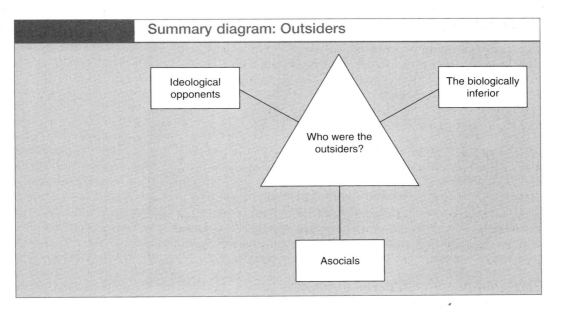

Summary diagram: Outsiders

Ideological opponents

The biologically inferior

Who were the outsiders?

Asocials

8 | Conclusion

Key question
Did Nazism's *Volksgemeinschaft* create a social revolution in the Third Reich?

Reaction
In this context suggesting a return to traditional established ways.

In a very obvious sense, the effects of the 12 years of the Third Reich had a dramatic impact on the German people. Yet, what was the exact nature of the social changes?

Some have seen it as social **reaction** of the worst kind. This was because it reinforced the traditional class structure and strengthened the position of the establishment élites – especially the powerful interests of the military and big business – at the expense of more popular institutions, such as trade unions. Others believe that the Nazi *Volksgemeinschaft* brought about a social revolution which caused the collapse of the social élites and the traditional loyalties and values which had dominated German life since the mid-nineteenth century and that it paved the way for the emergence of a liberal, democratic West Germany. Alternatively, some historians feel that Nazism simply led to 'a revolution of destruction'; that the real changes came about through the destruction wrought by the effects of total war, economic collapse, genocide and political division. Finally, it has been suggested that very few fundamental changes in values and attitudes had any real effect in the 12 years of Nazi rule. Prevailing cultural traditions and social institutions, such as the family and the Churches, did not break down overnight.

So, in conclusion, it should be noted that:

- Despite Nazi rhetorical support for the *Mittelstand* and the peasantry, both groups remained under social and economic pressure. In contrast, the traditional élites continued to dominate and property and industry stayed in private ownership. Indeed, big business prospered.
- Women were supposed to stay at home and have more children, but really their role was set by the economic demands of the situation.

'The one-pot meal'. One of the images cultivated by the Nazi leadership was the creation of the *Volksgemeinschaft* by encouraging people to eat a simple meal together.

- The Christian Churches were expected to wither away. However, the Churches survived and enjoyed the support of the vast majority of Christians, although active opposition to the regime was actually limited.
- Nazi culture was meant to establish new roots in the *Volk*, but it exerted little more than a negative, censorious role.
- It seems that the indoctrination of German youth did have some successes, especially in the pre-war years. However, even then the effects of Nazi education have been questioned on the grounds of imposing conformity without real conviction.
- If there was a 'revolutionary' core to Nazism, it is to be found in the obsessive nature and implementation of its racial policy, and that is the focus of the subject in Chapter 10.

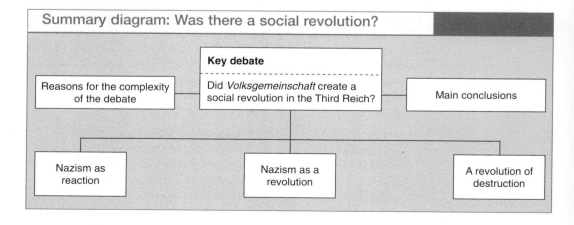

Summary diagram: Was there a social revolution?

Key debate

Did *Volksgemeinschaft* create a social revolution in the Third Reich?

Reasons for the complexity of the debate

Main conclusions

Nazism as reaction

Nazism as a revolution

A revolution of destruction

Study Guide: AS Question

In the style of Edexcel

To what extent did the German people benefit from Nazi social policies in the period 1933–9? (30 marks)

Exam tips

The cross-references are intended to take you straight to the material that will help you to answer the question.

- This question focuses mainly on the content of Chapter 9 and so it covers a lot of material, which can be found between pages 176 and 210.
- The question provides a specific end date with the year 1939. Remember a high mark depends on answering the actual question set, so you should not go beyond this date in your answer.
- It would be helpful to explain the aims of the Nazi social policies, e.g. *Volksgemeinschaft* (pages 93 and 177). You will need to be clear what Nazi policies were, and about what impact they had. What difference did they make to people?
- You could evaluate the various arguments for the 'benefits' of Nazi social policies and then compare with the arguments against. But that simple structure can lead to confusion between the different elements. So it is better to plan a structure that allows you to analyse effectively throughout by dividing the content into some main themes and considering the 'benefits' and 'disadvantages' for each theme. This thinking and planning will also help you to use your time effectively in an exam essay. See the table below as an example:

Themes	Benefits	Disadvantages	Assessment of each theme
Education/youth			
Women			
Religion			
Workers			
Conclusion			

It would be helpful to mention that some Germans could not benefit as they were 'outsiders'.

---

10 The Racial State

POINTS TO CONSIDER
The previous chapter considered many of the social themes covered by the concept of the *Volksgemeinschaft*, but the essential topic of Nazi racism will be the focus of this chapter. This topic can be broken down into three chronological stages, but it also raises a number of broader issues:

- The origins of anti-Semitism
- Gradualism 1933–9
- War and genocide 1939–45

Key dates

1933	April 1	First official boycott of Jewish shops and professions
1935	September 15	Nuremberg Race Laws introduced
1938	November 9–10	*Kristallnacht*: anti-Jewish pogrom
1939		Creation of the Reich Central Office for Jewish Emigration
1942	January	Wannsee Conference: 'Final Solution' to exterminate the Jewish people

1 | The Origins of Anti-Semitism

At the very centre of Nazi social policy was the issue of race and, specifically, anti-Semitism. Hitler's obsessive hatred of the Jews was perhaps the most dominant and consistent theme of his political career. The translation of such ideas into actual policy was to lead to racial laws, government-inspired violence and the execution of the **genocide** policy that culminated in what became known as the **Holocaust**. For historians, such questions pose immense problems.

Historical background

There is a long tradition of anti-Semitism in European history. It was not the preserve of the Nazis, and it certainly has never been just a purely German phenomenon. It was rooted in the religious

Key question
How was anti-Semitism in Nazi Germany rooted in the past?

Key terms

Genocide
The extermination of a whole race.

Holocaust
Term to describe mass slaughter – in this context it refers to the extermination of the Jews.

hostility of Christians towards the Jews (as the murderers of Jesus) that can be traced back to medieval Europe. And the reason went further than that. Jews being used as a scapegoat for society's problems was a long-established practice.

However, there emerged in Germany in the course of the nineteenth century a more clearly defined anti-Semitism based on racism and national resentment. By 1900 a number of specifically anti-Semitic *völkisch* political parties were winning seats in the *Reichstag* and, although they were comparatively few, their success shows that anti-Semitic ideas were becoming more prevalent and generally more respectable. One of the leaders of these right-wing anti-Semitic parties was the Imperial Court Chaplain, Adolf Stöcker, 1874–90. Some historians have seen this anti-Semitism as a by-product of the nationalist passions stirred up by the emergence of Imperial Germany as a world power under Kaiser Wilhelm II, 1888–1918. However, it should be remembered that a similar development had also taken place in German-speaking Austria, and there the political situation was very different.

Social factors

Key question
How did social changes affect the development of anti-Semitism?

In reality, the emergence of political anti-Semitism was a response to intellectual developments and changing social conditions. The Jews became an easy scapegoat for the discontent and disorientation felt by many people as rapid industrialisation and urbanisation took place. And, because many of the Jews were actually immigrants from eastern Europe, they were easily identifiable because of their different traditions. Moreover, although many members of the Jewish community were impoverished, they became the focus of envy because they were viewed as privileged. In 1933, for example, although Jews comprised less than 1 per cent of the German population, they composed more than 16 per cent of lawyers, 10 per cent of doctors and 5 per cent of editors and writers.

In the late nineteenth century, anti-Semitism also began to be presented in a more intellectual vein by the application of the racial theories of Social Darwinism (see pages 91–2). According to such thinking, nations were like animals and only by struggling and fighting could they hope to survive. In this way, an image of intellectual and cultural respectability was given to those anti-Semites who portrayed the Jews as an 'inferior' or 'parasitic' race and the German race as superior:

- Heinrich von Treitschke, the leading historian, who publicly declared 'the Jews are our misfortune'.
- Richard Wagner, the musician and composer whose operas glorified German mythology and often portrayed Jewish characters as evil.
- Houston Stewart Chamberlain, an Englishman, who in his book, the *Foundations of the Nineteenth Century*, celebrated the superiority of the German *Volk*.

Such thinking brings one of the leading historians of Nazi Germany, J. Noakes, to suggest that by 1914:

> In the form of a basic dislike of the Jews and of what they were felt to represent, it [anti-Semitism] had succeeded in permeating broad sections of German society from the Kaiser down to the lower middle class. Ominously, it was particularly strongly entrenched within the academic community, thereby influencing the next generation.

Nazi anti-Semitism 1919–33

Key question
What were the causes of anti-Semitism in Nazi Germany?

The emergence of right-wing racist *völkisch* nationalism was clearly apparent before 1914, but its attractions expanded in the aftermath of the First World War: the self-deception of the 'stab in the back' myth; the humiliation of the Versailles Treaty; and the political and economic weaknesses of the Weimar Republic. So, by the early 1920s, there were probably about 70 relatively small right-wing splinter parties, e.g. the Nazi Party.

In that environment Hitler was able to exploit hostility towards the Jews and turn it into a radical ideology of hatred. He was the product, not the creator, of a society that was permeated by such prejudices. Yet, it would be inaccurate to dismiss Hitler as just another anti-Semite. Hitler's hatred of Jews was obsessive and vindictive, and it shaped much of his political philosophy. Without his personal commitment to attack the Jews and without his charismatic skills as a political leader, it seems unlikely that anti-Semitism could have become such an integral part of the Nazi movement. He was able to mobilise and stir the support of the leading anti-Semitic Nazis:

- Göring (see page 168)
- Goebbels (see pages 237–8)
- Himmler (see pages 230–3)
- Streicher (see pages 88 and 216)
- Heydrich (see page 222).

It is all too easy to highlight the rhetoric of Nazi anti-Semitism as the reason for the success of the Party. Certainly, 37.3 per cent of the population may have voted for Hitler the anti-Semite in July 1932, but the vast majority of Germans were motivated by unemployment, the collapse of agricultural prices and the fear of communism. Indeed, in a 1934 survey into the reasons why people joined the Nazis, over 60 per cent did not even mention anti-Semitism.

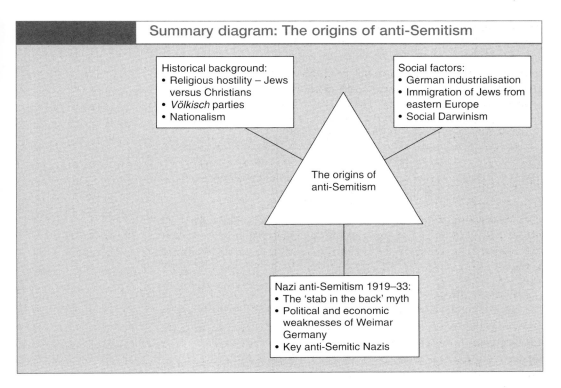

Summary diagram: The origins of anti-Semitism

Historical background:
- Religious hostility – Jews versus Christians
- *Völkisch* parties
- Nationalism

Social factors:
- German industrialisation
- Immigration of Jews from eastern Europe
- Social Darwinism

The origins of anti-Semitism

Nazi anti-Semitism 1919–33:
- The 'stab in the back' myth
- Political and economic weaknesses of Weimar Germany
- Key anti-Semitic Nazis

Key question
Did Nazi anti-Semitism change over time?

Key term
Gradualism
Changing by degrees; progressing slowly.

Key date
First official boycott of Jewish shops and professions: 1 April 1933

2 | Gradualism 1933–9

The Nazi approach to anti-Semitism was **gradualist**. The early moves against the Jews gave no suggestion of the end result. Indeed, for some Germans the discriminatory legislation was no more than the Jews deserved. For the more liberal minded, who found such action offensive, there was the practical problem of how to show opposition and to offer resistance. Once the apparatus of dictatorship was well established by the end of 1934, the futility of opposition was apparent to most people. Feelings of hopelessness were soon replaced by those of fear. To show sympathy for, or to protect the Jews, was to risk one's own freedom or one's own life. It was an unenviable dilemma.

Legal discrimination

Many radical Nazis were keen to take immediate measures against Jewish people and their businesses, but the Party's leadership was worried that it could get out of hand. And those concerns were confirmed when a one-day national boycott was organised for 1 April 1933. Jewish-owned shops, cafés and businesses were picketed by the SA, who stood outside urging people not to enter. However, the boycott was not universally accepted by the German people and it caused a lot of bad publicity abroad.

The Nazi leaders developed their anti-Semitism in a more subtle way. Once the Nazi regime had established the legal basis for its dictatorship (see pages 139–43), it was legally possible to initiate an anti-Jewish policy, most significantly by the creation of the Nuremberg Laws in September 1935. This clearly stood in contrast to the extensive civil rights that the Jews had enjoyed in Weimar Germany. The discrimination against the Jews got worse as an ongoing range of laws was introduced (see Table 10.1). In this way all the rights of Jews were gradually removed even before the onset of the war.

Nuremberg Race Laws introduced: 15 September 1935

Table 10.1: Major Nazi anti-Jewish laws 1933–9

Date		Law
1933	7 April	Law for the Restoration of the Professional Civil Service. Jews excluded from the government's civil service
	4 October	Law for the exclusion of Jewish journalists
1935	15 September	The Nuremberg Race Laws:
		Reich Citizenship Act. 'A citizen of the Reich is a subject who is only of German or kindred blood.' Jews lost their citizenship in Germany
		Law for the Protection of German Blood and German Honour. Marriages and extramarital relations between Jews and German citizens forbidden
1938	5 July	Decree prohibiting Jewish doctors practising medicine
	28 October	Decree to expel 17,000 Polish Jews resident in Germany
	15 November	Decree to exclude Jewish pupils from schools and universities
	3 December	Decree for the compulsory closure and sale of all Jewish businesses
1939	1 September	Decree for the introduction of curfew for Jews

Propaganda and indoctrination

Nazism also set out to cultivate the message of anti-Semitism; in effect to change people's attitudes so that they hated the Jews. Goebbels himself was a particularly committed anti-Semite and he used his skills as the Minister of Propaganda and Popular Enlightenment to indoctrinate the German people (see pages 237–8). All aspects of culture associated with the Jews were censored. Even more worrying was the full range of propaganda methods used to advance the anti-Semitic message, such as:

- posters and signs, e.g. 'Jews are not wanted here'
- newspapers, e.g. *Der Angriff*, which was founded by Goebbels himself; *Der Stürmer*, edited by the *Gauleiter* Julius Streicher, which was overtly anti-Semitic with a seedy range of articles devoted to pornography and violence
- cinema, e.g. *The Eternal Jew*; *Jud Süss*.

A particular aspect of anti-Semitic indoctrination was the emphasis placed on influencing the German youth. The message

Poster for the anti-Semitic film *The Eternal Jew*.

was obviously put across by the Hitler Youth, but all schools also conformed to new revised textbooks and teaching materials, e.g tasks and exam questions.

Terror and violence

In the early years of the regime, the SA, as the radical left wing of the Nazis, took advantage of their power at local level to use violence against Jews, e.g. damage of property, intimidation and physical attacks. However, after the Night of the Long Knives in June 1934 (see pages 150–2), anti-Semitic violence became more sporadic for two probable reasons. First, in 1936 there was a distinct decline in the anti-Semitic campaign because of the Berlin Olympics and the need to avoid international alienation.

Secondly, conservative forces still had a restraining influence. For example, Schacht had continued to express worries about the implications of anti-Semitic action for the economy (although he resigned in 1937 – see page 164).

However, the events of 1938 were on a different scale. First, the union with Austria in March 1938 resulted, in the following month, in thousands of attacks on the 200,000 Jews of Vienna. Secondly, on 9–10 November 1938 there was a sudden violent **pogrom** against the Jews, which became known as the 'Night of Crystal Glass' (*Kristallnacht*) because of all the smashed glass. *Kristallnacht* started in Berlin and spread throughout Germany with dramatic effects: the destruction of numerous Jewish homes and 100 deaths, attacks on 10,000 Jewish shops and businesses, the burning down of 200 synagogues and the deportation of 20,000 to concentration camps. The excuse for this had been the assassination of Ernst von Rath, a German diplomat in Paris, by Herschel Grünspan, a Jew, on 7 November. Goebbels had hoped that the anti-Semitic actions might also win Hitler's favour, and compensate for Goebbels' disreputable affair with a Czech actress. It should be noted that much of the anti-Semitic legislation (see also pages 216–17) came in the months after the pogrom.

Forced emigration

From the start of the Nazi dictatorship a number of Jews had decided to leave Germany voluntarily. Many Jews with influence, high reputation or sufficient wealth could find the means to leave. The most popular destinations were Palestine, Britain and the USA, and among the most renowned emigrés were Albert Einstein, the scientist, and Kurt Weill, the composer.

However, from 1938 a new dimension to anti-Semitism developed – forced emigration. As a result of the events in Austria in 1938, the Central Office for Jewish Emigration was established in Vienna, overseen by Adolf Eichmann. Jewish property was confiscated to finance the emigration of poor Jews. Within six months Eichmann had forced the emigration of 45,000 and the scheme was seen as such a success that, in January 1939, Göring was prompted to create the Reich Central Office for Jewish Emigration run by Heydrich and Eichmann (see Table 10.2).

> **Key term**
>
> **Pogrom**
> An organised or encouraged massacre of innocent people. The term originated from the massacres of Jews in Russia.

> **Key dates**
>
> *Kristallnacht*, anti-Jewish pogrom: 9–10 November 1938
>
> Creation of the Reich Central Office for Jewish Emigration: 1939

Table 10.2: The Jewish community in Germany 1933–45

	Jewish population	Emigrés per annum
1933	503,000	38,000
1939 (May)	234,000	78,000*
1945	20,000	N/A

* The cumulative figure of Jewish emigrés between 1933 and 1939 was 257,000

It is therefore estimated that the Nazi persecution led to about half of the Jewish population leaving before the war. Technically, the Jews had voluntarily emigrated but they were forced to leave behind all their belongings. Given those circumstances, the remainder decided to take their chances and stay in Germany, rather than lose their homes and all their possessions.

Conclusion

Despite the range of anti-Semitic measures of 1933–9, it is difficult to claim that the Nazis had pursued a planned overall policy to deal with 'the Jewish question'. In many respects the measures were at first haphazard. However, on one point it is very clear – the year 1938 marked an undoubted '**radicalisation**' of Nazi anti-Semitism. The legal laws, the violence connected with *Kristallnacht* and the forced emigration came together, suggesting that the regime had reached a pivotal year – a fact confirmed by the tone of the speech in the Reichstag by Hitler on 30 January 1939:

> If the international Jewish financiers in and outside Europe should succeed in plunging the nations once more into a world war, then the result will not be the Bolshevising [making communist] of the earth, and thus the victory of Jewry, but the annihilation of the Jewish race in Europe.

Key question
Why was the year 1938 so significant?

Radicalisation
A policy of increasing severity.

Key term

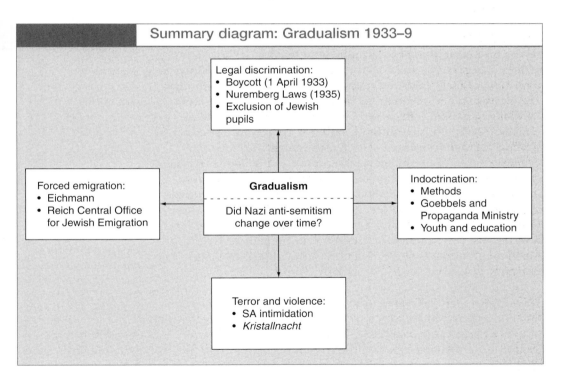

Summary diagram: Gradualism 1933–9

Legal discrimination:
• Boycott (1 April 1933)
• Nuremberg Laws (1935)
• Exclusion of Jewish pupils

Forced emigration:
• Eichmann
• Reich Central Office for Jewish Emigration

Gradualism
- - - - - - - - - - - -
Did Nazi anti-semitism change over time?

Indoctrination:
• Methods
• Goebbels and Propaganda Ministry
• Youth and education

Terror and violence:
• SA intimidation
• *Kristallnacht*

3 | War and Genocide 1939–45

At the time it was inconceivable to imagine that the Holocaust was possible. Who in 1939 could have predicted the scenario of the next six years? The suggestion that millions would be systematically exterminated would have defied belief. It is an event in modern European history that even now seems almost beyond rational comprehension, although it had a terrifying logic to it. For those who lived in occupied Europe it was easier and more comfortable to dismiss the rumours as gross and macabre exaggerations, the result of wartime gossip and Allied propaganda. Yet, the unbelievable did happen and it required not only the actions of a 'criminal' minority but also the passivity of the 'innocent' majority. In Germany the moral dimension has helped to make this historical debate a particularly impassioned one.

From emigration to extermination

Germany's victory over Poland in autumn 1939 (see page 246) meant that the Nazis inherited responsibility for an estimated three millions Jews. Moreover, the beginning of a general European war made emigration of Jews to independent countries more difficult. However, plans to 'resettle' so many people placed such a great strain on food supplies and the transportation system that, in the short term, the Nazi leadership in Poland were compelled to create a number of Jewish **ghettos**, e.g. Warsaw, Krakow and Lublin.

The invasion of Russia in summer 1941 marked a decisive development. From that time, it was seen as a racial war launched by the **SS** *Einsatzgruppen* that moved in behind the advancing armies. These four special 'Action Units' were responsible for rounding up local Jews and murdering them by mass shootings. During the winter of 1941–2 it is estimated that *Einsatzgruppen* had killed 700,000 Jews in western Russia, but the bloody process clearly raised the practical implications for the Nazi leadership of finding a '**Final Solution**' to the Jewish question.

Nevertheless, there remains uncertainty and debate over when exactly it was decided to launch the genocide of the Jews (see pages 223–4). Options were probably being considered during autumn 1941, but it was only agreed as a result of the Wannsee Conference on 20 January 1942. There, in no more than a few hours, a meeting, chaired by Heydrich and organised by Eichmann, outlined the grim details of the plan to use gas to kill Europe's 11 million Jews.

In the course of 1942, a number of camps were developed into mass extermination centres in Poland, most notably Auschwitz, Sobibor and Treblinka, which were run by the Death's Head Units of the *Waffen* SS (see page 231). Most of the Polish Jews were cleared from their ghettos and then 'transported' by train in appalling conditions to their death in gas chambers. It is believed that, of the original three million Polish Jews, only 4000 survived the war. In 1943–4 Jews from all over Europe were deported to face a similar fate – so that by 1945 it is estimated that six million European Jews had been murdered.

Key date

Wannsee Conference. 'Final Solution' to exterminate the Jewish people: 20 January 1942

Key question
How did Nazi anti-Semitism degenerate into genocide?

Key terms

Ghetto
Ancient term describing the area lived in by the Jews in a city. Under Nazi occupation the Jews were separated from the rest of the community and forced to live in appalling and overcrowded conditions.

SS *Einsatzgruppen*
'Action Units'. Four of the units were launched in eastern Europe after the invasion of Russia. Responsible for rounding up local Jews and murdering them by mass shootings.

Final Solution
A euphemism used by the Nazi leadership to describe the extermination of the Jews from 1941.

Table 10.3: The Nazi extermination of the Jews 1940–5

Date		Event
1940		First deportations of Jews from some German provinces
1941	June	Action squads (*Einsatzgruppen*) of SS moved into the USSR behind the advancing armies to round up and kill Jews
1941	1 September	All Jews forced to wear the Yellow Star of David
1942	20 January	Wannsee Conference. Various government and Party agencies agreed on the 'Final Solution' to the Jewish problem
	Spring	Extermination facilities set up at Auschwitz, Sobibor and Treblinka
1943	February	Destruction of Warsaw Ghetto
1943–4		Transportation of Jews from all over German-occupied Europe to death camps began
1945	27 January	Liberation of Auschwitz by Soviet troops

Henri Pieck, *Behind Barbed Wire*. Painting drawn in Buchenwald concentration camp.

Profile: Reinhard Heydrich 1904–42

1904		– Born at Halle in Saxony, Germany
1922–8		– Joined the navy but discharged (probably for a sexual offence against a woman)
1931		– Joined the NSDAP and the SS
1932		– Appointed leader of the newly created SD (the Party's intelligence security service, see pages 230–1)
1934	June	– Worked closely with Himmler in the Night of the Long Knives. Appointed SS Lieutenant-General
1936		– Appointed Chief of Secret Police (but still under Himmler's authority)
1939	January	– Created Reich Central Office for Jewish Emigration
	September	– Appointed Head of RSHA (Reich Security Head Office), but still under Himmler's authority
1941		– Reich Protector of Bohemia and Moravia (Czech lands)
1942	January	– Chaired the Wannsee Conference meeting to exterminate the Jews
	May	– Assassinated by the Czech resistance in Prague

Heydrich was undoubtedly talented – he was not only physically the image of the perfect Aryan but also a very good sportsman and a talented musician and linguist. Yet, his skills gave way to the dominating traits of selfishness, ambition and brutality that earned him the title of 'the butcher of Prague'. He advanced extremely quickly within the SS, so at the age of 32 he was appointed Chief of Secret Police. With his abilities he was responsible for:

- developing and running the policing system of surveillance and repression
- implementing the Nazi racial policy
- chairing the notorious meeting at Wannsee Conference which agreed on the Final Solution.

Gypsies

In addition to the Jews, the Gypsies (Sinti and Roma) were also subject to racial persecution and became victims of Nazi genocide. The Gypsies had been viewed as 'outsiders' throughout European history for several clear reasons:

- they were non-Christian and they had their own Romany customs and dialect
- they were non-white – because they had originated from India in the late medieval period
- their 'traveller' lifestyle with no regular employment was resented.

Key question
Why were the Gypsies persecuted?

So, even before the Nazi dictatorship and during Weimar's liberal years, there was official hostility towards the Gypsies and, in 1929, 'The Central Office for the Fight against the Gypsies' was established.

By 1933 it is believed that the number of Gypsies in Germany was about 25,000–30,000, and they, too, were beginning to suffer from the gradualist policy of Nazi discrimination:

- Gypsies were defined exactly like the Jews as 'infallibly of alien blood' according to the Nuremberg Laws of 1935.
- Himmler issued, in 1938, a directive titled 'The Struggle against the Gypsy Plague', which ordered the registration of Gypsies in racial terms.
- Straight after the outbreak of the war, Gypsies were deported from Germany to Poland – and their movements were severely controlled in working camps. Notoriously, in January 1940, the first case of mass murder through gassing was committed by the Nazis against Gypsy children at Buchenwald.

As with the Jews, the Gypsies during the war were the focus of ever increasing repression and violence but there was no real, systematic Nazi policy of extermination until the end of 1942. In the first months of 1943 Germany's Gypsies were sent to Auschwitz camp and over 1943–4 a large proportion of Europe's Gypsy population from south-eastern Europe was exterminated, a figure between 225,000 and 500,000.

Conclusion

Key question
Why did the
Holocaust happen?

The issue of the Holocaust remains one of the most fundamental controversies in history. For some historians Hitler remains the key, as he was committed to the extermination of the Jews at an early stage in his political career. It is argued that this was followed by a consistent gradualist policy, which led logically from the persecution of 1933 to the gates of Auschwitz. In the simplest form these historians suggest that the Holocaust happened because Hitler willed it. On the other hand, other historians have rejected the idea of a long-term plan for mass extermination. Instead, they have suggested that the 'Final Solution' came to be implemented as a result of the chaotic nature of government during the war. As a result, various institutions and individuals improvised a policy to deal with the military and human situation in eastern Europe by the end of 1941. Schleunes therefore describes the road to Auschwitz as a 'twisted one' and concludes, 'the Final Solution as it emerged in 1941 and 1942 was *not* the product of grand design'.

This controversy has generated a close scrutiny and analysis of the available evidence, particularly in the past 20 years. So, although the exact details are not clear, it seems fair to conclude the following points about the 'Final Solution':

- The initial arrangements for the implementation of the 'Final Solution' were haphazard and makeshift and the Nazi leadership did not have any clear programme to deal with the Jewish question until 1941.
- No written order for the killing of the Jews from Hitler has been found, although in January 1944, Himmler publicly stated that Hitler had given him 'a *Führer* order' to give priority to 'the total solution of the Jewish question' and clearly Hitler had often spoken in violent and barbaric terms about the Jews throughout his career.
- Probably around autumn 1941 it was decided by the top Nazi leadership to launch an extermination policy and this was agreed at the Wannsee Conference in January 1942 by a broad range of representatives of Nazi organisations.

In the light of these points the terrible outcome of the 'Final Solution' could be explained as a pragmatic (practical) response to the confusion and chaos of war in 1941–2, rather than the culmination of long-term ideological intent.

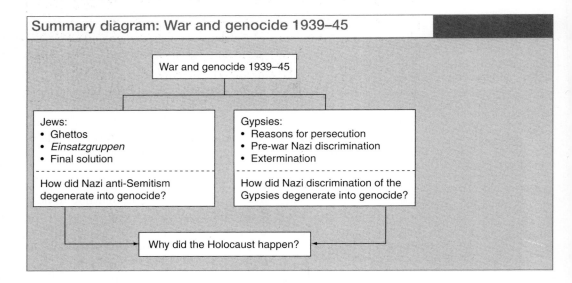

Summary diagram: War and genocide 1939–45

Study Guide: AS Question

In the style of Edexcel

How accurate is it to describe the Nazi persecution of the Jews in the years 1933–42 as increasing steadily in Germany? (30 marks)

Exam tips

The cross-references are intended to take you straight to the material that will help you to answer the question.

This question requires you to examine the pattern and nature of persecution during these years. Did it increase? Was the increase 'steady', or were there times of sudden change?

   You will need to display knowledge of the ways in which the Jews in Germany faced persecution (pages 216–19), and then consider whether this shows changing patterns of persecution. You could refer to:

- legal discrimination (pages 215–16)
- propaganda and indoctrination (pages 216–19)
- violence (pages 216–17)
- forced emigration (pages 218–19)
- the effects of the beginning of the war (pages 219–20)
- genocide – the SS killing squads and the Wannsee Conference decision of the 'Final Solution' (pages 219–20 and 223–4).

In coming to a judgement, look carefully at page 219. If 1938 marked an undoubted 'radicalisation' of Nazi anti-Semitism then you might well agree that persecution increased, but challenge the idea that the pattern was simply one of a steadily increasing trend. You could argue that 1938 marked a turning point.

The Nazi Regime

POINTS TO CONSIDER
It is all too easy to assume that the Nazi consolidation of power in 1933–4 led to Hitler creating an all-powerful personal dictatorship. Yet, there were various other important forces in the Nazi regime and the Third Reich, as well as political resistance, particularly during the war. The main areas to considered are:

- The role of Hitler
- The apparatus of the police state
- The propaganda machine
- Resistance

Key dates

1934	June 30	Night of the Long Knives
1935		Mass arrests by *Gestapo* of socialists and communists
1936	June	Appointment of Heinrich Himmler as Chief of the German Police
1938	September	Planned *putsch* by General Beck if war resulted from Czech crisis
1939	September	Creation of RSHA
1942		Red Orchestra discovered and closed down
1942–3	Winter	Military 'turn of the tide'; German defeats at El Alamein and Stalingrad
		White Rose student group; distribution of anti-Nazi leaflets
1944	July	Stauffenberg Bomb Plot on 20 July failed to overthrow regime. Army purged

1 | The Role of Hitler

In theory, Hitler's power was unlimited. Nazi Germany was a one-party state and Hitler was undisputed leader of that Party. In addition, after the death of Hindenburg in August 1934, the law concerning the head of state of the German Reich combined the posts of president and chancellor. Constitutionally, Hitler was

Key question
What was the role of Hitler in Nazi Germany?

Ein Volk, Ein Reich, Ein Führer. Hitler at the centre of Germany. This postcard is dated 13 March 1938, the day after the Nazi take-over of Austria.

also commander-in-chief of all the armed services. (This image of Hitler was very much presented in the postcard shown above: *Ein Volk, Ein Reich, Ein Führer*. 'One people, one empire, one leader.')

'*Führer* power'

However, if one studies contemporary documents, such as this extract from a leading Nazi theorist, E. Huber, it is clear that Hitler's personal dictatorship was portrayed in more than purely legal terms:

> If we wish to define political power in the *völkisch Reich* correctly, we must not speak of 'state power' but of '*Führer* power'. For it is not the state as an impersonal entity that is the source of political power, but rather political power is given to the *Führer* as the executor of the nation's common will. '*Führer* power' is comprehensive and total: it unites within itself all means of creative political activity: it embraces all spheres of national life.

Huber's grandiose theoretical claims for '*Führer* power' could not mask basic practical problems. First, there was no all-embracing constitution in the Third Reich. The government and law of Nazi Germany emerged over time in a haphazard fashion. Secondly, there was (and is) no way one individual could ever be in control of all aspects of government. Thus, Hitler was still dependent on sympathetic subordinates to put policy decisions into effect. And thirdly, Hitler's own personality and attitude towards government were mixed and not conducive to strong and effective leadership.

Hitler's character

Hitler certainly appeared as the charismatic and dynamic leader. His magnetic command of an audience enabled him to play on 'mass suggestion'; he portrayed himself as the ordinary man with the vision, willpower and determination to transform the country.

However, this was an image perpetuated by the propaganda machine and, once in government, Hitler's true character revealed itself, as is shown in the memoirs of one of his retinue:

> Hitler normally appeared shortly before lunch … When Hitler stayed at Obersalzberg it was even worse. There he never left his room before 2.00 pm. He spent most afternoons taking a walk, in the evening straight after dinner, there were films … He disliked the study of documents. I have sometimes secured decisions from him without his ever asking to see the relevant files. He took the view that many things sorted themselves out on their own if one did not interfere … He let people tell him the things he wanted to hear, everything else he rejected. One still sometimes hears the view that Hitler would have done the right thing if people surrounding him had not kept him wrongly informed. Hitler refused to let himself be informed … How can one tell someone the truth who immediately gets angry when the facts do not suit him?

Hitler liked to cultivate the image of the artist and really he was quite lazy. This was accentuated further by Hitler's lifestyle: his unusual sleeping hours; his long periods of absence from Berlin when he stayed in the Bavarian Alps; his tendency to become immersed in pet projects such as architectural plans. Furthermore, as he got older he became neurotic and moody as was demonstrated in his obsession with his health and medical symptoms, both real and imagined.

Hitler was not well educated and had no experience for any role in government or administration. As cynics say, Hitler's first real job was his appointment as chancellor. He followed no real working routine, he loathed paperwork and disliked the formality of committees in which issues were discussed. He glibly believed that mere willpower was the solution to most problems.

Key question
Was Hitler an
effective dictator?

Hitler's leadership

Surprisingly, Hitler was not always very assertive when it came to making a decision. Although he was presented to the world as the all-powerful dictator he never showed any inclination to co-ordinate government. For example, the role of the cabinet declined quite markedly after 1934. In 1933 the cabinet met 72 times, but only four times in 1936 and the last official cabinet meeting was held in February 1938. Consequently, the rivalry between the various factions in the Third Reich was rife and decision-making became, more often than not, the result of the *Führer*'s whim or an informal conversation rather than rational clear-cut chains of command.

Yet, Hitler somehow still played a decisive role in the development of the Third Reich. In a telling phrase, historian Norman Rich wrote: 'The point cannot be stressed too strongly. Hitler was master in the Third Reich' and this was because:

- Hitler ran a deliberate policy of 'divide and rule'.
- Hitler took responsibility for making the 'big' decisions that shaped the direction of Nazi Germany, e.g. foreign policy.
- Despite other power bases, Hitler preserved his own authority by tolerating only key Nazis, who were personally loyal, for example Himmler.

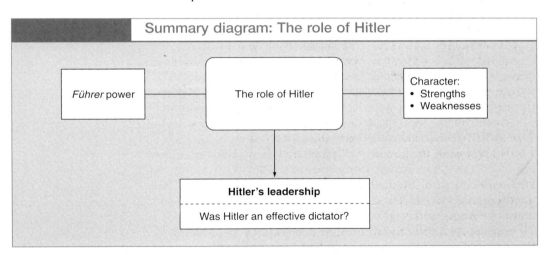

Summary diagram: The role of Hitler

Key question
How did the SS
emerge?

2 | The Police State

Although by July 1933 Germany had become a one-party state, in which the Nazi Party claimed sole political authority, there was really a whole array of Party and state institutions within the system of government:

- the Party with its own organisations, e.g. the Hitler Youth
- the state's institutions with its own organisations, e.g. the government ministries and the judiciary (see Figure 11.1).

However, amidst all the confusion of the state and Party structure there emerged an organisation that was to become the mainstay

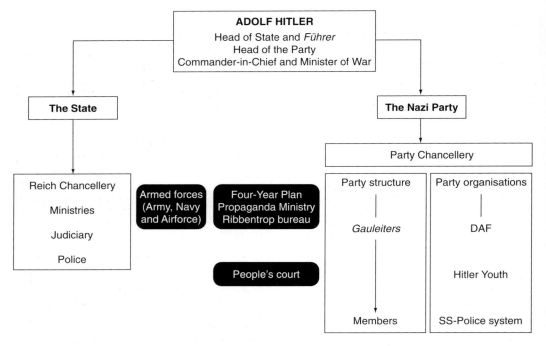

Figure 11.1: The structure of the Third Reich

of the Third Reich – the SS. The SS developed an identity and structure of its own which kept it separate from the state and yet, through its dominance of police matters, linked it with the state.

The emergence of Himmler and the SS

The SS had been formed in 1925 as an élite bodyguard for Hitler, but it remained a relatively minor section of the SA, with only 250 members, until Himmler became its leader in 1929. By 1933 the SS numbered 52,000, and it had established a reputation for blind obedience and total commitment to the Nazi cause.

Himmler had also created in 1931 a special security service, Sicherheitsdienst (SD), to act as the Party's own internal security police. In the course of 1933–4 he assumed control of all the police in the *Länder*, including the **Gestapo** in Prussia. Thus, Hitler turned to Himmler's SS to carry out the purge of June 1934 (see page 151). The loyalty and brutal efficiency of the SS on the Night of the Long Knives had its rewards, for it now became an independent organisation within the Party. Two years later all police powers were unified under Himmler's control as '*Reichsführer* SS and Chief of all German Police', including the *Gestapo*. In 1939 all party and state police organisations involving police and security matters were amalgamated into the **RSHA**, overseen by Himmler but actually co-ordinated by his deputy, Heydrich (see Figure 11.2 on page 231).

Gestapo
Geheime Staats Polizei: Secret State Police.

RSHA
Reich Security Office, which amalgamated all police and security organisations.

Key terms

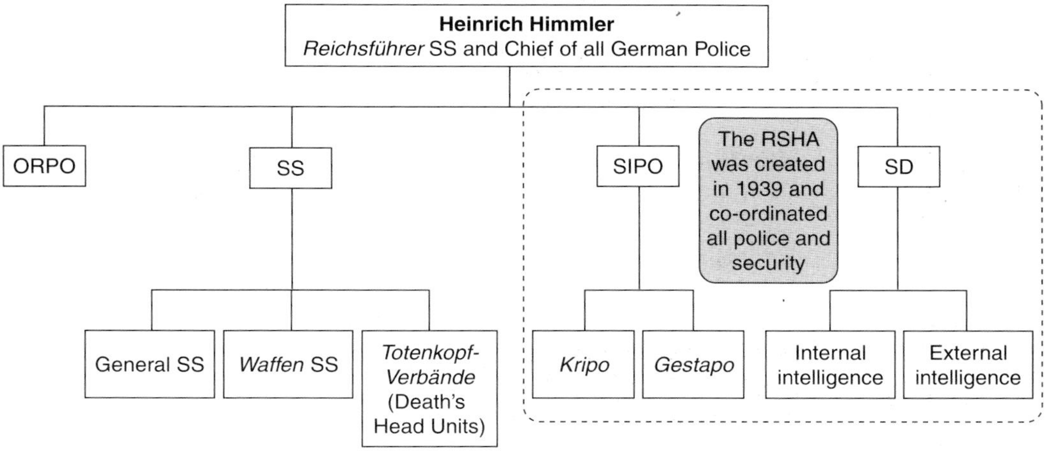

Key

ORPO	(*Ordnungpolizei*) – Regular police	*Waffen* SS – Military armed SS
SS	(*Schutz Staffel*) – Protection squad	Death's Head Units – Ran concentration camps
SIPO	(*Sicherheitspolizei*) – State security	*Kripo* – Criminal police
SD	(*Sicherheitsdienst*) – Party security	*Gestapo* – Security/surveillance

Figure 11.2: The SS-Police system in 1939

The SS-Police system that had been created, therefore, served three main functions:

- Intelligence gathering by the SD. It was responsible for all intelligence and security and was controlled by its leader Heydrich, but still part of the SS. All its responsibilities grew as occupied lands spread.
- Policing by the *Gestapo* and the *Kripo*. The *Kripo* was responsible for the maintenance of general law and order, e.g. dealing with asocials and thieves. In 1936 the *Kripo* was linked with the *Gestapo*. The *Gestapo* was the key policing organisation for upholding the regime by using surveillance and repression. It had a reputation for brutality and it could arrest and detain anyone without trial – although its thoroughness and effectiveness have been questioned (see page 233).
- Military action by the first units of the ***Waffen* SS**. Up to 1938 it consisted of about 14,000 soldiers in three units – but it was racially pure, fanatically loyal and committed to Nazi ideology. From 1938 its influence grew rapidly. This was affected by the political weakening of the German army and also by the more anti-Semitic policies (see pages 216–18).

It is important to keep in perspective the extent of the position of the SS in the years 1933–9. The embryonic power of the SS had definitely been created. With the take-over of territories in 1939 the creation of the '**New Order**' really began – it was from that time that the personnel and influence of the SS expanded enormously.

Key terms

***Waffen* SS**
Armed SS – the number of divisions grew during the war from three to 35.

New Order
Used by the Nazis to describe the economic, political and racial integration of Europe under the Third Reich.

Profile: Heinrich Himmler 1900–45

1900		– Born in Munich in Bavaria, Germany
1917–18		– Joined the cadets, but did not face action in First World War
1919–22		– Studied agriculture at the Munich Technical University
1923		– Joined the Nazi Party
1923	November	– Took part in the Munich Beer Hall *putsch*
1929		– Appointed leader of the SS
1930		– Elected as Nazi deputy of the *Reichstag*
1934	June	– Arranged the purge of the SA in the Night of Long Knives
1936		– Given responsibility as '*Reichsführer* SS and Chief of all German Police'
1939		– Created himself as the Commissar of the Strengthening of the German Nationhood – Formed the RSHA
1943		– Appointed Minister of Interior (replacing Frick)
1944		– Appointed as Commander-in-Chief of the Home Army
1945	May	– Arrested by British forces but committed suicide before trial

Himmler was in many respects a nondescript uninspiring character who before 1929 achieved little in his work or in the Party. Yet, with a reputation for an organised, obsessive, hard-working style, he became the leader of the brutally efficient SS machine which really held the Third Reich together.

When he was appointed leader of the SS he quickly converted the small group of 250 into a committed élite force of 52,000. Yet, until 1934 Himmler and the SS remained very much in the shadow of Röhm and the SA – it was his decision to take responsibility for the purge in the Night of the Long Knives that proved to be his real turning point.

From that time Himmler's political power continued to increase right until the collapse of the Third Reich. He must therefore undoubtedly take responsibility for:

- the development and control of the apparatus of terror which by surveillance and repression created the system of control
- the pursuit of his aim to create a German master-race and the development of élite institutions like *Lebensborn* and the *Ordensburgen* (see pages 203 and 187)
- the extermination of the subhuman races, such as the Jews and the Gypsies, in the concentration camps
- the exploitation of all the occupied lands for slave labour and arms production
- the development of the *Waffen* SS as an élite military force that matched the might of the German army by the end of the war.

Key dates

Night of the Long Knives: 30 June 1934

Appointment of Heinrich Himmler as Chief of the German Police: June 1936

Creation of RSHA: September 1939

Key question
How powerful was
the SS?

Key term

State within a state
A situation where
the authority and
government of the
state are threatened
by a rival power
base.

The SS state

As *Reichsführer* SS, Himmler controlled a massive police apparatus
that was answerable only to Hitler. The SS system had grown into
one of the key power blocs in the Third Reich. The SS-Police
system became, in effect, in the words of E. Kogon, a '**state within
a state**'. It was a huge vested interest, which numbered 250,000 in
1939 and had begun to eclipse other interest groups in terms of
power and influence. With the onset of war this tendency was
accentuated further. As German troops gained control over more
and more areas of Europe, the power of the SS was inevitably
enhanced:

- Security. All responsibilities of policing and intelligence
  expanded as occupied lands spread. The job of internal
  security became much greater and SS officers were granted
  severe powers to crush opposition.
- Military. The *Waffen* SS increased from three divisions in
  1939 to 35 in 1945, which developed into a 'second army' –
  committed, brutal and militarily highly rated. By 1944
  the SS was so powerful it rivalled the power of the German
  army.
- Economy. The SS became responsible for the creation of the
  'New Order' in the occupied lands of eastern Europe. Such a
  scheme provided opportunities for plunder and power on a
  massive scale, which members of the SS exploited to the full.
  By the end of the war the SS had created a massive commercial
  organisation of over 150 firms, which exploited slave labour to
  extract raw materials and to manufacture textiles, armaments
  and household goods.
- Ideology and race. The racial policy of extermination and
  resettlement was pursued with vigour and the system of
  concentration camps was widely established and run by the SS
  Death's Head Units (see also Chapter 10, page 220). The
  various 'inferior' races were even used for their economic value.

The SS was not immune to the rivalries and arguments which
typified Nazi Germany. Disagreements often arose, particularly
with local *Gauleiters* and the governors of the occupied territories.
Moreover, despite the traditional image of Nazism as an
all-knowing totalitarian police state, *Gestapo* policing had
clear limitations:

- It only had no more than 40,000 agents for the whole of
  Germany, so a large city, like Frankfurt, with about half a
  million people, was policed by just about 40–50 agents.
- Most of the work for the *Gestapo* was actually prompted by
  public informers, which were caused more often by gossip and
  generated enormous paperwork for limited return.
- The *Gestapo* had relatively few 'top agents', so it coped by
  over-relying on the work of the *Kripo*.

The oppression of Jews began early in Hitler's regime. Especially persecuted were the *Ostjuden* (Jews from eastern Europe, who had settled in Germany). Here, plainclothes *Gestapo* agents take Jews into custody.

Nevertheless, the SS state under Himmler not only preserved the Nazi regime through its brutal, repressive and often arbitrary policies of law enforcement, but gradually extended its influence. In this way it evolved over time into the key power group in the Third Reich.

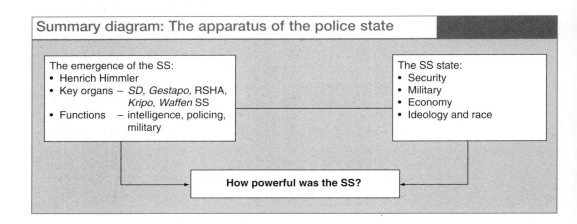

Summary diagram: The apparatus of the police state

The emergence of the SS:
- Henrich Himmler
- Key organs – *SD*, *Gestapo*, RSHA, *Kripo*, *Waffen* SS
- Functions – intelligence, policing, military

The SS state:
- Security
- Military
- Economy
- Ideology and race

How powerful was the SS?

Key question
How did Nazi propaganda use the media?

3 | The Nazi Propaganda Machine

Despite the power of the Nazi police apparatus, it would be too simple to suggest that the regime maintained itself in power simply by the use of terror and repression. From the very start both Hitler and Goebbels recognised how important propaganda could be as a vital cog in the Nazis state. As Goebbels stated at his very first press conference on 15 March 1933:

> I view the first task of the new ministry as being to establish co-ordination between the government and the whole people … If the means achieves the end, the means is good. Whether it always satisfies stringent aesthetic criteria or not is immaterial.

As a result considerable resources were directed towards the development of the propaganda machine in order to achieve the following aims:

- to glorify the regime
- to spread the Nazi ideology and values (and by implication to censor the unacceptable)
- to win over the people and to integrate the nation's diverse elements.

Under the Nazis all means of public communication were brought under state control.

Radio

Goebbels (and Hitler) had always recognised the effectiveness of the spoken word over the written and they had already begun to use new technology during the election campaigns of 1932–3. Up until this time, German broadcasting had been organised by regional states. Once in power, Goebbels efficiently brought all broadcasting under Nazi control by the creation of the Reich Radio Company. Furthermore, he arranged the dismissal of 13 per cent of the staff on political and racial grounds, and replaced them with his own men. He told his broadcasters in March 1933:

> I am placing a major responsibility in your hands, for you have in your hands the most modern instrument in existence for influencing the masses. By this instrument you are the creators of public opinion.

Yet, control of broadcasting was of little value in terms of propaganda unless the people had the means to receive it. In 1932 less than 25 per cent of German households owned a wireless – though that was quite a high figure compared to the rest of the world. Consequently, the Nazi government made provision for the production of a cheap set, the People's Receiver (*Volksempfänger*). Radio was a new and dynamic medium and access increased markedly. By 1939, 70 per cent of German homes had a radio – the highest national figure in the world – and it became a medium of mass communication controlled completely by the regime.

Ganz Deutschland
hört den Führer

mit dem Volksempfänger

'All Germany hears the *Führer* on the People's Radio'. The cheapness and popularity of the People's Radio made it easier for the Nazis to spread their propaganda.

Broadcasting was also directed at public places. The installation of loudspeakers in restaurants and cafés, factories and offices made them all into venues for collective listening. 'Radio wardens' were even appointed, whose duty it was to co-ordinate the listening process.

Press

Control of the press was not so easily achieved by Goebbels. Germany had over 4700 daily newspapers in 1933 – a result of the strong regional identities which still existed in a state that had only been unified in 1871. Moreover, the papers were all owned privately, and traditionally owed no loyalty to central government; their loyalty was to their publishing company, religion or political party.

Profile: Josef Goebbels 1897–1945

1897		– Born in the Rhineland. Disabled by a clubbed foot which affected his walking
1914–18		– Excused military service on the grounds of his disability
1917–21		– Attended the university of Heidelberg and graduated with a doctor of philosophy
1924		– Joined the Nazi Party. Originally, a supporter of the radical Nazi Gregor Strasser
1926		– Broke with Strasser and sided with Hitler
		– Hitler appointed him as *Gauleiter* of Berlin
1927		– Created the Nazi newspaper *Der Angriff*
1928		– Appointed member of the *Reichstag*
1930		– Put in charge of Party propaganda
1933	March	– Joined the cabinet and appointed Minister of Public Enlightenment and Propaganda, a post which he held until 1945
	May	– Encouraged the burning of 'un-German books'
1938		– His affair with Lida Baarova undermined his position with Hitler
	November	– Issued the orders for the anti-Semitic attacks of *Kristallnacht*
1943	February	– Called for 'total war' to rouse the nation after the defeat at Stalingrad
1945	April	– Committed suicide after poisoning his children and shooting his wife

Goebbels was a man from a humble background with many talents who became one of the few intellectuals in the Nazi leadership. However, he suffered from a strong inferiority complex over his physical limitations and he became an embittered and committed anti-Semite.

He was always a radical Nazi and, originally, a supporter of the Strassers, although he became a long-term loyal supporter of Hitler from 1926. As propaganda chief of the party from 1930, he played a crucial role in exploiting every possible method to sell the Nazi image in the series of elections, 1930–3.

Once he became Minster of Propaganda, he developed the whole range of the regime's propaganda techniques that were frighteningly ahead of their time. Unscrupulous and amoral in his methods, he was mainly responsible for:

• using all possible methods to advance the idea of Nazi totalitarianism
• censoring all non-Nazi culture and media
• promoting all the main ideological ideas of Nazism.

He was a very highly skilled orator and he remained a central figure until the final collapse of the regime, though other leading Nazis, such as Göring and Ribbentrop, distrusted him. His rivals also exploited his many love affairs to undermine his position and he became quite isolated in the years 1938–42. But with his personal leadership and his organisational skills he played an important part in the final two years of the war in making the nation ready for total war:

- he organised help for people in the bombed cities
- he took the initiative and gave the orders to put down the July Bomb Plot (see pages 242–3)
- he maintained civilian morale against all the odds, e.g. by visiting bombed cities (unlike Hitler)
- he took the responsibility to mobilise the last efforts to resist the Allied advance.

Various measures were taken to achieve Nazi control.

- First, the Nazi publishing house, *Eher Verlag*, bought up numerous newspapers, so that by 1939 it controlled two-thirds of the German press.
- Secondly, the various news agencies were merged into one, the DNB. This was state controlled, with the result that news material was vetted even before it got to the journalists.
- Thirdly, Goebbels introduced a daily press conference at the Propaganda Ministry to provide guidance on editorial policy.
- Finally, by the so-called Editors' Law of October 1933, newspaper content was made the sole responsibility of the editor; it became his job to satisfy the requirements of the Propaganda Ministry, or face the appropriate consequences. In this way, as one historian has explained, 'There was no need for censorship because the editor's most important function was that of censor.'

To a large extent, the Nazis succeeded in muzzling the press so that even the internationally renowned *Frankfurter Zeitung* was forced to close in 1943. However, the price of that success was the evolution of a bland and sterile journalism, which undoubtedly contributed to a 10 per cent decline in newspaper circulation before 1939.

Nazi ritual

One final aspect of the Goebbels propaganda machine was the deliberate attempt to create a new kind of social ritual. The *Heil Hitler* greeting, the Nazi salute, the **Horst Wessel** anthem and the preponderance of militaristic uniforms were all intended to strengthen the individual's identity with the regime. This was further encouraged by the establishment of a series of public festivals to commemorate historic days in the Nazi calendar (see Table 11.1).

Key term

Horst Wessel
A young Nazi stormtrooper killed in a fight with communists in 1930. The song he wrote became a Nazi marching song and later virtually became an alternative national anthem.

Key question
How did Nazism try to create a new social ritual?

Table 11.1: Historic days in the Nazi calendar

30 January	The seizure of power (1933)
24 February	Party Foundation Day (1925)
16 March	Heroes' Remembrance Day (War Dead)
20 April	Hitler's birthday
1 May	National Day of Labour
2nd Sunday in May	Mothering Sunday
21 June	Summer solstice
2nd Sunday of July	German culture
September	Nuremberg Party Rally
October	Harvest festival
9 November	The Munich *putsch* (1923)
Winter solstice	Pagan festival to counter Christmas

Conclusion

Key question
How effective was
Nazi propaganda?

Although control of the press and radio was Goebbels's major objective, he gradually extended his influence so that film, music, literature and art all came under the control of the Reich (as was shown in Chapter 9, pages 204–7). However, it is very difficult for historians to assess the effectiveness of Nazi propaganda. The extent of its influence clearly has massive implications for the whole thorny issue of public opinion.

Historians initially assumed rather too glibly that Nazi propaganda was a major achievement because it was possible to highlight the way Goebbels exploited all the means for propaganda – photographs, Party rallies, sport, festivals. This view was underlined by Herzstein's book in the 1960s, *The War That Hitler Won*. However, more recent research from oral history of local studies has raised serious doubts about its effectiveness and tended to show that the degree of success of propaganda varied according to different purposes. Very generally it is felt that propaganda succeeded in the sense that it:

- cultivated the 'Hitler myth' of him as an all-powerful leader
- strengthened the Nazi regime after Germany's economic and political crisis, 1929–33
- appealed effectively to reinforce established family values and German nationalism.

On the other hand, propaganda failed markedly in its attempt:

- to denounce the Christian Churches
- to seduce the working classes away from their established identity through the ideal of *Volksgemeinschaft*
- to develop a distinctive Nazi culture (see pages 204–7).

Such points give backing to the view that the propaganda machine was of secondary importance compared to the power and influence of the SS-Police system in upholding the Third Reich.

Summary diagram: The Nazi propaganda machine

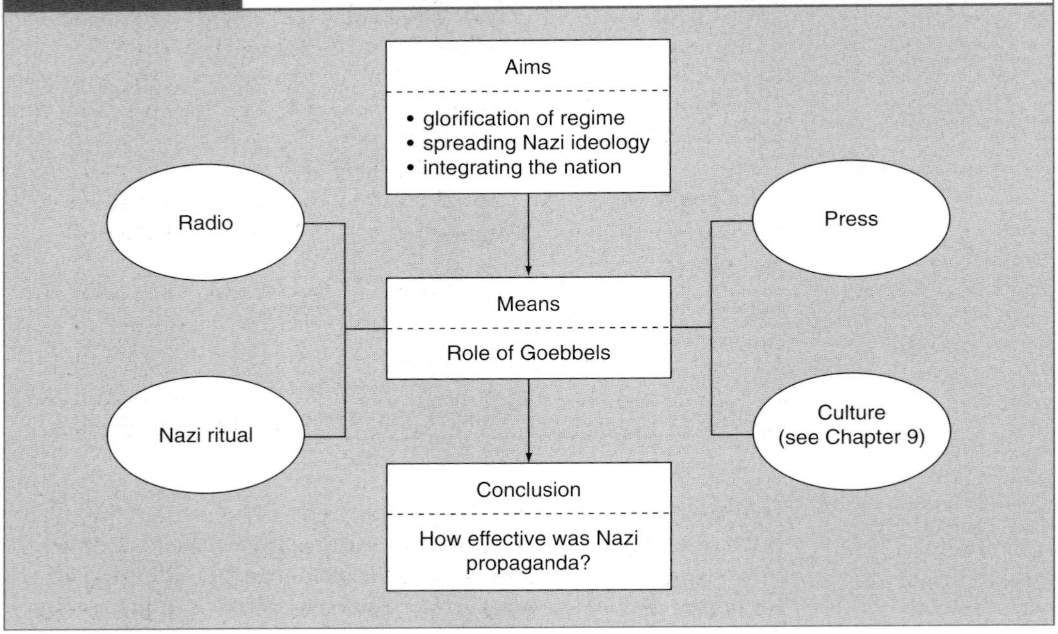

Aims

- glorification of regime
- spreading Nazi ideology
- integrating the nation

Radio

Press

Means

Role of Goebbels

Nazi ritual

Culture
(see Chapter 9)

Conclusion

How effective was Nazi
propaganda?

4 | Resistance

Active resistance to the Nazi regime failed and the Third Reich
only collapsed when Germany was defeated by the Allies. So
those who organised activities aimed at subverting the regime –
however gloriously and heroically portrayed – made enormous
personal sacrifices without making any real impression on the
Nazi stranglehold of power. The real question is why did they fail?

Communists

Although the Communist Party (KPD) had a mass membership of
300,000 and polled 17 per cent of the popular vote in 1932, it
felt the full force of Nazi repression from the very start (see
page 142). Over half of its members were interned during the
first year of Nazi rule. By 1935 the *Gestapo* had infiltrated the
remains of the party, which had tried to continue with the
distribution of printed pamphlets and posters and involvement in
minor acts of sabotage.

There followed a series of mass trials, although the communist
underground movement was never entirely broken in spite of this
onslaught. Many small communist cells continued to be formed
by Wilhelm Knöckel in many of the large German cities. The
most famous of the communist cells was the so-called Red
Orchestra (*Rote Kapelle*), a spy network that successfully
permeated the government and military through the aristocratic
sympathiser Schulz-Boysen. From 1938 to 1942 it transmitted
vital information back to Moscow – but all the members were
eventually caught and tortured appallingly.

Key question
Why was active
communist resistance
to the Nazi state so
limited?

Key dates

Mass arrests by
Gestapo of socialists
and communists:
1935

Red Orchestra cell
discovered and
closed down: 1942

Spanish Civil War
The 1936–9 conflict between Republicans, who supported the democratic government, and the Nationalists/Fascists (financially and militarily backed by Italy and Germany).

However, the impact of communist activities should not be overstated and German communists failed because:

- Leading activists after 1936 were also drawn away from Germany to fight for the Republicans against the Fascists in the **Spanish Civil War** in the belief that such a gesture was a more worthwhile way of resisting fascism.
- They took their orders from Moscow and yet in the 1930s Stalin purged elements of the whole communist movement.
- They were fatally compromised by the **Nazi–Soviet Pact** of 1939–41.
- Even when the USSR and Germany did end up at war with each other in June 1941 the resistance groups remained isolated.

Active communist resistance to the Nazi state was limited and in the end it really became more geared towards self-preservation, so that it was ready for the day when Nazism would be defeated and the Soviet 'liberation' could take place.

Students: the White Rose Group

Key question
Did the White Rose Group achieve anything?

The White Rose student resistance movement is probably the most famous of the youth groups because it went beyond mere dissent. It was led by brother and sister Hans and Sophie Scholl. *The White Rose* (the symbol of peace) was the name given to a series of leaflets printed in 1942–3 and distributed initially amongst the students of Munich University but in time to many towns in central Germany. The content of the leaflets was highly political and openly condemned the moral and spiritual values of the Nazi regime. One of the early leaflets was entitled 'Isn't every decent German today ashamed of his government?'

White Rose student group and the distribution of anti-Nazi leaflets: 1942–3

The group represented a brave gesture of defiance and self-sacrifice. However, from the start the group's security was weak and it was only a matter of time before the *Gestapo* closed in. In February 1943 the six leaders were arrested, tortured and swiftly executed. Sophie Scholl openly said to the court:

Nazi–Soviet Pact
A non-aggression pact between the USSR and Germany that opened the way for the invasion of Poland.

> What we wrote and said is in the minds of you all. You just don't say it aloud.

Conservative élites

Key question
Why did Germany's 'active resistance' fail to undermine the Third Reich?

It might seem surprising that the most influential active resistance emerged from the ranks of Germany's upper classes, who dominated the civil service and, most particularly, the officer corps. After all, these were the very same conservative nationalists who had given sympathetic backing to Nazi authoritarianism (see page 134). Yet, the army as an institution was never fully 'co-ordinated' (until the summer 1944) and therefore it enjoyed a degree of freedom from Nazi control. Moreover, with its access to arms, the army had the real capacity to resist. For these reasons the development of the active resistance of the German élites formed around the army, although once again it was to fail in its primary objective.

The opposition of the conservative élites emerged slowly. At first, most of them could give qualified support of Nazism for:

- its attacks on the left-wing movement
- its dismantling of the democratic system and the restoration of an authoritarian rule
- its hostility towards the Treaty of Versailles
- its demands for rearmament.

Most significantly, the army gave its blessing to the Night of the Long Knives which fatally linked itself with the regime (see pages 150–2). At first, then, the conservative élites did not recognise – or did not want to recognise – the true radical nature of Nazism. They unwittingly strengthened the regime to such an extent that resistance afterwards became much more difficult.

Diplomatic and military success 1938–42
The year 1938 marked the emergence of a real conservative resistance. Ulrich von Hassell, the ex-ambassador in Rome, and Carl Goerdeler, Mayor of Leipzig and a one-time member of Hitler's early government, both joined the Nazi opposition at this time. More significantly, Ludwig Beck, formerly Chief of the General Staff, became convinced by the summer of 1938 that Hitler's intention to invade Czechoslovakia could only lead to a continental war against Britain and France. Plans were drawn up to stage a *coup* and overtures were also made to the British Foreign Office. As it happened, the Allied **appeasement** of Hitler at Munich cut the ground from beneath the conspirators and the planned revolt was dropped while Hitler took the glory for his diplomatic gains.

Planned *putsch* by General Beck if war resulted from Czech crisis: 1938

Appeasement Making concessions in order to satisfy an aggressor. In this context, it refers to the Anglo-French policy of the 1930s towards Hitler's territorial demands.

Military failings 1942–4
Effective resistance began to re-emerge in the winter months of 1942–3 with the military disasters at El Alamein and Stalingrad (see page 249). The so-called Kreisau Circle was a wide-ranging group of officers, aristocrats, academics and churchmen who met at the Kreisau estate of Helmut von Moltke. The conferences discussed ideas about plans for a new Germany after Hitler and, in August 1943, a programme was drawn up. The principles of the Kreisau Circle were politically conservative and strongly influenced by Christian values. Indeed, there were pacifist elements in the group who were opposed to a *coup* against Hitler.

Nevertheless, some individual members were supporters of what became the most far-reaching act of resistance to Hitler's Germany – the Bomb Plot of 20 July 1944. A number of the civilian resistance figures made contact with dissident army officers, such as Beck and Tresckow, in order to plan the assassination of Hitler and the creation of a provisional government. In the words of Tresckow just before the attempted assassination:

> The assassination must take place, whatever the cost. Even if it should fail, the attempt to seize power in Berlin must take place. The practical consequences are immaterial. The German resistance must prove to the world and to posterity that it dares to take the decisive step.

Eventually, the lead was taken by Colonel von Stauffenberg, who came to believe that the assassination of Hitler was the only way to end the Nazi regime. He himself placed a bomb in Hitler's briefing room at his headquarters in East Prussia on 20 July 1944. Unfortunately for the conspirators, the briefcase containing the bomb was moved a few yards just a minute before it exploded. Hitler thus sustained only minor injuries. In the confused aftermath the generals in Berlin fatally hesitated, thus enabling a group of Hitler's loyal soldiers to arrest the conspirators and re-establish order. About 5000 supporters of the resistance were killed in the aftermath, including Stauffenberg, Beck, Tresckow, Rommel, Moltke and Goerdeler.

The conservative élites proved incapable of fundamentally weakening the Nazi regime and in that sense their active resistance failed. Among the reasons for this are:

- They only recognised the need to resist the regime after the crucial developments of 1934 and 1938, by which time it was too well established.
- The military oath tied the army to the Nazi regime and its leader.
- Hitler's diplomatic and military successes in 1938–42 undoubtedly blinded the élites. Even after the '**turn of the tide**' and the growing knowledge of brutal actions, the majority of army generals did not work with the resistance.
- Planning and organisation of effective action was always fraught with difficulties. Their long-term political aims lacked clarity and practical plans were inhibited by the environment of suspicion and uncertainty in a police state.

In the end the bad luck and confusion of the Bomb Plot of 20 July reflected these difficulties.

Turn of the tide
Used to describe the Allied military victories in the winter of 1942–3, when the British won at El Alamein in North Africa and when the Russians forced the surrender of 300,000 German troops at Stalingrad.

A photo taken of the room after Stauffenberg's bomb exploded. Despite the destruction Hitler was only slightly injured.

Profile: Claus von Stauffenberg 1907–44

1907	– Born in Bavaria, Germany, the descendant of an aristocratic military family
1926–30	– Joined the Bavarian Cavalry Regiment and commissioned as a lieutenant
1936–8	– Joined the army's War Academy in Berlin and graduated first in his class
1939–43	– Fought in Poland, France, Russia and Africa
1942	– Witnessed atrocities in Russia. Started to associate with the resistance of the Kreisau Circle along with Tresckow
1943 January	– Promoted to lieutenant-colonel
	– Badly injured when his staff car ran into a minefield in Africa. Lost his eye, two left-hand fingers and his right forearm
1944	– After his recuperation he decided to kill Hitler and draw up the plan codenamed 'Operation Valkyrie'. Several attempts were aborted in the first half of the year
July 20	– Detonated the bomb at Hitler's headquarters at Rastenburg, in eastern Germany. Hitler was only injured. Stauffenberg was arrested and shot in the late evening

Stauffenberg was an able and committed soldier who, like so many, initially admired Hitler. However, his strong Catholic moral outlook shaped his increasing doubts about the regime by 1941. He remained on the fringes of the Kreisau Circle in 1942–3, but he gave the resistance a real purpose from early 1944. Stauffenberg personally took the initiative to carry out the assassination, but for his failure he paid the ultimate price – along with his brother.

Summary diagram: Active resistance

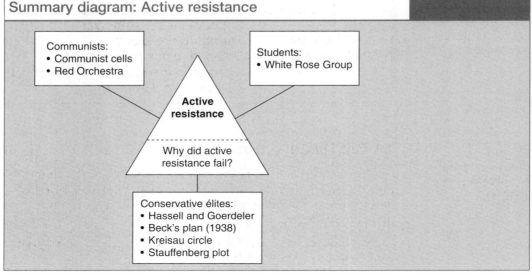

POINTS TO CONSIDER

There is a lot of detail in this chapter and you must be careful not to get too lost in the military history. Moreover, quite a lot of its aspects are connected with the discussion on Nazi domestic policy in Chapters 9–11. The following main themes need to be considered:

- Germany's military war
- Germany's defeat
- The 'Home Front'
- The condition of Germany in 1945

Key dates

1939	September 1	German invasion of Poland
	September 3	Britain and France declared war
1941	June 22	'Operation Barbarossa' – German invasion of USSR
	December 11	German declaration of war on USA following Pearl Harbor – continental war 'globalised'
1942	February	Speer's reforms to mobilise the war economy
	November	German defeat at El Alamein
1943	January	German surrender at Stalingrad
	February 18	Goebbels' speech rallied the people for a 'total war'
	July 24	Hamburg fire-storm
1944	June 6	Allied landings in Normandy
1945	May 7	German surrender: occupation and division of Germany

Key question
Why was Germany so successful in 1939–41?

1 | The Military War

In *Mein Kampf* Hitler openly stated his ambitions for foreign policy. Indeed, some historians believe that Hitler had a clearly defined set of objectives, which amounted to a 'stage-by-stage plan' (*Stufenplan*):

- The destruction of the Treaty of Versailles and the restoration of Germany's pre-1914 boundaries.

- The union of all German-speaking peoples such as Austria, western Poland, the borders of Czechoslovakia (the Sudetenland) and provinces in Hungary and Romania.
- The creation of *Lebensraum* – the establishment of a Nazi racial empire by expanding into eastern Europe at the expense of the Slavic peoples, particularly in Poland and Russia.

In the years 1935–8 Germany rapidly made some key gains which changed the continental balance of power:

- The Treaty of Versailles was challenged by the creation of an airforce and by the introduction of a conscripted army of 55,000 (March 1935).
- The remilitarisation of the Rhineland (March 1936).
- The *Anschluss* ('union') with Austria (March 1938).
- The Munich Agreement which ceded the German-speaking Sudetenland to Germany (September 1938).

However, once Nazi Germany had militarily occupied the non-German lands of Czechoslovakia in March 1939, Britain and France found it difficult to tolerate further German expansionism and immediately guaranteed to uphold the independence of Poland. Thus, when the German armed forces attacked Poland on 1 September 1939 Britain and France were obliged to declare war.

Although Germany found itself committed to a major war in the autumn of 1939, which Hitler had not expected to wage until the mid-1940s, Germany was not militarily destined to fail from the start. The string of victories from September 1939 to November 1941 bears witness to the military power exerted by the Nazi war-machine and suggests that Germany did not have to go down the road to total collapse. However, by early 1943 Germany faced serious military reverses, but Germany's eventual defeat was not inevitable. It has to be explained, not merely assumed.

Key dates

German invasion of Poland: 1 September 1939

Britain and France declared war on Germany: 3 September 1939

Initial victories

Without direct help from Britain or France, Poland was crushingly defeated by Germany's *Blitzkrieg* tactics within a few weeks. This gave the Germans access to valuable raw materials and labour as well as the aid received from the USSR under the terms of the Nazi–Soviet Pact. Hitler was, therefore, keen to maintain the military momentum and planned for an invasion of France to take place as early as November 1939. But the German attack was postponed several times, mainly because of the lukewarm attitude of senior army generals towards such an operation.

Phoney war

The German attack on the Western Front did not finally take place until May 1940, thus prolonging the Anglo-French '**Phoney War**' for eight months. Hitler's thinking seems to have revolved around the idea of removing the threat posed by the Western democracies before turning east again. To that end Germany needed to 'destroy France' and to make Britain accept German aspirations on the continent. In this way it was hoped to force Britain, under the pressure of military circumstances, into a 'deal' with Germany.

Key term

Phoney war
Used to describe the war period from September 1939 to May 1940 because there was no real aggressive activity on the Western Front.

The Low Countries and France

The German defeat of the Low Countries (Belgium and the Netherlands) and France within six weeks was a dramatic triumph for both the armed forces and Hitler. Diffident generals could hardly fail to be impressed by the *Führer*'s military and political handling of events. German popular opinion was relieved and triumphant. Hitler ruled not only in Berlin but also in Paris, Oslo, Vienna, Prague and Warsaw, while the Third Reich was bordered by the three 'friendly' powers of Spain, Italy and the USSR. It was assumed by many that the war was as good as over.

The Battle of Britain

If self-interest had prevailed, Britain would have settled with Germany. However, the new British prime minister, Churchill, refused even to consider negotiations. The implications of this stubbornness for Germany were clear-cut: Germany needed to secure air superiority in order to invade Britain and to disable its military and strategic potential. Thus, Germany's failure to win the **Battle of Britain** in the autumn of 1940 was significant. Yet, even more so was Hitler's personal decision to switch the military focus, and to start preparing for the invasion of the USSR even before Britain had been neutralised.

Battle of Britain
Name given to the air battle fought over the skies of southern England between the RAF and the Luftwaffe, July–October 1940.

Operation Barbarossa

On 18 December 1940 Hitler issued Directive No. 21 for 'Operation Barbarossa', stating that 'The German armed forces must be prepared to crush Soviet Russia in a quick campaign even before the end of the war against England.' This decision can only be explained by Hitler's belief that *Blitzkrieg* tactics could also succeed in bringing a quick victory against the USSR, as they had against Poland, France and the Low Countries.

The German invasion of the Soviet Union eventually took place on 22 June 1941. It was delayed by the need to invade Yugoslavia and Greece in order to secure Germany's southern flank. At first all went well. Vast tracts of Russian territory were occupied and thousands of prisoners were taken, so that by November 1941 German troops were only miles from Moscow and Leningrad.

'Operation Barbarossa' – German invasion of USSR: 22 June 1941

German declaration of war on USA following Japanese attack at Pearl Harbor – continental war 'globalised': December 1941

Reasons for success

The German military advance was the high-point of the war and in the years 1939–41 it was phenomenally successful for the following reasons:

- France and Britain failed to take the initiative and Poland was left to fight alone.
- Germany's *Blitzkrieg* strategy of rapid advances outmanoeuvred all of its enemies in the first two years.
- The French defensive strategy was based on the Maginot Line and it proved to be powerless in the face of German *Blitzkrieg* tactics. As a result the French political and military leadership lost the will to resist.
- Germany's expansion (from 1938) allowed it to exploit all the labour and resources of those countries for its own purposes.

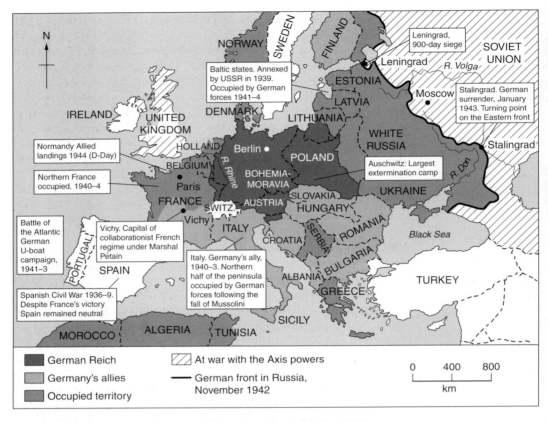

Figure 12.1: Europe, showing Nazi Germany at its height in 1942

• The USSR was taken by surprise by the German attack and was not really prepared.

However, despite Germany's successes, the military advance halted in December 1941. The Soviets had never lost the will to carry on fighting while Anglo-American aid and the snows of Russia combined to consolidate the Eastern Front. Hitler's gamble to break the USSR by launching a *Blitzkrieg* invasion had failed and Germany was now faced with the prospect of a long war on two fronts.

The 'turn of the tide'

December 1941 was significant in another sense too, for, in that month, the Japanese attack on the USA's naval base at **Pearl Harbor** 'globalised' the conflict. Although he was not obliged to do so, Hitler aligned Germany with Japan and declared war on the USA. This move was perhaps prompted by the USA involvement in the **Battle of the Atlantic** even before Pearl Harbor. However, it did not fit easily with Germany's existing strategy and above all it turned the industrial capacity of the world's greatest power against it. It is tempting therefore to suggest that by the end of 1941 Hitler had lost the military and diplomatic grasp which had previously allowed him to shape

Pearl Harbor
A US military base in the Pacific.

Battle of the Atlantic
The naval struggle between the Allied convoys and the German U-boats in the northern Atlantic.

Key question
When and why did the military balance turn against Germany?

international developments. Events were now very much running out of the *Führer*'s control.

German defeat at
El Alamein: November
1942

German surrender at
Stalingrad: January
1943

Yet, although it appears that the events of December 1941 were the vital turning point for German fortunes in the war, this was certainly not apparent at the time. Throughout 1942 German forces pushed deep into the Caucasian oilfields with the objective of capturing Stalingrad, while the Afrika Korps drove the British back across North Africa into Egypt. It was the eventual failure of these two offensives that enabled contemporaries to see the winter of 1942–3 as the 'turn of the tide': the British victory at El Alamein eventually led to the ejection of German forces from North Africa; and the encirclement and surrender of 300,000 troops at Stalingrad marked the beginning of the Soviet counter-offensive.

Key question
Why couldn't
Germany resist the
Allied advance?

Defeat

From 1943 Germany's strategy was essentially defensive. Hitler was determined to protect 'Fortress Europe' from Allied invasion, but possibly his strategic and political thinking was losing touch with reality. Increasingly it became shaped by his belief in German invincibility and his own ideological prejudices about race and communism. For example, in spite of all the military difficulties, the creation of the new racial order continued – there was no postponement of the Final Solution. Hitler deluded himself into thinking that the alliance of the USSR and the Western Allies could not last and that this would then allow Germany to play off one against the other.

The ruins of Berlin in May 1945.

However, Allied military co-ordination continued to work reasonably well. By the end of 1943 Anglo-American forces had linked up in Africa and had then established a hold on southern Italy, while Soviet forces had reconquered much of the Ukraine after the great tank victory at the battle of Kursk in July 1943. The war had also begun to have an impact on Germany itself. The massive bombing raids caused destruction and dislocation, although their exact strategic value has been questioned over the years. It was becoming clear that the war could not be won by Germany and that it faced total devastation unless the Allied demand for '**unconditional surrender**' was accepted.

Such realities prompted the attempted assassination of Hitler in July 1944 (see pages 243–4). Its failure meant that the war would have to be fought to the bitter end. Thus, strong German resistance forced the Western Allies to fight extremely hard in order to break out of the beach-head established in Normandy, France, in 1944, while in the east the Soviet advance progressed through eastern Europe in the face of desperate defensive measures. Yet, even then a blind optimism still prevailed in the minds of some Germans. It was not until 30 April 1945 that Hitler committed suicide when Soviet soldiers had advanced to within a mile of the Chancellery in Berlin. Only then was the German nation freed from the *Führer*'s command and only then could the war end.

Unconditional surrender
Roosevelt and Churchill's statement in 1943 that the Allies would not accept a negotiated peace.

Allied landings in Normandy: 6 June 1944

German surrender: occupation and division of Germany: May 1945

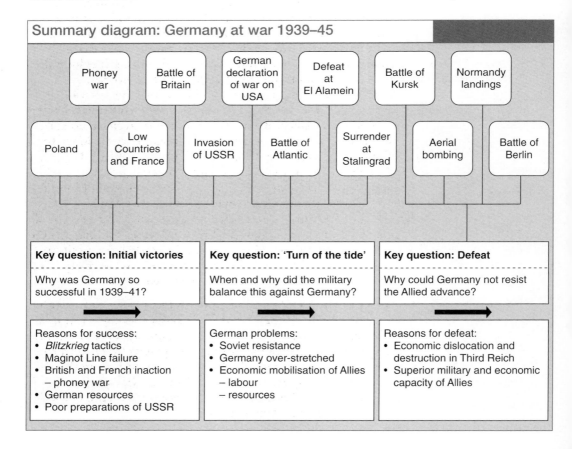

Summary diagram: Germany at war 1939–45

| Phoney war | Battle of Britain | German declaration of war on USA | Defeat at El Alamein | Battle of Kursk | Normandy landings |

| Poland | Low Countries and France | Invasion of USSR | Battle of Atlantic | Surrender at Stalingrad | Aerial bombing | Battle of Berlin |

Key question: Initial victories	**Key question: 'Turn of the tide'**	**Key question: Defeat**
Why was Germany so successful in 1939–41?	When and why did the military balance this against Germany?	Why could Germany not resist the Allied advance?
Reasons for success: • *Blitzkrieg* tactics • Maginot Line failure • British and French inaction – phoney war • German resources • Poor preparations of USSR	German problems: • Soviet resistance • Germany over-stretched • Economic mobilisation of Allies – labour – resources	Reasons for defeat: • Economic dislocation and destruction in Third Reich • Superior military and economic capacity of Allies

Key question
Did Germany have to
lose the war?

2 | Germany's Military Defeat

By May 1945 Germany lay in ruins. Nazi foreign policy had
reached its destructive conclusion. Its ambitions had been
extensive:

- To establish a 'greater Germany', which went well beyond
  Germany's 1914 frontiers.
- To destroy Bolshevik Russia.
- To create a new order based on the concept of Aryan racial
  supremacy.

The means to these ends had involved the acceptance of violence
and bloodshed on a massive scale.

On a superficial level, Hitler's final failure in his ambitions
could be explained by his strategic bungling. Hitler had always
believed (along with most generals going back to Imperial
Germany) that a war on two fronts had to be avoided. To this end
he needed an alliance with Britain and/or France – or at least their
neutrality – so that he could be free to launch an unrestrained
attack in the east. Consequently, when Germany failed to secure
either British neutrality or a British surrender in 1940–1, before
attacking the USSR, the foundations for defeat were laid.

Germany had become engaged in a conflict for which it was not
fully prepared. As has been seen in Chapter 8, at the start of the
war Germany did not exploit fully the available resources and
manpower. The alliance with Mussolini's Italy was also of little
gain. Indeed, Italian military weakness in the Balkans and North
Africa proved costly, since it diverted German forces away from
the main European fronts. Yet, Hitler was driven on ideologically
to launch an attack on the USSR with another *Blitzkrieg*.

The failure to defeat the Soviet Union before the onset of
winter in 1941, combined with the entry of the USA into the war,
now tipped the balance. Britain was still free to act as a launch-
pad for a Western Front and also, in the meantime, could strike
into the heart of Germany by means of aerial bombing. The
USSR could maintain the Eastern Front by relying on its
geography and sacrificing its huge manpower. As Stalin himself
recognised, the Allied victory could be summarised in his words:
'Britain gave the time; America the money; and Russia the blood.'

Hitler had militarily misjudged the antagonists, and now all the
resources and the industrial capacity of the world's two political
giants were directed towards the military defeat of Germany. The
following economic factors counted against Germany:

- The Four-Year Plan. In 1936 it was meant to make Germany 'fit
  for war within four years' but the German economy was not
  really ready for a long war in 1939. Its capacity was only strong
  enough to sustain a couple of short campaigns (see page 170).
- Anglo-American bombing. German industry peaked in the
  production of weapons in summer 1944, yet the German
  armed forces could not fully benefit from this because of the
  detrimental effect of Allied air raids.

- From the start Germany was short of labour. Millions of workers were required to keep up the industrial and agricultural production, and the gaps were only partially filled by forced labourers and an increase in female employment.
- Germany was deeply in debt. The reserves in gold and foreign currencies were almost completely used up by 1939 and the Nazi state had run up a debt of roughly 42 billion *Reichsmarks*.
- The US economy was just too powerful. In 1944 the ratio of Germany's fuel supply compared to the supply of the Western allies was 1:3. The USA sent massive support to the Allies, especially to the USSR which received 13,000 tanks and 15,000 planes.
- Soviet resources. The Soviet economy had undergone a ruthless industrialisation programme in the 1930s under Stalin and despite its limitations, Russia had vast resources of human manpower and raw materials, e.g. oil, coal and iron.

Such explanations might make historical analysis of Germany's defeat in the Second World War seem like a relatively straightforward exercise. However, before accepting such a simple view, it should be borne in mind that, even in 1942, Germany came very close indeed to capturing Stalingrad and to defeating Britain in Egypt. Such successes would have changed the course of the war and the final outcome might have been very different.

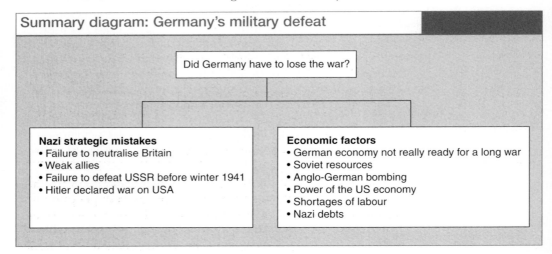

Summary diagram: Germany's military defeat

Did Germany have to lose the war?

Nazi strategic mistakes
- Failure to neutralise Britain
- Weak allies
- Failure to defeat USSR before winter 1941
- Hitler declared war on USA

Economic factors
- German economy not really ready for a long war
- Soviet resources
- Anglo-German bombing
- Power of the US economy
- Shortages of labour
- Nazi debts

3 | The 'Home Front'

Many of the features of the Nazi dictatorship affecting the German people have been covered in earlier chapters. Table 12.1 summarises some of the key points and important references.

Generally, the onset of the war underlined the totalitarian nature of the Nazi regime. The leadership no longer needed to show any regard for international opinion. However, within Germany the Nazis remained very aware of public opinion and the importance of keeping up the nation's morale.

Key question
How did the war change the German people's attitudes?

Table 12.1: The 'Home Front'

Features	References	Major developments in the war
Role of Hitler	pages 226–9	'Hitler myth' was glorified even more during initial victories Personal authority retained almost to the end
War economy	pages 170–4	Despite *Blitzkrieg* victories economic mobilisation was limited at start of war Speer's reforms from 1942 expanded arms production Effects of 'blanket bombing' by Allies
Propaganda	pages 235–9	Increased government censorship Failure of propaganda to compensate for declining military situation Glorification of war through films, e.g. Kolberg
Security/policing	pages 229–34	SS extended its power and influence and resorted to ever more brutal and arbitrary policies Limitations of *Gestapo* personnel

Youth	pages 185–90	HJ compulsory by 1939 and increased emphasis on
		  military drill and discipline
		HJ appeal increasingly polarised between fanatics and the
		  disaffected
		During the war the standard of teachers and HJ leaders
		  declined

Women	pages 171–2,
	198–203
		Contradiction between theory and practice of female
		  employment
		Increased personal pressures: work, home, bombing and
		  absentee husbands

Opposition	pages 196–7, 240–4	Dissent increased, e.g. Christians, youth Active resistance failed, e.g. Stauffenberg plot
Churches	pages 192–8	Initially cautious policy on the Churches Persecution intensified from 1941 Religion remained a sensitive political issue, as shown by the increase in church attendance
Jews and outsiders	page 208 and Chapter 10	Radicalisation of racial policies against Jews leading to genocide Gypsies and other outsiders Euthanasia stopped in response to Catholic opposition

The declaration of war in September 1939 was not met with the patriotic frenzy of August 1914. Rather the mass of people seemed to be resigned and apprehensive. However, the German strategy of *Blitzkrieg* was incredibly successful and the victories of 1939–40 gave the impression of military and economic strength. Most of the people's doubts about Hitler were, therefore, put to one side. On his return journey from France back to Berlin he was met by ecstatic crowds, which were cleverly recorded in the newsreels.

The Nazi economy was not really ready for a major war from 1939 (see page 170) and as a result, from the earliest days the Nazis had to introduce the rationing of food, clothes and basics like soap and toilet paper. Although the German population was adequately fed – even up until early 1944 its rations were about 10 per cent above the minimum calorific standard – the diet was very boring and restricted. By 1942 consumer goods began to decline and in the final 12 months of the war the situation

Ein Kampf ein Wille, ein Ziel:

Sieg um jeden Preis!

'One battle, one will, one goal: victory at any cost!'
Propaganda poster from May 1942. It conveys the image of ordinary men, women and children on the home front supporting German soldiers fighting on the military front.

worsened very dramatically with clear human consequences. For example:

- food rationing led to real shortages (and real hunger by 1945)
- clothes rationing was ended, but only because of the decline in clothes production
- boots and shoes were in short supply
- small luxuries, like magazines and sweets, were stopped.

By 1942 Germany found itself at war with Britain, the USSR and the USA and it faced a long drawn-out conflict. Under the leadership of Speer, the minister of armaments, the German economy was geared even more to fighting a 'total war' (see pages 171–2). This meant that every part of German society was focused on the war effort and would have to make real sacrifices:

Speer's reforms to mobilise the war economy: February 1942

key date

- industry was organised more efficiently
- working hours were increased
- more women were drafted into work
- millions of foreign workers were encouraged to work (but under controls)
- non-essential businesses were closed.

During the winter 1942–3 it became impossible for Nazi propaganda and censorship to disguise the reality of the military defeats of Stalingrad and El Alamein. Moreover, on the home front, the Anglo-American bombing began to hit the great urban centres day and night. Most famously, on the night of 24 July

By 1943 Allied bombing of German cities had increased to the level that children in cities were being encouraged to go to the countryside for safety. The poster encourages parents to register their children aged 3–14 years for the programme, which was not compulsory.

1943 a massive raid on Hamburg created a fire-storm that killed 30,000 civilians and left an estimated one million homeless. By 1945 it is estimated that as a result of the air-raids:

- 300,000 Germans were killed
- 800,000 were wounded
- 3.6 million homes were destroyed (20 per cent of the total housing).

The effects of the Allied bombing on the German civilian (as opposed to the effects on industry, see pages 173–4) have been the subject of considerable discussion. Some have claimed that despite the difficult circumstances faced by most Germans in the final two years of the war, there was no real sign of a decline of morale leading up to the collapse of the regime itself. Indeed, in the face of Allied mass bombing many people came together against the enemy. Rumpf therefore claims, 'Under the terrible blows of that terror from the skies the bonds grew closer and the spirit of solidarity stronger.'

However, research of the reports from the SD which carried out reports on civilian morale and public opinion from 1939 tends to confirm that, from 1943, people became increasingly resigned to the coming disaster and by 1944 there had developed a major loss of confidence in the regime. There was a growing mood of grumbling and complaint. Very interestingly, the source below highlights the deepening cynicism in the nation about the political and military situation after Stalingrad and there was broad criticism of the state and Hitler.

> A large section of the nation cannot imagine how the war will end and the telling of vulgar jokes against the state, even about the *Führer* himself, has increased considerably since Stalingrad. (An SD report, 1943)

So although it is true that active resistance to the war remained very limited (see pages 240–4), popular dissent in various forms developed, as Welch writes in his conclusion on *The Third Reich: Politics and Propaganda*:

> The debacle of Stalingrad undoubtedly affected the morale of the German people. It forced them to question Nazi war aims and led to a crisis of confidence in the regime amongst broad sections of the population.

Table 12.2: Three phases of the war in Germany

Main phases	Key military events	Developments in Germany
1939–41 The years of Nazi victories	Nazi control over Poland and northern and western Europe German invasion of USSR leading to control of most of western USSR	Introduction of food/clothes rationing Casualties limited
1941–3 The 'turn of the tide'	German declaration of war on USA following Japanese attack at Pearl Harbor German defeat at El Alamein German surrender at Stalingrad	'Final Solution' started to exterminate Jews Speer's reforms to mobilise the war economy More resistance developed, but isolated Creation of Kreisau Circle White Rose group of students at Munich
1943–5 'Total war' and defeat	Western Allies' invasion of France: D-Day USSR gained control of eastern Europe, including Berlin German surrender Western Allies' occupation of western Germany	Goebbels' speech rallied the people for a 'total war' Allied mass bombing of Germany, e.g. Hamburg fire-storm Manufacture of clothes ended and clothes rations suspended Stauffenberg's 'July plot' failed Auschwitz liberated by USSR Food only available on black market Dresden bombing: thousands killed in two nights by Allies Hitler's suicide in Berlin

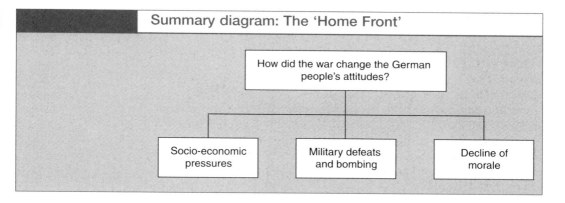

Summary diagram: The 'Home Front'

How did the war change the German people's attitudes?

- Socio-economic pressures
- Military defeats and bombing
- Decline of morale

Key question
How serious was Germany's condition by 1945?

4 | Germany in 1945

In the weeks before the capital fell to the Russians a typical Berliner's joke began to circulate: 'Enjoy the war while you can! The peace is going to be terrible.'

It is no exaggeration to say that the German state had ceased to exist by May 1945. Hitler and Goebbels and a number of other Nazi leaders had committed suicide, while others had fled or been captured and arrested (see the profiles of the main characters). Therefore, central government had broken down. Instead, Germany and Berlin had been divided by the Allies into four zones, each one with their own military commander giving orders and guidelines for the local economy and administration.

But, in the short term, the most telling problem facing Germany in that spring was the extent of the social and economic crisis.

Population displacement

At the end of the war it is estimated that one in two Germans were on the move:

- roughly 12 million German refugees fleeing from the east
- 10 million of the so-called 'displaced persons', who had done forced labour or had been prisoners in the various Nazi camps
- over 11 million German soldiers, who had been taken as prisoners of war: 7.7 million in camps in the west were soon released, whereas the 3.3 million in the USSR were kept in captivity until the 1950s, of whom one-third did not survive.

All these people posed a serious problem to the British and the Americans because of the lack of food.

Urban destruction

Major German cities, especially Cologne, Hamburg and Berlin, had been reduced to rubble because of Anglo-American bombing and Soviet artillery firing (see the photograph on page 249). Twenty per cent of housing had been completely destroyed, and a

further 30 per cent badly damaged, which led many to accept
sheltered accommodation or to escape to the countryside.

Food and fuel shortages

Food was the immediate problem, but it was soon to be
exacerbated by the onset of winter at the end of 1945. The
average recommended calorie consumption of 2000 calories sank
to 950–1150 and, if it had not been for emergency relief from the
Western Allies and care parcels from charities, starvation would
have been far worse. This level of malnourishment led to illnesses
such as typhus, diphtheria and whooping cough.

Economic dislocation

Surprisingly, the economy had not completely broken down, but it
was very badly dislocated. Industrial capacity had obviously
declined dramatically, but its destruction was exaggerated at the
time. Moreover, the infrastructure of bridges and railways and the
utilities, like gas and water, had broken down during the end of
the war. Also, the state had massive debts, so Germany was once
again facing the problem of a rising inflation causing a major
black market in the supply of food and other goods.

  The Third Reich had been destroyed in May 1945, but that left
Germany in ruins. Violence, destruction and dislocation had
brought it to **zero hour**.

Zero hour
Used in German
society to describe
Germany's overall
collapse at the end
of the Second
World War.

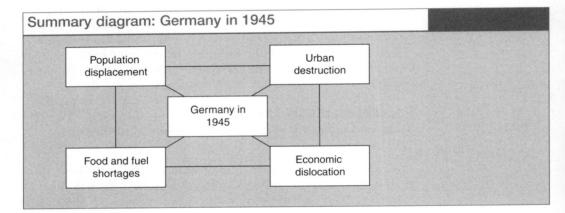

Summary diagram: Germany in 1945

In 1934 he became leader of the country after the death of Hindenburg.

Führerprinzip 'The leadership principle'. Hitler upheld the idea of a one-party state, built on an all-powerful leader.

Gauleiter Means 'leader of a regional area'. The Nazi Party was organised into 35 regions from 1926.

Genocide The extermination of a whole race.

Gestapo Geheime Staats Polizei: Secret State Police.

Ghetto Ancient term describing the area lived in by the Jews in a city. Under Nazi occupation the Jews were separated from the rest of the community and forced to live in appalling and overcrowded conditions.

Gleichschaltung 'Bringing into line' or 'co-ordination'.

GNP Gross national product is the total value of all goods and services in a nation's economy (including income derived from assets abroad).

Gradualism Changing by degrees; progressing slowly.

Great Depression The severe economic crisis of 1929–33 that was marked by mass unemployment, falling prices and a lack of spending.

Guns or Butter? A phrase used to highlight the controversial economic choice between rearmament and consumer goods.

Hard currency A currency that the market considers to be strong because its value does not depreciate. In the 1920s the hardest currency was the US dollar.

Holocaust Term to describe mass slaughter – in this context it refers to the extermination of the Jews.

Horst Wessel A young Nazi stormtrooper killed in a fight with communists in 1930. The song he wrote became a Nazi marching song and later virtually became an alternative national anthem.

Hyper-inflation Hyper-inflation is unusual. In Germany in 1923, it meant that prices spiralled out of control because the government increased the amount of money being printed. As a result, it displaced the whole economy.

Imperial Germany The title given to Germany from its unification in 1871 until 1918. Also referred to as the Second Reich (Empire).

Imports Goods purchased from foreign countries.

Indoctrination Inculcating and imposing a set of ideas.

Junkers The landowning aristocracy, especially those from eastern Germany.

Kaiser Emperor. The last Kaiser of Germany was Wilhelm II, 1888–1918.

Kulturkampf 'Cultural struggle'. Refers to the tension in the 1870s between the Catholic Church and the German state, when Bismarck was chancellor.

Labour exchanges Local offices created by the state for finding employment. Many industrialised countries had labour exchanges to counter mass unemployment.

League of Nations The international body initiated by President Wilson to encourage disarmament and to prevent war.

Lebensborn Literally 'spring' or 'Fountain of Life'. Founded by Himmler and overseen by the SS to promote doctrines of racial purity.

Lebensraum 'Living space'. Hitler's aim to create an empire by establishing German supremacy over the eastern lands in Europe.

Mandates The name given by the Allies to the system created in the Peace Settlement for the supervision of all the colonies of Germany (and Turkey) by the League of Nations.

Marxism The political ideology of Karl Marx. His two major books, *Communist Manifesto* and *Capital*, outline his beliefs that the working classes will overthrow the industrial classes by revolution and create a classless society.

Mass suggestion A psychological term suggesting that large groups of people can be unified simply by the atmosphere of the occasion. Hitler and Goebbels used their speeches and large rallies to particularly good effect.

Mein Kampf 'My struggle'. The book written by Hitler in 1924, which expresses his political ideas.

Mittelstand Can be translated as 'the middle class', but in German society it tends to represent the lower middle classes, e.g. shopkeepers, craft workers and clerks. Traditionally independent and self-reliant but increasingly felt squeezed out between the power and influence of big business and industrial labour.

Mutual guarantee agreement An agreement between states on a particular issue, but not an alliance.

National Opposition A title given to various political forces that united to campaign against Weimar. It included the DNVP, the Nazis, the Pan-German League and the *Stahlhelm* – an organisation of ex-soldiers. The 'National Opposition' was forged out of the Young Plan in 1929 to oppose all reparations payments.

Nationalisation The socialist principle that the ownership of key industries should be transferred to the state.

Nationalism Grew from the national spirit to unify Germany in the nineteenth century. Supported a strong policy to embrace all German-speakers in eastern Europe.

Nazi–Soviet Pact A non-aggression pact between the USSR and Germany that opened the way for the invasion of Poland.

New functionalism A form of art that developed in post-war Germany which tried to express reality with a more objective view of the world.

New Order Used by the Nazis to describe the economic, political and racial integration of Europe under the Third Reich.

Night of the Long Knives A crucial turning point when Hitler arranged for the SS to purge the SA leadership and murder about 200 victims, including Ernst Röhm, Gregor Strasser and Kurt von Schleicher.

November criminals Those who signed the November Armistice and a term of abuse to vilify all those who supported the democratic republic.

Pan-German League A movement founded at the end of the nineteenth century campaigning for the uniting of all Germans into one country.

Paramilitary units Informal non-legal military squads.

Passive resistance Refusal to work with occupying forces.

Pearl Harbor A US military base in the Pacific.

Phoney war Used to describe the war period from September 1939 to May 1940 because there was no real aggressive activity on the Western Front.

Plebiscite A vote by the people on one specific issue – like a referendum.

Pogrom An organised or encouraged massacre of innocent people. The term originated from the massacres of Jews in Russia.

Polarisation The division of society into distinctly opposite views (the comparison is to the north and south poles).

Population policy In 1933–45 the Nazi government aimed to increase the birth rate.

Proletariat The industrial working class who, in Marxist theory, would ultimately take power in the state.

Proportional representation A system that allocates parliamentary seats in proportion to the total number of votes.

Protestant General name for the reformed Churches created in sixteenth-century Europe that split from the Roman Catholic Church. There were 28 different Protestant Churches in Germany, of which the largest was the Lutheran (the German state Church, like the Church of England).

Putsch The German word for an uprising (though often the French phrase, *coup d'état*, is used). Normally, a *putsch* means the attempt by a small group to overthrow the government.

Radicalisation A policy of increasing severity.

Rapallo treaty This was not an alliance, but a treaty of friendship between Germany and the USSR.

Rationalisation Decree An intended reform of the economy to eliminate the waste of labour and materials.

Reaction In this context suggesting a return to traditional established ways.

Reactionary Opposing change and supporting a return to traditional ways.

Real wages The actual purchasing power of income taking into account inflation/deflation and also the effect of deductions, e.g. taxes.

Red Threat A 'Red' was a loose term used to describe anyone sympathetic to the left and it originated from the Bolshevik use of the red flag in Russia.

Reichstag The German parliament. Although created in 1871, it had very limited powers. Real power lay with the Emperor.

Revolution from below The radical elements in the Party, e.g. the SA, that wanted to direct the Nazi revolution from a more local level rather than from the leadership in Berlin.

RSHA Reich Security Office, which amalgamated all police and security organisations.

Rule of law Governing a country according to its laws.

SA *Sturm Abteilung* became known in English as the Stormtroopers. They were also referred to as the Brownshirts after the colour of the uniform. They supported the radical socialist aspects of Nazism.

Schlieffen plan Its purpose was to avoid a two-front war by winning victory on the Western Front before dealing with the threat from Russia. It aimed to defeat France within six weeks by a massive German offensive in northern France and Belgium.

'A second revolution' Refers to the aims of the SA, led by Ernst Röhm, which wanted social and economic reforms and the creation of a 'people's army' merging the German army and the SA. The aims of 'a second revolution' were more attractive to the 'left-wing socialist Nazis' or 'radical Nazis', who did not sympathise with the conservative forces in Germany.

Self-determination The right of people of the same nation to decide their own form of government. In effect, it is the principle of each nation ruling itself. Wilson believed that the application of self-determination was integral to the

Peace Settlement and it would lead to long-term peace.

Siegfriede 'A peace through victory' – referring to Germany fighting the First World War to victory and making major land gains.

Social Darwinism A philosophy that portrayed the world as a 'struggle' between people, races and nations. Hitler viewed war as the highest form of 'struggle' and was deeply influenced by the theory of evolution based upon natural selection.

Socialist republic A system of government without a monarchy that aims to introduce social changes for collective benefit.

Soviet A Russian word meaning an elected council. Soviets developed during the Russian Revolution in 1917. In Germany many councils were set up in 1918, which had the support of the more radical and revolutionary left-wing working class.

Soviet republic A system of government without a monarchy that aims to introduce a communist state organised by the workers' councils and opposed to private ownership.

Spanish Civil War The 1936–9 conflict between Republicans, who supported the democratic government, and the Nationalists/Fascists (financially and militarily backed by Italy and Germany).

SS *Schutz Staffel* (protection squad); became known as the Blackshirts, named after the uniform.

SS *Einsatzgruppen* 'Action Units'. Four of the units were launched in eastern Europe after the invasion of Russia. Responsible for rounding up local Jews and murdering them by mass shootings.

'Stab in the back' myth The distorted view that the army had not really lost the First World War and that unpatriotic groups, such as socialists and Jews, had

undermined it. The myth severely weakened the Weimar democracy from the start.

State within a state A situation where the authority and government of the state are threatened by a rival power base.

Tariffs Taxes levied by an importing nation on foreign goods coming in, and paid by the importers.

Teutonic paganism The non-Christian beliefs of the Germans in ancient history (heathens).

Toleration Acceptance of alternative political, religious and cultural views.

Total war Involves the whole population in war – economically and militarily.

Turn of the tide Used to describe the Allied military victories in the winter of 1942–3, when the British won at El Alamein in North Africa and when the Russians forced the surrender of 300,000 German troops at Stalingrad.

25-Points programme Hitler drew up the Party's 25-points programme in February 1920 with the Party's founder, Anton Drexler.

Unconditional surrender Roosevelt and Churchill's statement in 1943 that the Allies would not accept a negotiated peace.

Unilateral disarmament The disarmament of one party. Wilson pushed for general (universal) disarmament after the war, but France and Britain were more suspicious. As a result only Germany had to disarm.

Unrestricted submarine warfare Germany's policy of attacking all military and civilian shipping in order to sink supplies going to Britain.

Vernunftrepublikaner 'A rational republican' – used in the 1920s to define those people who really wanted Germany to have a constitutional monarchy but who, out of necessity, came to support the democratic Weimar Republic.

Volk   Often translated as 'people', although it tends to suggest a nation with the same ethnic and cultural identities and with a collective sense of belonging.

Völkisch   Nationalist views associated with racism (especially anti-Semitism).

Volksgemeinschaft   'A people's community'. Nazism stressed the development of a harmonious, socially unified and racially pure community.

Waffen **SS**   Armed SS – the number of divisions grew during the war from three to 35.

War bonds   In order to raise more money to pay for the war, Imperial Germany encouraged people to invest into government funds in the belief they were helping to finance the war and their savings would be secure.

Wehrmacht   The German army.

Weimar Republic   Took its name from the first meeting of the National Constituent Assembly in Weimar. The Assembly had moved there because there were still many disturbances in Berlin. Weimar was chosen because it was a town with a great historical and cultural tradition.

Weltpolitik   'World policy' – the imperial policy of Kaiser Wilhem II to make Germany a great power by overseas expansion.

White-collar workers   Workers not involved in manual labour.

White Terror   The 'Whites' were seen as the opponents (in contrast to the Reds). The 'White Terror' refers to the suppression of the soviet republic in Bavaria in March 1919.

Zero hour   Used in German society to describe Germany's overall collapse at the end of the Second World War.

Index